# DIVINE MAN OR MAGICIAN?

# SOCIETY
# OF BIBLICAL
# LITERATURE

---

# DISSERTATION SERIES

William Baird, Editor

---

**Number 64**

DIVINE MAN OR MAGICIAN?
Celsus and Origen on Jesus

by
Eugene V. Gallagher

Eugene V. Gallagher

# DIVINE MAN OR MAGICIAN?
## Celsus and Origen on Jesus

*Scholars Press*

Published by
Scholars Press
101 Salem Street
P.O. Box 2268
Chico, CA 95927

# DIVINE MAN OR MAGICIAN?
## Celsus and Origen on Jesus

Eugene V. Gallagher

Ph.D., 1980
University of Chicago

Advisor:
Jonathan Z. Smith

© 1982
Society of Biblical Literature

**Library of Congress Cataloging in Publication Data**

Gallagher, Eugene V.
    Divine man or magician?
    (Dissertation series / Society of Biblical Literature ;
no. 64) (ISSN 0145-2770)
    Originally presented as the author's thesis (Ph.D.)—
University of Chicago, 1980.
    Bibliography: p.
    1. Jesus Christ—Person and offices—Early church,
ca. 30-600. 2. Gods. 3. Celsus, Publius Juventius. 4.
Origen. I. Title. II. Series: Dissertation series (Society of
Biblical Literature) ; no. 64.
BT198.G29    1981        232'.8     81-16542
ISBN 0-89130-542-4      AACR2

Printed in the United States of America

## TABLE OF CONTENTS

# CHAPTER I

## THE "DIVINE MAN" AND THE PROBLEM OF CLASSIFICATION

*Introduction*

During the past two decades, the study of Ancient Mediterranean Religions has been marked by a resurgence of interest in
the "divine man." Originally promoted by members of the
"religionsgeschichtliche Schule" as a means of getting at the
similarities between Jesus and other holy men and thus of assessing the relative indebtedness of early Christianity to its
cultural milieu, the revived concept has been put to various
uses, some of which still recall its scholarly origins. H.D.
Betz, H. Koester, T. Weeden, and others have found traces of a
"divine man Christology" in the canonical gospels; D. Georgi
has seen it as the key which unlocks the identity and theology
of Paul's opponents in II Corinthians; others have linked the
divine man to a literary genre, the "aretalogy," and have pursued the relations of that genre to the earliest Christian documents.[1] To a great extent, contemporary research has cast the
divine man as a pivot on which the relations between early
Christianity and other religions of Late Antiquity turn.[2]

Given the importance which the concept has assumed in the
scholarly literature, it is unfortunate that its use has been
continually beset by methodological problems. M. Smith's recent
brief history of the research only hints at the gravity and
diversity of the difficulties.[3] The methodological confusion
has not paralyzed the field; indeed, it has fostered a prolifera-
tion of competing theories. But that only confirms the urgent
need for a clear and precise method. This call has been sounded
before. It is, in fact, one of the hallmarks of the resurgent
interest in the divine man that scholars feel compelled to exhort
their peers to methodological clarity. That it has not been
achieved should not preclude its pursuit. Some fundamental presuppositions of previous research must be re-examined, and
challenged where necessary. Until they are, any assessment of
the utility of the divine man concept for the investigation of
the relations among various Hellenistic religions is premature.

Research on divine men is currently organized by three
inter-locking foci:  the figure itself, the genre of the texts
in which it is encountered, and the contexts of activity in which
such figures and texts are to be understood.  Those foci in
turn depend upon three assumptions which have determined and, I
will argue, distorted the course of research.  They are:

1) that there was a native category (elsewhere "Hellenistic
   belief," "type," "device," "pattern," or "concept") of
   the divine man, and

2) that the evidence of such a native category is to be
   found in certain biographical texts, which

3) were written for the purpose of religious propaganda.

Since they have been very influential, basic questions need to
be proposed and answered about each of those assumptions:

1) Was there a *Hellenistic* concept of the divine man?
   If so, what were its contours, variations, etc.?

2) Was that concept expressed solely, or primarily, in
   biographical texts?  That is, is there a necessary connection between the divine man and certain types of
   literature, such as the "aretalogy"?

3) In what contexts and to what ends were such texts produced, circulated, and received?  Is there a necessary
   connection between divine men, aretalogies, and religious
   propaganda?

When the questions are phrased in that fashion, it becomes clear
that the entire matter depends upon the figure of the divine man.
Before reports of their activities can be considered, and before
the context or function of those reports can be discussed, the
divine men themselves must be found.  The answers to the first
question are crucial.

*The Figure of the Divine Man*

In modern scholarship, the concept of the divine man has
been employed primarily for two related purposes:  the construction of typologies of divine figures and the comparison of
figures subsumed under those types.  Many scholars, each in a
different way, have sought an answer to this question:  is
there a type, the divine man, whose variations can be traced and
compared in several Hellenistic religious traditions?  Since the

typological and comparative enterprises have had a long and complex history both in this specific field and in the general
study of religions, it should prove worthwhile to view the current state of the question in light of that history.

As early as 1910, in the first edition of his *Hellenistische
Mysterienreligionen*, R. Reitzenstein mentioned "eine *allgemeine
Vorstellung* von dem θεῖος ἄνθρωπος" of which Apollonius of Tyana
and Alexander of Abonuteichos were specific examples. Reitzenstein's use of the "divine man" fits well with his overall intention to describe the shared characteristics of Hellenistic
religions through comparisons of individual incidences.[4] For
Reitzenstein, the divine man who displays a higher nature, personal sanctity, deep wisdom, and mantic and thaumaturgic abilities exemplifies the individualistic tenor of Hellenistic piety.
The prevalence of divine men is to be reckoned, along with the
increased incidence of "personal mysteries" such as those portrayed in the Hermetic texts, as a consequence of the appearance
of each Hellenistic religion in diasporic as well as native
forms.[5] Reitzenstein argues that the incorporation of specific
social groups into world empires or into their spheres of cultural influence had specific consequences for national religions.
Political and cultural events, by submerging or suppressing the
importance of national identity, provoked on one hand a greater
focus on the individual, and, on the other hand, a broadening
of focus to include all humanity. So that

> . . . in propaganda and Diaspora any religion must
> become different, infinitely more personal than it
> is within a self-contained national constituency in
> which participation in it is taken for granted and
> no personal decision is placed upon the individual,
> and yet again it also must become more universal,
> intended for the whole of humanity, not for a single
> nation alone.[6]

In such a situation, the divine man who combined in his person
both specific personal appeal and the intimation of universal
competence became an important factor on the religious scene.
Indeed, it is to the activity of such figures that Reitzenstein
traces the spread of the various Oriental mysteries. Reitzenstein does not see the wandering servants of individual Oriental
deities as official priests of native temples; rather he views

them as priests and prophets who "validate their proclamations
by means of the ecstatic spirit of their discourse and by means
of prediction and miracle."[7]  He portrays the Oriental missionaries as "divine men," and the situation which gave rise to
their activity forms the background for his "allgemeine Vorstellung."

Certain aspects of Reitzenstein's approach need to be high-
lighted.  First of all, his comments on the "general conception"
of the divine man represent only a portion of Reitzenstein's
larger project, the development of a composite picture of
Hellenistic piety in all its aspects by extracting common characteristics from a group of diverse examples.  Further, he
chooses his examples specifically from the Hellenistic world.
Thus, his general conception will be pertinent only to that
field.  Reitzenstein attempts to avoid the criticism that his
definition of the field is arbitrary by arguing that a variety
of political, social, and cultural factors made the Hellenistic
world an organic unity.  Because of that unity, he can speak
of a *Hellenistic* type of the divine man, although he rests content with that and does not elaborate any sub-types.  To be
sure, Reitzenstein does not follow a rigid step-by-step format
in his discussion.  His remarks are frequently allusive and
fragmentary.  Nevertheless, he does articulate his presuppositions, primarily those concerning the cultural unity of the
Hellenistic world, and attempts to secure a basis for comparison
of various divine men.

Of the many studies that followed in the wake of Reitzenstein, and which were indebted to him in varying degrees, only
a few can be mentioned.  In discussing them particular attention will be devoted to two questions:  what is the source of
each author's conception of the divine man, and how is it used
in comparative studies?

G.P. Wetter's 1916 monograph, *Der Sohn Gottes*, deals primarily with the gospel according to John, though it intends to
provide as well "a contribution to the knowledge of the savior-
figure in antiquity."  While the specifics of Wetter's argument
are not strictly relevant here, the context in which they are
interpreted is.  He writes that

> . . . the conception of the Son of God flows
> together with another which is widespread in
> Hellenism:  the divine man (θεῖος ἄνθρωπος),
> or, as it is expressed among the Christians,
> the man of god (ὁ ἄνθρωπος τοῦ θεοῦ).  But with
> that we find ourselves in an area which lies too far
> from our subject, and which we can not follow
> here.[8]

In that passage Wetter seems to accept the idea that there was
a Hellenistic ("einer im Hellenismus viel allgemeineren") concept of the divine man.  He then edges toward an investigation
of sub-types in his distinction between the Hellenistic and
Christian designations for the general figure.  In itself, that
poses few problems and even promises an advance over Reitzenstein's monochromatic portrait, but Wetter does not stop there.
The area which he hesitates to enter and only briefly describes
is marked off for Wetter by the Melanesian term *mana*.  Taking his
cue from the overwhelming popularity which the term enjoyed in
contemporary anthropology and comparative religions as a designation for power of many sorts, he attempts to set the figures with
whom he had been occupied into a broader context.  He notes that
"mana" played an important role in early Semitic piety and
especially in primitive religions, and that it is not lacking
even in higher forms ("in den höheren Formen") of religion.
As Wetter's mention of Saul and Muhammad suggests, he suspects
that the type of the "son of god" which he found in the Hellenistic world is of much wider distribution.  His implicit typology
is not limited by cultural or temporal boundaries as Reitzenstein's was.  In the concept of mana, Wetter finds the basis for
the assimilation of personalities as diverse as Saul, Muhammad,
Melanesian chiefs, and Jesus into a single type.  Insofar as the
designation "son of god" or its equivalent can be understood to
describe a possessor of mana, they can all be treated as examples
of the same general type.

Wetter also introduces an historical dimension into his
brief discussion:

> This conception of the Son of God probably had
> a long history before it reached the Hellenistic
> world and was brought into connection with its
> thought.  But then it certainly underwent a
> transformation.  Of course, not a few concrete,

> real characteristics remain, and the Son of
> God himself stands in his thoroughly primitive
> form before us, but in the same way a certain
> spiritualizing has taken place just as it always
> happened with Oriental thought in Hellenism.[9]

In transposing his comparison into an historical framework,
Wetter was again of the same mind as many of his contemporaries.
R.H. Codrington's discussion of mana in his 1891 publication of
*The Melanesians* had provided evolutionary theorists with a useful tool. R.R. Marett, for example, in replying to E.B. Tylor's
theory that the earliest stages of religious belief could be
described as a belief in souls or "animism," posited an even
earlier stage which is exemplified in the Melanesian concept of
mana as a power that penetrates all things and which may be found
concentrated in certain objects or persons.[10] Wetter seems
to have endorsed the assumption shared by many of his anthropologist colleagues that *simple* societies, such as that of
Melanesia, could be taken to represent accurately the social
forms and beliefs of *early* societies, such as that of Greece
before Homer. But he seems to have been unaware of the difficulties that assumption entailed.

Wetter correctly suspected that any further discussion of
mana would have led him too far from his central theme. But
his admission that the concept of mana informs his conception
of the "Gestalt" of the Son of God begs further clarification.
The brief allusions to Saul, Muhammad, and Melanesian chiefs
lead one to inquire after a typology which highlights their
mutual relations. None, however, is to be found. Nor is the
relation between the Christian and Hellenistic perceptions of
the Son of God figure specified. With his appeal to mana Wetter
has ushered many more figures into the discussion. But he has
done little to clarify their similarities and differences.
Despite his remarks about differentiation, he presents a type,
but no typology.

The dangers courted in extending the typology of the divine
man beyond the confines of the Hellenistic world are clearly displayed in O. Weinreich's 1926 article "Antikes Gottmenschentum."
Weinreich shares several of Wetter's presuppositions and
expresses them in a clearer form:

> We intend to examine the type of the "Godman,"
> the θεῖος ἄνθρωπος, and to consider a few of its
> ancient representatives, in order to comprehend
> the kind and range of this history-of-religions
> phenomenon in Antiquity.[11]

Weinreich finds it appropriate to investigate the "primitivsten
Grundlagen der ganzen Erscheinung" before proceeding to individual examples. Like Wetter, he finds those foundations in the
concept of mana, noting his debt to the contemporary phenomenol-
ogy of religion. For Weinreich, the specific relevance of mana
is secured by the observation that ancient religions had a similar primitive conception of power as expressed in words like
δύναμις, ἀρετή, and *virtus*. He is also more explicit about the
comparative and evolutionary framework of his treatment:

> We begin with the Homeric world. Of course we
> should not expect to find in Homer's epic many
> traces of the mana of the primitive ruler or king.
> The Homeric world does not stand at the same stage
> of development as those of Oceania or the Sioux
> Indians.[12]

Weinreich also invokes a notion of survivals to bridge the gap
between the dark primitive past and the artistically stylized
world of the Homeric epic. Again, while the concept of mana
seems to provide the basis for an all-inclusive "phenomenolog-
ical" category of the divine man, its low rank on the evolutionary scale simultaneously furnishes the means for distinguishing
the more primitive manifestations from the "higher forms," as
Wetter also proposed. Mana becomes the essential kernel which
is found unadorned only in the most primitive contexts, while
elsewhere it is found encrusted with art, philosophy, and theology. The use of the concept of mana allowed Weinreich to
extend the scope of the category of the divine man, but only
at the risk of blurring the differences between individual
possessors of mana and obscuring their relationships to specific
cultures. For example, his discussion of the marvelous aspects
of the life of Pythagoras frequently lists parallel motifs from
others' lives, but Weinreich does not pursue the specific
meanings of those parallels in their own contexts. Pythagoras'
descent into Hades is mentioned in the same sentence as those of
Herakles, Theseus, and Jesus; Pythagoras' ability to calm

wild animals with a single word or with a movement of his hand
is briefly compared to similar abilities manifested by Orpheus,
and Buddhist and Christian saints.[13] Because he does not locate
those parallels in their particular contexts, Weinreich is left
with a single over-arching "type" of massive distribution. His
"type" is so general as to be of little help in the analysis
of specific texts.

Like Weinreich, H. Windisch is explicit about his conception
of the divine man. He identifies it as a central category in
the history of ancient religions and traces the roots of the
Greek view to the world-wide concept of power or mana. Frazer's
*Golden Bough* and van der Leeuw's *Phänomenologie der Religion*,
as well as Weinriech's article, are adduced as support.[14] In
Windisch's work the transition between Melanesia and the
Mediterranean is less jarring, but it is still undergirded by
an evolutionary scheme. He numbers among the sources of the
Greek conception of the divine man folk religion, philosophical
thought in general, and Plato who combined and transformed
elements from the other two sources. Socrates is described,
for example, as "an entirely new form of θεῖος ἀνηρ."[15] More
specific to Windisch's overall purpose is the observation that
the various Greek θεῖοι constitute a "Typenkreis" in which can
also be located the NT figures of Jesus and Paul. At times,
it seems that other members of the "Typenkreis" represent sub-
types. There is, for example, a discussion of "der Typos des
Pythagoras," of which the figure of Empedocles represents a
"Paralleltypus." Apollonius of Tyana is seen as uniting all
previously known types in himself, while he and Jesus of Nazareth
are described as belonging to the same type.

It is difficult to identify and sort out Windisch's intentions. Though his opening discussion of power and mana suggests
that he is working with a category of wide applicability, his
later comments suggest that he envisages a specifically
"Hellenistic" type which is subject to temporal and geographical
limitations. Further, his discussion of Pythagoras, Empedocles,
Apollonius, and Jesus as types in themselves threatens the entire
enterprise by elevating each individual to the status of a type.

When the path of some pioneers of divine man research, from Reitzenstein to Windisch at least, is retraced, the most important questions to emerge and remain unsolved concern the principles by which typologies were constructed and the uses to which they were put. Reitzenstein's location of the Hellenistic divine man within a specific cultural matrix proved intriguing, but he did not pursue variations in either the figure or the matrix, thus leaving his readers with a single "type" rather than typology. Wetter suggested that the question might be put into a broader framework of comparison, but his description of that framework, animated by the prevailing winds of anthropological thought, raised serious questions about the scope and manageability of his typology. Nor did Wetter venture a full presentation of his implicit typology. Weinreich seems to follow Reitzenstein in identifying a single type and Wetter in setting that type within an evolutionary scheme. More subtle, yet more confusing, is Windisch's attempt to account for both universality and specificity by detailing the forms of appearance of the divine man which were typical in the history of ancient religions. But Windisch's endeavor is weakened by his tendency to identify individuals as the sole representatives of sub-types of the divine man; Empedocles, for example, represents the "Empedocles-type." Nor are the implications of Apollonius' unification of a variety of types spelled out. A typology which merely reproduces actual diversity is not helpful. Finally, Windisch fails to clarify the relations between his most general level of description (possessors of mana), the culture-specific level (possessors of mana in ancient Mediterranean religions), and the possible variations within a given culture (a Pythagoras-type, etc.). None of those scholars has been able to strike a balance between the concerns for unity (the identification of the divine man type) and diversity (individual exemplars of that type) by bringing general and intermediate categories into some sort of logical relationship.

The failure to be clear and specific about the procedures and goals of typological analysis has hindered the study of divine men. Wetter, Weinreich, and Windisch have chosen to depict divine men as specific manifestations of a larger

phenomenon in the history of religions, but brief allusions to
mana and apparently random lists of possessors of it failed to
make the relationships between individual figures and the general
category sufficiently precise.  Because there were no clear
principles for the choice and ordering of examples, what resulted
was a collection, not a typology.  Since the principles of or-
ganization are weak in such groupings, the relations among their
members are difficult to discover.  It is not clear in Wetter's
scheme, for example, just what Jesus and Muhammad, or any other
possessor of mana, do or do not have in common.  Even when the
attempt to situate the divine man in the general history of
religions is not pursued, similar problems develop.  Those, like
Reitzenstein and, largely, Windisch, who would limit the inquiry
to the Hellenistic world have also failed to articulate clear
and discrete sub-types and to specify the relations among them,
as the confusion over Windisch's classification of Pythagoras,
Empedocles, Jesus, and Apollonius suggests.  Finally, Reitzenstein seems not to have been directly concerned with typology.
Suppressing the differences among individual figures, he sought
rather to unite them in a single category, for purposes other
than the study of divine men themselves.  Thus, he provides a
shaky foundation for typological studies.

The construction of typologies can be a useful tool for
the location and preliminary analysis of data.  Used improperly,
however, typologies can create more problems than they solve.
Such was the impact of the concern with "types" on the early
studies of divine men.  Some researchers saw a way of relating
their specific concerns with divine men to the general study of
religions, but the tools that they chose for that task did not
serve them well.  More importantly, terms like "type" and
"typology" were employed with wide variability and often dis-
maying imprecision.  The problems raised by those early attmepts
continue to influence the study of divine men, and they have
needlessly complicated it.

L. Bieler's ΘΕΙΟΣ ΑΝHP: *das Bild des "göttlichen Menschen"
in Spätantike und Frühchristentum* (1935 and 1936) provides a
refreshing dose of methodological rigor.  Bieler admits from
the outset that he is not interested in historical development

but rather in the "Gesamttypus" or even the Platonic idea of
the divine man.[16]  Individuals will never manifest in perfection
all the essential characteristics of the type, but they all,
more or less, bear its stamp.  Since that type appeared in both
the late classical and the early Christian sources, Bieler's
investigation will contribute to the history of ancient religions,
but it also will provide "structural-psychological" insights into the structure of the religious personality.[17]  Bieler's
concerns are clearly set forth.  He pursues the question of the
divine man both because it will furnish insight into the history
of certain religious traditions and because it will allow him
to comment on problems of general interest in the study of religions.  How does Bieler arrive at that type?

     Since he is interested more in a general conception than
in individuals, Bieler looks first for typical rather than distinguishing characteristics.  He claims that such traits become
more pronounced the further in time a biographical report is
distanced from its subject.  In folklore, saga, and mythology a
levelling process occurs in which the sharp, individualistic
edges are worn down and rounded off; specific instances come more
and more to conform to the outline of an implicit type.  Indeed,
the surest confirmation that a trait is typical is its appearance
in folklore, saga, and myth.[18]  Instead of combing the extant
materials for traces of historical personages, Bieler takes the
opposite route:

> . . . on the contrary, we should utilize the
> tradition without hesitation:  the image by which
> the folk and posterity are uplifted is still
> subjected to the force of a type to a much greater
> extent than an individual life, and the more so
> the farther from its historical source it is
> distanced in time.  Popular tradition preserves
> the memory of historical personages because it
> patterns them after general human types.[19]

The characteristics with which people are endowed in folktales,
sagas, and myths indicate what their audience knew or expected
to hear about them; Bieler is concerned not with the "historical
Apollonius" or the "historical Alexander of Abonuteichos" but
with how they have been viewed.  He illustrates his approach
elsewhere by claiming that what Suetonius and Nicolaus of Damascus

say about the emperor Augustus is not "historically accurate
but essentially correct."[20]

Bieler makes no assumptions about the fundamental similarities among all possessors of mana, but neither does he limit
his results to the Hellenistic world. His method of arriving
at a type deserves careful consideration. As it stands, it
resembles Max Weber's use of the ideal type in historical research. Bieler, however, does not appeal directly to any theoretical discussion of ideal-type analysis nor does he mention
Weber. But a brief review of Weber's theory should make Bieler's
affinities to it clear. For Weber, one function of the ideal
type is "to facilitate the presentation of an otherwise immensely
multifarious subject matter by expediently constructed rational
types."[21] M. Hill describes the Weberian ideal type as an ab-
straction from aspects of concrete reality rather than a comprehensive empirical account of that reality; it enables one to
disentangle and explain complex realities by making the analysis
of each component in an empirical mix easier.[22] The ideal
type approach can be seen as a way of filtering out extraneous
factors in order to enhance the precision of analysis. In his
first volume Bieler attempts to reduce the otherwise multifarious
wonder-workers, philosophers, wandering teachers, et al. to a
single type, that of the θεῖος ἀνήρ, by extracting from the
voluminous literature about them the typical career, personality,
knowledge and abilities, teaching and works, followers and
school, reception by the world, and relationship to god of the
divine man. Though the type itself is complex, it represents
an attempt to order an even more disparate reality.

For Bieler, however, the type is not wholly of his own
making. From his discussion of folklore, it appears that the
type also exists, somehow, in the mind of the people. Again,
Bieler does not provide full scholarly background for his conception of folklore, but he seems to subscribe to a view similar
to that proposed by A. Olrik in his 1908 article "Epic Laws of
Folk Narrative": "everything superfluous is suppressed and only
the essential stands out salient and striking."[23] If myths and
folktales are means of reducing the many to the one, the multifarious reality to the striking example, it remains for the

researcher to make explicit the patterning process in the tales themselves. That is precisely what Bieler sets out to do by combining his implicit theory of folk literature with ideal type analysis.

The aim of such analysis is not solely the formulation of a type. In themselves, the many parallel instances which make up a type indicate nothing, or, rather, too many things.[24] Bieler exhorts the reader to seek after the meaning of those parallels. Real parallels are to be found only when the function of the specific motif is the same in each instance; stories and individual characteristics can wander here and there--they are only "Baustoff."[25] It is the "Geist" which animates the "Gestalt" which is essential and original.[26] Here Bieler not only resembles Weber in his appeal to "Geist" but also in his insistence that the ideal type is useful only in so far as it promotes comparison. In Weber's words:

> Such constructions make it possible to determine the typological locus of a historical phenomenon They enable us to see if, in particular traits or in their total character, the phenomena approximate one of our constructions:  to determine the degree of approximation of the historical phenomenon to the theoretically constructed type.[27]

To that end, Bieler devoted a second volume to examining the relative congruence between his general type and individual divine men; he conceived of that volume as the proof of the theoretical approach of the first.[28]

The connection between those two volumes has often been disregarded by those who accuse Bieler of formulating too general a type; and the firm theoretical grounding of his ideal type analysis has not often been appreciated. More than any of his predecessors or contemporaries, Bieler has been misunderstood. The current impasse in divine man studies can be traced in part to that misunderstanding.

Bieler's thesis has not fared well recently. Typical is the position of W. Von Martitz: "the generous use of θεῖος ἀνηρ in Bieler, *passim*, gives the wrong idea that there was a designation and fixed concept in this early period."[29] Von Martitz denies that θεῖος ἀνηρ ever functioned as a technical term in

Hellenistic literature.  More sweeping is the condemnation of
P. Achtemeier, who writes in support of the arguments of
D. Tiede, which

> ought to put an end to the too widespread prac-
> tice of assuming that one can lump together every
> virtue attributed to any revered figure in the
> ancient world and obtain the hellenistic "ideal"
> of the "divine man."  That method, used by L.
> Bieler in his ΘΕΙΟΣ ΑΝΗΡ (first published in
> 1935-36), ought finally to be dropped.[30]

It would seem only fair, however, to request that Bieler's method
be understood correctly before it is so unceremoniously dropped.
Neither quoted argument is convincing.  Von Martitz does recall
a common misunderstanding in typological studies when he notes
that Bieler's ideal type can foster the mistaken impression
that θεῖος ἀνηρ was a technical term in Hellenistic literature.
But he does not appreciate the precautions which Bieler took to
avoid that eventuality;[31] his quarrel lies more with the subsequent use of Bieler than with Bieler himself.  On the other
hand, Achtemeier's assertion that Bieler merely "lump[ed] together every virtue attributed to any revered figure in the
ancient world" disregards the theoretical principles on which
Bieler based his argument.

Also, Achtemeier's complaints about the "too widespread"
use of the concept of the divine man as a catch-all shows that
it is the use of Bieler as much as Bieler himself which provokes
criticism.  If the comments of Von Martitz and Achtemeier are
an accurate barometer, one should expect to find a rather skewed
perception of Bieler's method in current studies of the divine
man.  Actually, several of the errors which they decry are more
evident in the work of their contemporaries than in Bieler's.

Prominent in modern work is the *assumption* that a *type* of
the divine man in the Hellenistic world did indeed exist.  Little
effort is devoted to the establishment of that type; neither
Reitzenstein's depiction of it as the product of certain cultural
and political forces, nor Wetter's and Weinreich's dependence
on other disciplines for the outlines of a typology, nor
Windisch's tentative steps towards a culture-specific typology
have been followed in recent studies.  The study of the divine
man has been cut loose from its theoretical moorings.  While the

abandoning of "mana" as a key to the figure of the divine man
might be hailed as a salutary escape from an imprecise concept
and an evolutionary framework of investigation, nothing has
really been offered in its place. The assumption of the existence
of the divine man type and the rejection of the theoretical underpinnings that once supported it constitute more of a problem
than a solution.

The problem is particularly evident in some works that seek
a "divine man Christology" in the New Testament. H.D. Betz, for
example, claims that Christology borrows motifs from "the
Hellenistic concept of the Divine Man (θεῖος ἀνηρ)."[32] While
Bieler arrived at his concept by a careful search through the
extant materials and by adopting a view of myth and folklore
which emphasized their own interest in the typical, Betz does
not really disclose his procedure. He notes that the context
of the belief is to be found in Hellenistic anthropology which
saw man as hovering between the divine and the animal, and he
gives a brief sketch of the character of the divine man, but
he also cautions that the concept is open to considerable variation according to context. Because the term θεῖος ἀνηρ fails to
occur in the New Testament, Betz claims that the influence of
the Hellenistic concept was mediated by Hellenistic Judaism,
again without specific demonstration. Furthermore, he urges
that "we must recognize that within the New Testament itself
the concept of the Divine Man Jesus has undergone far-reaching
theological developments, so that even there we encounter a
variety of expressions of it."[33] Betz finds as many as five different "divine man Christologies" in the gospels and their
sources. His interpretative strategy echoes those of his predecessors in a disturbing way. Though he makes no appeal to
mana or to an explicit evolutionary scheme, Betz nevertheless
sets off a large segment of his category as qualitatively inferior. The corollary of his treatment of the New Testament may
well be that the Hellenistic forms of the divine man which pre-
ceded the New Testament and which exerted an influence on its
images of Jesus were *not* subject to "far-reaching theological
developments." More importantly, apart from a distinction
between Christian and non-Christian manifestations of divine

men, no clear typology is proposed by Betz, nor are the mutual
relations of the five different "divine man Christologies" in
the gospels fully developed.

H. Koester also tries to establish a "divine man Christology" as one of the earliest ways of looking at Jesus:

> Gospels in the form of aretalogies, such as the
> miracles sources of Mark and John, proclaim that a
> particular divine power is present and available
> in these powerful acts of Jesus. Belief in
> this "gospel" implies that the benefits of such
> miraculous acts are accessible, or even that
> these acts can be repeated in the religious
> experience of the believer. Jesus is the "divine
> man" (θεῖος ἀνηρ). . . .[34]

In keeping with his view that such works were produced for the
purposes of religious propaganda, Koester also claims that
the concept of the divine man proved to be an "appealing device"
for Jewish missionary activity and that "the events of Jesus'
life and ministry were easily cast into this pattern."[35]  Though
he footnotes Bieler as the "standard work," Koester's understanding of how the events of Jesus' life could be made to conform with a pre-existent pattern of the divine man seems at
odds with Bieler's approach. Clearly lacking is any locus for
that pattern, or any full description of the "appealing device"
and the manner of its appropriation. The existence of a pattern
is *assumed* not demonstrated. Bieler's approach does not support
Koester's comments.

By misapprehending Bieler's use of the ideal type and by
appealing to his work as support for the existence of a
*Hellenistic* type of the divine man, scholars like Koester and
Betz have perpetrated an historical anachronism.[36]  Such a type
*may* be there, but that is not exactly what Bieler was getting
at. For Bieler, it takes the efforts of the scholar to raise
the disparate indications in the Hellenistic literature to the
level of a useful research tool by extracting from them common
features and recurrent patterns. Such theoretical models are
useful in their "explanation of the *virtual* tendencies of a
system, in light of which *actual* discrepancies may be investigated."[37]  In their use of Bieler, recent studies have frequently
mistaken his model of virtual tendencies for a description of

empirical reality.  Moreover, from Bieler's point of view it is
not a question of "far-reaching theological developments" of
the Hellenistic concept of the divine man in the gospel traditions, nor is it a question of the early Christian adaptation
of an appealing device from the Jewish missionary tradition.
Rather, it is a question of how each "actual" appearance of the
figure of the divine man conforms to and departs from the model
of "virtual" tendencies which Bieler has constructed.  By
retrojecting Bieler's ideal type into the Hellenistic world,
scholars have obfuscated both the gains and limitations of typological analysis.

Much of the confusion in the current study of divine men
stems from a basic misapprehension of the nature and functions
of ideal types in historical research.  As a recent commentator
on Weber states:

> . . . strictly speaking, ideal types do not pro-
> vide a description of any set of empirical phenomena;
> rather, they describe constellations or sequences
> of phenomena which would frequently exist if (1)
> people always decide to act in certain ways in cer-
> tain kinds of situations (although actually they do not),
> and if (2) all empirical instances of these kinds
> of situations had the same features (which they
> actually have not).  Thus, they describe hypothetical
> constellations of events, that is, mental constructs.
> [Further] (1) Statements about the model must
> not be treated as if they constituted a theory of
> a class of empirical phenomena.  (2) The construction
> or selection of a suitable model and its applica-
> tion to a particular case must not be confused
> with the testing of empirical hypotheses.[38]

To be sure, the earlier theorists did not always address the
question of whether they were advancing hypothetical constructs
or descriptions of empirical reality.  Bieler, however, did.
Those who have used his work as a rich mine of material have
often misconstrued the theoretical principles by which he col-
lected and organized it.

Bieler's typology is a hypothetical construction.  In his
first volume he deliberately ignored historical variations and
sought to construct "die platonische Idee" of the divine man.
That figure in itself told him little; it was through comparison
of specific occurrences of the type that he sought to arrive at
the distinctive "Geist" which animated each new coining of the

type. The "lumping together" of a range of historical figures
was scarcely the final goal of Bieler's project; its end was
not simply the construction of the "ideal" of the Hellenistic
"divine man." Nor did he intend, as recent scholars seem to
assume, to provide a full and accurate picture of empirical
reality. The final goal of ideal type analysis is not the construction of the type, but the comparison of specific instances
to the type. Bieler is quite clear on that point.[39]

M. Hill has observed that in social theory the elaboration
of a large and all-inclusive typology is frequently followed by
the development of sophisticated webs of sub-types;[40] it would
seem that Bieler was preparing the way for that in his comments
at the end of the first volume and in the individual studies
which comprise his second. But volume 2 remains "eine Reihe
kleinerer Arbeiten" and he never presses towards an elaboration
of sub-types based on the particular "Geist" which animates individual texts, or, for that matter, on any other criterion.
Bieler cannot be faulted completely for leaving work to be done,
but those who take up that work can be held accountable to the
principles by which it should proceed.

In *The Charismatic Figure as Miracle Worker*, D.L. Tiede upbraids Bieler for excessive generality. He describes his own
study as "a negative evaluation of the interpretative significance of the generalized portrait of the θεῖος ἀνηρ which has
been extensively defended by Ludwig Bieler among others."[41]
Tiede rejects Bieler's "synthetic portrait" as well as Reitzenstein's general conception,[42] because they do not take sufficient
account of the variations in traditions about Hellenistic divine
men. But Tiede also betrays little awareness that Bieler intended his ideal type to get at just those variations. Tiede,
confusing scholarly tools with empirical reality, complains that

> Bieler aggregated so many features into his
> composite portrait of the "typical divine man"
> that it would be difficult to find any hero
> in antiquity to whom at least several of these
> qualities were not attributed . . . the diver-
> sity that was recognized in the sources was
> treated by Bieler as of secondary importance
> compared with the general conception of the
> "divine man" which he believed he could identify
> in a wide variety of contexts. . . .[43]

That Bieler devoted more energy to the development of his ideal
type than to the discussion of its shadings and variations
merits mention, but that his one-sidedness provides sufficient
ground for refuting his whole approach is doubtful.  Instead of
attempting a more sophisticated description of sub-types as a
complement to Bieler's work, Tiede insists on dispensing with
the ideal type entirely.  The "alternative method" which he proposed in its place should be considered.

In opposition to the "many scholars [who] have been oper-
ating under the false impression that the term θεῖος ἀνηρ was a
fixed concept in the Hellenistic world,"[44] Tiede *tries* to demonstrate that the "complete aggregate portrait of the divine man"
which is found in later Hellenistic authors like Philostratus
and Porphyry is the result of the fusion of two originally distinct forms.  Writing of aretalogical traditions Tiede contends
that

> Although all of these forms of praise share a
> propagandistic function, it is vital to the
> methodology of this essay to demonstrate that
> the origins of the following two traditions are
> discrete . . . the aretalogies of the divine man
> and of the miracle worker. . . .[45]

Tiede's argument thus takes an historical form; he intends to
show that two originally distinct images of the divine man were
later combined.  It is difficult to see how such an approach
would undermine any of Bieler's conclusions, given his explicit
abstention from any historical questions.[46]  Thus Tiede seems
to be following more in the steps of Reitzenstein and Windisch;
he is looking for the ways in which one type of the divine man
was distinguished from another in the Hellenistic world.
Certainly comments like this should be read in that light:

> . . . in the Hellenistic world, diverse attempts
> to authenticate the divine stature or power of a
> charismatic figure can be identified, and the
> criteria which were used to evaluate such claims
> can be distinguished.[47]

Tiede wants to separate two primary sets of criteria, originally
discrete.  Following M. Hadas, he advances the "suffering
Socrates" as "one of the most potent models of the 'divine man'
of the philosophical tradition,"[48] but he sets forth no single

figure as a model for the "type" of the divine miracle worker.
In fact, while Tiede frequently mentions "traditional" or
"Hellenistic" images of his primary types, they are usually
found in combination.  Thus Pythagoras is nominated as "the
prototype of the synthetic Hellenistic 'divine man'."[49]  Most
often Tiede describes reworkings of, reactions to, and combinations of his purportedly traditional types, as in the case of
Apollonius of Tyana "where it is possible to observe a diversity
of opinion and a tension between those who think his miracles
are the primary means of authenticating his divinity and those
who see his wisdom as a philosopher as demonstrating his supernatural character."[50]

Tiede has assembled some interesting texts, but his alternative method, due to its imprecision, cannot mold them into a
coherent picture.  Again, the failure to specify the status of
the types under scrutiny weakens the argument.  Though Tiede
wants to claim the original separation of the divine wise man
and the divine miracle worker, the evidence, especially from the
Hellenistic period, seems to tell against that distinction.  M.
Smith has proposed that the synthetic picture of the omnicompetent divine man, both philosopher and miracle worker, is historically prior to any specialized portraits which emphasize either
one of those traits.[51]  Smith's position casts severe doubt on
Tiede's historical reconstruction.  Yet it does not account, nor
does Tiede's thesis in its present form, for some of the more
interesting facts which Tiede has brought to light.

There can be little doubt that Tiede is correct in noticing
that there were sharp differences among their contemporaries on
how certain figures on the ancient religious scene were to be
understood.[52]  Philostratus' *Life of Apollonius*, for example, is
intended at least in part to defend its subject against the
charge that he was a magician and charlatan.[53]  Charges and
counter-charges of many varieties followed such figures wherever
they went.  Tiede rightly claims that there is ample evidence
for the reconstruction of the criteria by which claimants to
divinity were judged; he is less convincing in claiming that
those criteria can be reduced to two primary categories, and
that those sets of criteria were originally distinct.  Those

restrictions lead him to take a narrow view of the material he
introduces. For example, it is not readily apparent that
Artapanus' portrait of Moses, which Tiede characterizes as "in
direct competition with traditional Egyptian benefactors who
gained immortality and divine status because of their practical
sagacity (σύνεσις) and benefits to men (εὐεργεσία): Diodorus
I 13.1)"[54] can be readily subsumed under either the divine wise
man or the divine miracle worker "type." Rather it seems that
there was a multiplicity of types, or at least a range of categories which could be combined into types, into which their contemporaries tried to fit the perplexing mob of would-be divine
men. I will attempt to show later in the chapter that such
attempts at classification do figure prominently in literature
about divine men. Their contemporaries do not seem to have been
content to treat each of them as unique historical individuals.
Tiede demonstrates some awareness of that complex situation, but
his theoretical framework does not allow him to exploit it fully.

Tiede's distaste for Bieler's excessive generality might
have led him to develop a full classification of empirical phenomena, but he seems to think that his two "types," the divine wise
man and the miracle worker, exhaust the possibilities. Tiede's
failure to support his argument on either empirical or theoretical grounds and his failure to entertain the existence of other
"types" or sub-types of divine men seriously undermine the
typological dimension of his argument. He has not provided a
compelling alternative to Bieler's approach. Tiede's categories
and types hover uncertainly between ideal type analysis and
description of empirical reality. Despite his disclaimers,
Tiede's two types of divine man come closer to being abstrac-
tions from aspects of concrete reality than to being comprehensive empirical accounts of that reality. The difficulty encountered in isolating the types in their pure state reveals their
abstract nature. Thus Tiede seems to be working at cross purposes. While he disapproves of Bieler's style of analysis, he
supplants it with a similar scheme. While he recognizes the
wealth of material at his disposal for the elucidation of
Hellenistic ways of perceiving divine men, he reduces that rich-
ness to a false duality. His implicit combination of history

and morphology recalls the problems inherent in the works of
Wetter, Weinreich, and Windisch.

As the review of some representative positions shows, none
of the attempts to establish a typology of divine men in the
Hellenistic world has been wholly satisfying.  Reitzenstein
showed the importance of the figure for the Hellenistic world,
but he did not pursue the question further.  Those who chose to
rely on categories derived from anthropology and comparative
religions were hindered by the weaknesses of the models they
adopted; they failed to produce convincing typologies.  Bieler
proposed a methodologically consistent ideal typology which has
been all too frequently misapplied and misunderstood.  Perhaps
understandably, more recent contributions have abstained from
explicit theorizing of any sort, although their assumptions are
often clear enough.  Some theories, such as the evolutionary
view of which mana formed a part, have clearly proven to be
dead-ends; others, such as the culture-specific approach initi-
ated by Reitzenstein and taken up haltingly but intriguingly by
Windisch, have not yet been pursued as far as they might be;
others, like that of Bieler, have fallen into disfavor and stand
in need of rehabilitation.  The current student of divine men
stands before a theoretical choice, and the decision not to
choose is not an option.  Not to choose means only to conceal
one's theoretical assumptions; it is impossible to pursue scholarship without such a basis.

Tiede's interest in the authentication of divine stature
and the criteria which were used to evaluate claims to divine
stature has been echoed by C. Talbert.  In "The Concept of Immortals in Mediterranean Antiquity," he argues that in the ancient world there were two separate categories of divinity which
were applicable to mortals:

> On the one hand, certain men were believed in
> their historical existence to have displayed
> the divine presence in some special way and were
> hence regarded as θεῖοι ἄνδρες.
>    On the other hand, a more select group of
> men were believed at the end of their careers
> to have been taken up into heaven, to have
> attained immortality, and to have received a
> status like that of the eternal gods.  Such
> figures were designated immortals.[55]

Talbert claims that the immortals are to be understood in contrast to another type of divine beings who had no beginning in
history, the eternals.  Zeus is a typical eternal, while Heracles
and Dionysos are typical immortals.  He finds evidence for such
an indigenous typology particularly in Diodorus of Sicily, where
the following statement occurs:

> As regards the gods . . . men of ancient times
> have handed down to later generations two differ-
> ent conceptions:  certain of the gods, they say,
> are eternal and imperishable. . . .  But the
> other gods, we are told, were terrestrial be-
> ings who attained to immortal honor and fame
> because of their benefactions to mankind, such
> as Heracles, Dionysos, Aristaeus, and the others
> who were like them.[56]

Talbert traces the influence of the concept of the immortals
through several traditions and concludes with some observations
on the distinction between θεῖοι ἄνδρες and immortals:  "not
every θεῖος ἄνηρ was believed to have become an immortal."[57]
Moreover, Talbert contends that some traditions and individuals
found the concept of the immortals less congenial than others.
Porphyry, for example, seems content with the idea of Pythagoras
as a divine man, but resists portraying him as an immortal.
Similarly in Hellenistic Judaism, "both Josephus and Philo find
suitable that variety of the θεῖος ἄνηρ in which divine presence
is understood in terms of virtue, though neither approves of
the mythology of the immortals.  They deliberately keep the two
conceptions separate."[58]  Like Tiede, Talbert views Philostratus'
*Life of Apollonius* as a composite, but where Tiede saw the fusion
of the divine wise man and the divine miracle worker, Talbert
sees the integration of the mythology of the immortals into the
account of "a wise and virtuous θεῖος ἄνηρ during his earthly
career."[59]  While this is not the appropriate place to debate
the relative merits of those assessments of Philostratus' *Life*,
it can be noted that Talbert provides, at least in outline, a
fuller, clearer, and more internally consistent typology than
heretofore encountered.  It can be diagrammed like this:

DIVINITY

*eternals*                                    *immortals*

                                              (Sub-types of
                                              the θεῖος ἄνηρ?)

There are, however, some problems with Talbert's proposal.
His typology is incomplete and the status of sub-types, such as
that "variety of θεῖος ἀνηρ" which Josephus and Philo found ap-
proriate to their purposes, begs further explanation.  The argument that θεῖος ἀνηρ in general was an ancient category of
divinity also needs further textual support.  It cannot be based
on Bieler's presentation.  Most importantly, Talbert has not
taken sufficient account of the polemical dimension of Diodorus'
classificatory scheme.  A distinction between eternals and immortals is presented by Diodorus, but it is clearly based on
Euhemerist principles.[60]  Osiris, for example,

> . . . by reason of the magnitude of his benefac-
> tions received the gift of immortality with the
> approval of all men and honour equal to that of
> the gods of heaven.  After this he passed from
> the midst of men into the company of the gods and
> received from Isis and Hermes sacrifices and every
> other highest honour.  These also instituted rites
> for him and introduced many things of a mystic
> nature, magnifying in this way the power of the
> god.[61]

Similar explanations are offered of the reception of divine
honors by Heracles and Isis.[62]

In light of that polemical dimension of Diodorus' "mythology
of the immortals," perhaps more caution should be exercised before it is proposed as a basic feature of religious thought in
Late Antiquity.  Though Plutarch cites Euheremus as evidence for
such a mythology,[63] it appears that Plutarch may have held a
somewhat different conception of that mythology than Diodorus.
For example, Plutarch rejected Euhemerism out of hand, claiming
that Euhemerus

> spread atheism over the whole inhabited earth by
> obliterating the gods of our belief and converting
> them all alike into generals, admirals, and kings,
> who, forsooth, lived in very ancient times and are
> recorded in inscriptions written in golden letters
> at Panchon.[64]

In place of the Euhemerist position Plutarch prefers "the judgement of those who hold that the stories about Typhon, Osiris,
and Isis are records of experience of neither gods nor men, but
of demigods."[65]  Demigods, according to Plutarch, possess a

greater than human nature, yet they do not possess an uncontami-
nated divine nature; they occupy a category midway between gods
and ordinary mortals.  Osiris, among others, became a god on
account of his virtue.[66]

Plutarch's portrait of a demigod who receives divine honors
on account of virtue and Diodorus' portrait of a man who receives divine honors on account of philanthropy differ at least
in their particulars.  They suggest that a native Hellenistic
"mythology of the immortals" was flexible enough to allow changes
according to the demands of the polemical context.  In this case,
Plutarch's rejection and Diodorus' acceptance of the Euhemerist
argument were the decisive factors.

Despite its disregard for context of classificatory schemes,
particularly in Diodorus, Talbert's approach is suggestive for
those who would disclose the varieties of conceptions of divinity
in the Hellenistic world.  But what will such an approach yield?
For an answer to that question, a brief return to the potentially
helpful, yet hazardous, field of social theory is in order.

Prominent in recent anthropological thought is the concern
with order and the systems by which it is imposed on what M.
Douglas has called "an inherently untidy experience."[67]  She, and
others, intend to discover the techniques developed *within* cultures for the reduction of what Weber called "multifarious reality" to manageable dimensions.  Where Weber saw that as the task
of historical research and the function of ideal type analysis,
anthropologists have recently stressed that similar processes
can be identified within cultural systems, though they are likely
not to correspond to those systems of ordering with which the
outside observer is familiar.  Their work proceeds from the
shared assumption that attention to native systems of classification, such as the distinction between immortals and eternals
in Diodorus, will not only aid in the solution of culture-
specific problems, such as the character and status of the Hellenistic divine man, but will also open up the broader horizons
of native cultures as viewed from within.  The research treats
reality as "socially constructed" and presumes that any "picture" or fragment of that reality "carries in itself at any
given moment the social configurations of that time and place."[68]

Thus schemes of classification have embedded in them both a view
of the world and a reflection of the social reality that shaped
that view.  They provide a point of entry into the social and
symbolic life of the culture under scrutiny.  Though Talbert
makes no specific appeal to this current of contemporary anthropological thought, his approach is compatible with it.  That
suggests that his discussion of Hellenistic typologies of
divine men may not only reveal how their contemporaries thought
about them, but also how they thought about, and created, the
entire world in which they lived.  One might wonder whether im-
porting foreign theories into the discussion should be resisted
on the principle of "once burned, twice careful," but previous
failures do not in themselves preclude future success and the
claim to have no theory whatsoever is untenable.[69]

The comparative study of divine men in the Hellenistic
world has, for the most part, led to a series of dead ends (the
divine man as a possessor of mana in Wetter, Weinreich, and
Windisch), and confusing intersections (Windisch's and Tiede's
implicit combinations of ideal and empirical types).  A promising
early route (Bieler's) has found few followers.  The study of
the divine man is currently at an impasse because there are no
clear paths to take.  They may yet be developed.  But before
that, a brief look at the texts and contexts in which the activity
of divine men is reported is necessary.

*The Literary Evidence*

Talbert's work on native classification of candidates for
divine status implicitly undermines the tacit assumption that
information about divine men is to be found primarily in biographical literature.  If clear indication of indigenous conceptions of types of divinities can be found in Diodorus, for example, there should be no inherent reason why other kinds of
literature might not be examined as well.  Indeed, the common
restriction of the inquiry to a recognizable "canon" of biographical texts (the lives of Pythagoras, Lucian's satirical
lives, Philostratus' *Life of Apollonius*, etc.) contradicts the
frequently voiced opinion that the Hellenistic world knew a
"mob of divine or deified men and their many varieties."[70]

If it did, it is unlikely that they were met only in biographical writings.

The linking of the divine man to a specific type of text
derives in part from the perennial interest of scholars to bring
their research to bear upon the figure of Jesus and the genre
of the canonical gospels. By linking divine men to "aretalogies"
they could pursue both questions simultaneously. Given a definition of the aretalogy "as a formal account of the remarkable
career of an impressive teacher that was used as a basis for
moral instruction,"[71] its application to the study of the gospels
becomes readily apparent. Koester makes that application precise when he speaks of "gospels in the form of aretalogies, such
as the miracles sources of Mark and John."[72] While such statements promise intriguing results, they depend upon a series of
unproven assumptions. Initially, they rest on the extension of
the term "aretalogy" to cover not only the report of the mighty
deeds of a deity but also collections of such reports or even
fuller biographical accounts.[73] Also, the search for historical
antecedents of the gospel accounts or sources which could have
furnished a pattern for their composition[74] depends on hypothetical "aretalogies" in the developed form. Those sources are not
extant. Finally, they depend on the assumption that one must
look to aretalogies in order to study divine men. H. Kee sums
up the problem of aretalogies:

> The confusion has come from the extension of
> this term by some scholars to include (a)
> collections of miracle stories and (b) biographies
> of supernaturally endowed persons. The terminolog-
> ical confusion is compounded by logical confusion
> when, as corollaries, it is further assumed that
> (1) one who does a miracle is a θεῖος ἀνηρ, and that
> (2) the aim of a biographical account of such a
> miracle-worker is to demonstrate his divine na-
> ture . . . the pattern of the biographical so-called
> "aretalogy" . . . is not nearly so fixed as its
> proponents claim, . . . the components of these
> lives of miracle workers (or the collection of
> miracle stories on which they are based) do not
> always or even regularly have as their aim the
> demonstration of the divine nature of the performer
> of the miracles.[75]

If there are no compelling reasons to locate divine men solely
in a quasi-biographical genre, the field of investigation is

widened considerably.  Any text would be admissible, since there
are no *a priori* considerations which would rule it out.  To
some extent, the texts chosen will depend on an assessment of
the context in which they are to be understood.  To that I now
turn.

*The Contexts of Divine Man Activity*

    Kee's caution that lives of miracle workers need not neces-
sarily have as their aims the demonstration of the divine nature
of their subjects, strikes close to a long-held assumption.  In
its simplest form (Koester's "Aretalogies were normally written
for the purposes of religious propaganda,"[76] for example), it
ascribes a common intention to all such literary products.
That view of the literature mirrors a common view of the figures
themselves--a view which goes back at least to Reitzenstein,
who asserted that the activity of divine men is to be understood
in the context of the religious propaganda carried on especially
by Oriental cults in the  Roman world.[77]  Further, he claimed
that it was the individual propagandist's appearance as a divine
man which confirmed his preaching, a position later developed
by D. Georgi in his study of Paul's opponents in II Corinthians.
Thus, the activity of the divine men and their partisans is
seen as an important factor in religious competition.[78]  That
devotees of various cults engaged in propagandizing is hard to
deny; that at least some of them attempted to confirm their
messages through striking performances also seems secure, but
that the performance of miracles was at the heart of Hellenistic
religious propaganda overstates the case.  To claim that the
recording and proclamation of the performance of miracles in-
variably served the purposes of propaganda also begs proof.
Again, the presumed direct relationship between miracle-working,
aretalogies, and propaganda has set the question in too narrow
a context.  A review of some important characteristics of propaganda in the Hellenistic world can broaden that context and re-
introduce complexity into the relationships between figures,
texts, and contexts.

    Propaganda, "the more or less systematic effort to manipu-
late other people's beliefs, attitudes, or actions by means of

symbols,"[79] was only one aspect of a complex of closely related
religious activities. It occupied the opposite side of the
coin from apologetics, the more or less systematic effort to
fend off the manipulation of one's beliefs, attitudes, or actions. Both take their place in the larger missionary scenario
which was so much a part of Hellenistic religious life. Their
interaction centers on the issue of conversion:  where propaganda
would promote it, apologetics would forestall it. The close relationship of apologetics and propaganda sometimes makes it
hard to pin down the point at which one shades over into the
other. In the Hellenistic world, the competition for religious
adherents was fought through propaganda and apologetics.

Significantly, each presumes a social relationship. Neither
can be conducted in isolation; another individual or group must
be envisaged as the "target population." That social background
leaves a strong imprint on either type of argument. Apologists,
for example, must walk a thin line between two worlds. They can
not rely solely, or even too strongly, on esoteric doctrine and
its systematic explication; they must use common parlance to
make a point while concurrently striving to remain faithful to
their own views. An effective defense or appeal can not be
couched wholly in terms shared with the intended audience and
still adequately represent the nuances of the speaker's own
tradition, nor can it be framed in language wholly foreign to
the intended audience and still elicit a response. Propagandists
and apologists alike face the task of staking out a middle position between their own views and those of the people whom they
would convince. That attempt to strike a balance between concession to the perceived demands of an audience and the preservation of a precise articulation of a message defines the propagandistic and apologetic enterprises.

In the process of conversion the movement of individuals
between those two poles can be traced. Several Hellenistic conversion stories begin with the subject's anxiety and uncertainty
which is then brought to a head by a confrontation with an
authoritative teacher and/or set of writings, and is finally
resolved by adherence to the system espoused by that teacher
or set of writings. For example, in the conversion account of

Justin, a second century Christian, the movement from object to
author of propaganda is clear.  Not only does the process of
conversion suggest the working of propaganda and apologetics
on individual lives, it highlights the constant process of
sifting, weighing, and deciding that accompanies them.  Though
the transition from one state to another is smoothed over in
retrospective accounts of conversions, such as Justin's which
was composed some twenty-five years after the fact, the criteria
by which the alternatives were to be judged are nevertheless
clearly set forth.  Take, for example, the speech of Justin's
mentor:

> There existed, long before this time, certain men
> more ancient than all those who are esteemed
> philosophers, both righteous and beloved by God,
> who spoke by the Divine Spirit, and foretold
> events which would take place, and which are now
> taking place.  They are called prophets.  These
> alone both saw and announced the truth to men,
> neither reverencing nor fearing any man, not
> influenced by a desire for glory, but speaking
> those things alone which they saw and heard,
> being filled with the Holy Spirit.  Their writings
> are still extant, and he who has read them is
> very much helped in his knowledge of the beginning
> and end of things and of those matters which the
> philosopher ought to know, provided he had be-
> lieved them. . . .[80]

The passage is studded with a series of criteria by which the
prophets, and their books, can be adjudged authoritative.  Acceptance of the message implies an assent to the validity of
those criteria.  Though Justin does not portray himself, in
retrospect, as having carefully pondered each item before deciding to accept the Christian "philosophy," the criteria on
which such a decision could be based are prominent in his account.  The process of conversion, which is often sparked by
propaganda (Justin's mentor, e.g.) and which frequently issues
in apologetics (Justin's retrospective account) and can lead to
propaganda by the recent convert (Justin's appeal to Trypho) can
be conceived as a series of decisions.  Conditioned to be sure,
and often less than fully conscious, those decisions were nonetheless implicitly based on certain criteria.  Individual's
accounts of their own conversions furnish a glimpse at those
criteria.

Similarly, individual's accounts of the activity of claimants to divinity may also provide a glimpse at the criteria by
which such claimants were evaluated. Tiede's "criteria which
were used to evaluate the diverse attempts to authenticate the
divine stature or power of a charismatic figure" will be found
both in arguments for and against specific figures. To focus
simply on propaganda is to miss the complex nature of the issue.
Propaganda seeks, even demands, a response. Apologetic arguments
are frequently marshalled in opposition to propaganda. Statements of individuals caught in the crossfire can reveal the influence of each side. When the complexity of the ideological
milieu and sociological background of missionary religions in
the Hellenistic world is brought to the fore, certain implications follow. The assumption that accounts of divine men were
propagandistic in intent and the restriction of the inquiry to
biographical texts are not compatible.

Justin's conversion story suggests that the criteria for a
decision are most readily apparent when the attractiveness of
one alternative has to be asserted at the expense of another.
The prophets and their books were *more* ancient, *more* close to
god, *more* righteous, *more* capable of foretelling the future,
etc. Justin portrays them as *superior* to those teachers with
whom he had formerly been involved. The criteria on which their
superiority is decided is stressed in the argumentative context.
The attraction of the prophetic books is asserted in relation to
the lesser attraction of other books. Since, like Justin's
mentor, divine men and their partisans frequently sought adherents, the decisions involved might provide an analogy to those
involved in the evaluation of claimants to divine status. The
criteria by which such claimants were judged will be accessible
in argumentative contexts, in situations where their relative
superiority is asserted and supported. Windisch anticipated
as much when he wrote that

> . . . a θεῖος ἄνθρωπος who really deserves the
> name is always one who knows, who is inspired,
> who brings salvation, who is "sent": one who
> stands above man.[81]

The argument about who really deserved to be called a θεῖος
ἄνηρ can provide a range of criteria by which claimants to

divinity were evaluated and a range of lower-level categories
compatible with those elicited by Talbert. Those criteria and
categories will not only detail a sharper view of the indigenous
perception of the divine man, but might also uncover world-
views in which individual divine men made sense.

Since the proposed approach has serious implications for
the ways in which the study of the divine man is undertaken, it
might be helpful to give a brief example of some results that
have already been achieved and their theoretical underpinnings.
They center on the evaluation of purported thaumaturgical activity. In the texts, the fervent proclamation of miracle working
ability is frequently countered by the ascription of the results
to magic. Where the supporters of a given figure would perceive
his actions as miraculous, his detractors would see them as
magical. Representatives of the French sociological school, Durk-
heim, Mauss, and particularly Hubert, were particularly interested in that question. In his article "Magia," Hubert proposed
that anything considered abnormal, impure, or foreign ran the
risk of being branded "magical" in the Hellenistic world. Magic
was a characteristic activity of strangers; it was something
done by *someone else:*

> . . . an uprooted religion is magic up to the
> point when it receives the legal sanction of
> the city, officially or officiously, where it
> has been transplanted. It follows that magic
> is not to be distinguished from religion by
> the miraculous character of its results or by
> the mechanism of its procedures, but by that
> which it presents as abnormal at a given point
> of space or time and as incompatible with the
> received system of ideas and customary images.[82]

Hubert's position is repeated by Nock: "What gets the name of
magic is a varied complex of things, mainly *qua* professional
or *qua* criminal in intent or *qua* alien."[83] Those specific observations coincide with Mauss' general remark that "we can conclude that a magician has, in so far as he has one, a social
status which may be defined as abnormal."[84] What the French
sociologists stressed, that the issue was less the performance
of certain actions than the evaluation of those actions, comes
through clearly in this statement from Mauss:

> We might go so far as to say that there are
> evil spells which are evil only in so far as
> people fear them. The fact of their being
> prohibited provides a delimitation for the
> whole sphere of social action.[85]

Among more recent scholars, M. Smith has argued in a similar vein
that "son of god," "θεῖος ἄνηρ," and "magician" refer to a single social type, viewed from different perspectives.[86] With
that, the polemical context of the debate over magic and miracles
in the Hellenistic world becomes established. Consequences follow for the search for criteria by which claimants to divine
status were evaluated. Especially in argumentative literature,
the apparently straight-forward proposals, like those offered
by Diodorus, are less likely to be found. It will not be the
performance of certain actions, but the evaluation of them, that
will provide keys to a range of criteria. The deed which demonstrates divinity for one audience may well demonstrate the
malign influence of demons for another. In dealing with the
criteria, judgments rather than actions should be paramount.

If the activity of divine men and their partisans can be
located within the ideological context of missionary activity
in the Hellenistic world, then not only biographical, or even
historical, texts need to be considered. Texts which capture
most clearly the discussions and arguments sparked by missionary
activity need also to be studied. Indeed, such texts will be
of crucial importance for uncovering the "diverse attempts to
authenticate the divine stature or power of a charismatic
figure . . . and the criteria which were used to evaluate such
claims."[87]

## Description and Method of the Study

In order to uncover those criteria, I will concentrate on
the classifications implicit in a group of religious texts from
the second through fourth centuries. Each treats a religious
leader who founded a movement or cult and who tried to claim the
allegiance of significant numbers of people as patrons or followers. The authors consider the religious leaders less with
the passion of initial personal encounter than with the detached reflection of those whose decision has long since been

made.  The implicit and often fragmentary taxonomies which the
texts reveal were composed and wielded for specific purposes.
Each leader was tried and found either acceptable or wanting
not as an abstract enterprise but because the allegiance of great
numbers of people was tied to the assessment of his character.
The classifications were developed for explicitly polemical purposes; they were formed as a result of the interplay of propaganda and apologetics.  They were intended to provide not only
guidelines for the evaluation of certain figures, but also for
actions taken on the basis of that evaluation.  By concentrating
on biographical literature scholars have missed much of the
give-and-take which characterizes Hellenistic thought about divine men.  Propagandistic biographies were only links in a complex chain which included apologetic responses to propaganda as
well as more detached attempts at evaluation.

Provided the polemical context of the texts in question is
recognized, current anthropological literature about native
systems of classification can still aid the student of the divine man by suggesting certain questions and modes of procedure.
Certainly, the divine man appeared to his Hellenistic contemporaries as an extraordinary individual.  Perhaps as much as the
pangolin among the Lele and the cassowary among the Karam, which
have exercised the imagination of M. Douglas and R. Bulmer, respectively, in their studies of "primitive" systems of classification,[88] the divine man provoked an identification crisis.
Bulmer was led to ask "Why the Cassowary is not a Bird" among
the Karam; it can also be asked "Why the Divine Man is not a
Man" for his Hellenistic contemporaries.  In each case the
question provides a point of entry into native systems of classification, the presuppositions on which they are based, and
the ways in which they contribute to the construction of a meaningful world.

Where might the native categories and principles of clas-
sification which bore upon would-be religious leaders in the
Hellenistic world be found?  Freed from questions of genre, the
"lives" of various figures such as Apollonius of Tyana, Jesus of
Nazareth, and Alexander of Abonuteichos remain important sources.
Regardless of genre, to the extent that they are purposefully

presenting a specific image of their subjects they can be desig-
nated as missionary in intent.  Typically the lives argue for
a particular understanding, or range of possible understandings,
of their subjects, be it θεῖος ἀνήρ, intimate of the god(s),
philosopher, sage, examplar of moral virtues, or conversely,
charlatan, magician, deceiver, fiend, or demoniac.  Whatever the
details of the portrait, it is presented to the audience as
*the* correct point of view.

Furthermore, that general characterization indicates that
such works are not all that distant from the enterprise of classification itself.  That leads to

Proposition 1:  TO THE EXTENT THAT THEY ARGUE FOR
A PARTICULAR PERCEPTION OF THEIR SUBJECTS, THE
HELLENISTIC "LIVES" ARE INVOLVED IN CLASSIFYING
THEIR SUBJECTS ACCORDING TO IMPLICIT CRITERIA.

Those criteria are, simply, the reasons adduced for the prefer-
ence of one point of view over any others.  If the lives contain
statements along the lines of "X should be considered Y," in
which X designates the subject and Y the quality, the implicit
principles of classification are to be found in the latter part
of the basic statement:  "because Z," Z designating the rea-
son(s) *why* "X should be considered Y."

In such a case the outlines of a *system* of classification
are only faintly present; they are *implicit*.  But if such a
system presumes that there be classes, entities which are to be
assigned to those classes, and principles by which that assignment can be undertaken, and if statements along the lines of
"X should be considered Y because Z" are to be found in the
lives, then they can be treated as exercises in classification,
albeit partial and polemical.  Thus, the sources out of which
Bieler developed his ideal type of the divine man and into which
others retrojected their misconstructions of the notion of the
ideal type can also be of use to those who would seek the outlines of indigenous attempts at sorting out the "mob" of divine
men into discrete classes.

Thus, a reorientation of the research into divine men promises to identify and demonstrate new uses for familiar sources.
It can also bring new or under-utilized sources more fully into
the discussion.  As noted above, it is the *argumentative*

character of the lives which suggests that they may contain implicit systems of classification.  It is the "because" of the
statement "X should be considered Y because Z" that is crucial
in this respect:  it converts or attempts to convert the force
of "should" to "must."  But frequently, as arguments strive to
be convincing, they confront alternative categories and principles of assignment.

An example:  "X should be considered *wise* (a class designation) because $Z_1$ . . . $Z_n$ (a series of stories which demonstrate
the wisdom of X in action)."  That is the skeletal structure of
the propagandistic life: a series of anecdotes arranged to
prove a point about the subject.  The principles of classification employed is that repeated demonstration of wisdom in discrete incidents warrants the conclusion that X should indeed be
considered wise.  But that hypothetical case presents only a
single category and a single principle of classification, and
it minimizes the difficulty involved in determining which events
or actions can be seen to demonstrate wisdom.  The introduction
of alternative categories would take this form:  "if $Z_1$ . . . $Z_n$
demonstrate Y (wisdom), not Q (another class designation, ignorance, e.g.), then X should be considered Y, not Q."  As that
shows, the introduction of even a single alternative complicates
the proceedings and highlights the argumentative nature of the
text.  It demands that the connection between certain actions
and wisdom (or ignorance) be specified; it demands reasons and
those reasons reveal implicit principles of classification.
"Y not Q" is the basic structure of the apology.  The fact that
it is not the performance of certain acts ($Z_1$ . . . $Z_n$), but the
evaluation of them ($Z_1$ . . . $Z_n$ do or do not demonstrate Y),
which is at stake is crucial in the understanding of the subject (X).  The introduction of alternative categories makes both
the categories themselves and the principle of assignment more
explicit.  That leads to

> Proposition 2:  SITUATIONS OF CONTROVERSY WILL
> ELICIT THE CLEAREST EXPRESSIONS OF THE PRINCIPLES
> OF CLASSIFICATION PRESUMED BY THE STATEMENT "X
> SHOULD BE CONSIDERED Y."

It follows that controversial texts can be used to supplement the evidence of biographical texts for systems of

classification of claimants to divine status.  They differ from
biographies in the extent to which the consideration of alternative categories is explicitly undertaken.  That indicates that
a range of alternative categories (class designations) and principles of assignment (Y because . . .; Q becuase . . .; not
Q but Y because . . .;) will be more clearly apprehended.  If
that is so, it should turn out that controversial texts will become a primary source for native systems of classification of
the divine man, and that they can help clarify the less explicit
attempts at pigeon-holing present in biographical and historical
texts.  Greater attention to controversial texts would reorient
the study of the divine man in the Hellenistic world.

If the outlines and fragments of systems of classification
can be uncovered, and if some of their categories and principles
of assignment can be described, it should be possible to detail
not only the native perceptions of the divine man but also the
view of the larger world which those perceptions fit, and possibly even the social reality which shaped them.  The setting
of the divine man in the context of missionary activity and the
intellectual give-and-take which characterized it, though it
presumed certain social relationships, was actually more ideological in its orientation.  Social reality took a back seat to the
implications of certain ideological stances.  Outside of some
scattered attempts,[89] few have sought to locate that ideology
within a distinctive social matrix.  Anthropological approaches
to native classificatory systems can lead that question to be
posed anew, but they cannot provide the answers.

One interesting, though limited, answer has been set forth
by P. Brown in his article on "The Rise and Function of the
Holy Man in Late Antiquity."  He contends that the often spec-
tacular thaumaturgical performances of late Roman holy men have
distracted attention from the more mundane foundations of their
remarkable power and social prestige:

> It was through the hard business of living his
> life for twenty-four hours in the day, through
> catering for the day-to-day needs of his local-
> ity, through allowing his person to be charged
> with the normal hopes and fears of his fellow
> men, that the holy man gained the power in
> society that enabled him to carry off the

occasional *coup de théâtre*. Dramatic interven-
tions of holy men in the high politics of the
Empire were long remembered. But they illus-
trate the prestige that the holy men had already
gained, they do not explain it. They were rather
like the cashing of a big cheque on a reputation;
and, like all forms of power in Late Roman society,
this reputation was built up by hard, unobtrusive
(and so, for us, partly obscure) work among those
who need constant and unspectacular ministrations.[90]

Brown then claims that those constant and unspectacular ministrations were modelled on the relations between a rural patron and
his clientele. He sees patronage as a fact of late Roman life
and, relying on Libanius, presents the career of the typical
patron in some detail. The *patronus* was a man who could exercise power on the spot: "villagers needed a hinge-man, a man
who belonged to the outside world and yet could place his
δύναμις, his know-how and (let us not forget) his culture and
values at the disposal of the villagers."[91] In a similar fashion, the successful holy man appears in the sources as a power-
wielding outsider; his location outside and (sometimes literally)
above the village situation enabled him to exert a considerable
influence on local affairs of all sorts.

Brown would distinguish the late Roman holy man from the
earlier Hellenistic θεῖοι ἄνδρες, who, in his estimation, found
their source of power through occult wisdom which was located
within society,[92] but other recent work can be used to question
the basis of that distinction. D. Georgi, for example, in a
brief and allusive article identifies the *polis* as the world
from which sprang the concept of the divine man.[93] Though he
treats no single case in detail, Georgi asserts that the socioeconomic make-up of the polis demanded the intervention of outside benefactors for continuing survival, particularly during
times of stress. Those who did intervene to the benefit of the
populace were rewarded with various types of divine honors.
There is ample evidence from inscriptions and literary texts
alike that kings and wealthy benefactors received statues, cultic observances, and games in their honor for having alleviated
shortages in time of famine, for having provided buildings,
medical care, education, and other services for needy cities.[94]
Approaching the question from the other side, W. Burkert has

traced the pejorative use of γόης to the fear and mistrust of
the polis-dweller for the outsider, the individual, the person
who was out of step with the general populace.[95] Γόης,
εὐεργέτης, and other terms which were used to describe civic
benefactors and malefactors, and the typical pattern of social
relations between benefactors and recipients can be found several
hundred years earlier than Brown's analysis suggests. That
indicates that the social reality which shapes the conception
and activity of the late Roman holy man may also have influenced
the earlier Hellenistic θεῖοι ἄνδρες. If it has, it can be expected to have left its mark on the categories which were developed, and displayed in the literature, for the understanding
of such figures. That it has will be demonstrated in a later
portion of this study.

This particular investigation will center on Origen's *Contra
Celsum*, specifically on the argument between Celsus and Origen
about the life and character of Jesus of Nazareth, which occupies
most of books I and II. Since it is a controversial text, considerations of method (cf. Proposition 2) lead to the suspicion
that the criteria, categories, and principles of classification
which undergird the argument about Jesus will be particularly
accessible. The text should provide material out of which at
least one model of a system of classifying would-be divine men
can be constructed. (Two--if the adversaries presume different
systems.) *Contra Celsum* is well-suited to this method because,
unlike many other controversial or apologetic texts, it preserves ample evidence of both viewpoints.[96]

The text presents the fullest consideration of the divine
man, up to its time, in the Christian tradition. Justin's treatment of Jesus vis-a-vis other purported divinities is fragmentary and one-sided; Tertullian's is scarcely as full. That
*Contra Celsum*'s treatment of the question is also influential
for later Christian tradition (as is Celsus' for later anti-
Christian tradition) is indicated by Eusebius' explicit quotation and thorough-going reliance on it in his *Against Hierocles*.
Thus, the focus on *Contra Celsum*, and the texts directly related
to it, will illuminate the ways in which divine men were understood throughout the first three centuries of this era. There

is no argument or strategy in contemporary texts which is not
displayed at least as fully and clearly in *Contra Celsum*.

In the following chapters I will attempt to uncover the
full range of categories and principles of classification used
by both Celsus and Origen in their discussion of Jesus and other
would-be divine men.  By seeking similar materials in a series
of closely related texts, I will try to discern whether such
categories and principles were idiosyncratic or whether they
were set in a widespread view of the world and of human activity
within it.  Finally, I will ask whether those categories,
principles, and world-views of which they were part had any
basis in contemporary social reality.  I will attempt to show
that there were indeed certain distinctively Hellenistic ways
of looking at claimants to divine status and that a full appreciation of them can inform both typological and comparative
studies in the future.

CHAPTER II

CELSUS AND ORIGEN ON DIVINE MEN, I

*Introduction*

Due partially to the influence of the aretalogy hypothesis, the evidence about divine men in CC has not provoked extensive scholarly discussion. Reitzenstein, Wetter, and Windisch did call attention to the information preserved by Celsus (CC VII. 9, esp.) about second-century prophets who used the *ego eimi* formula to announce their own divinity.[1] Duly noted were the possible parallels to the language of the gospel according to John. Similarly, several researchers noted the importance of the topic of magic for both Celsus and Origen.[2] In both cases, the evidence provided by the adversaries is treated as a disparate group of unrelated scraps; its role in the argument of either is rarely considered. CC is seen more as a rich mine of second and third century beliefs than as an integral work in itself.

A few scholars did discuss the function of comments on divine men and related topics in CC. In *Celsus und Origenes: das Gemeinsame ihrer Weltanschauung* A. Miura-Stange devotes over 35 pages to Celsus' attack on Jesus, which she identifies as "der Kernpunkt und das Leitmotiv" of his treatise.[3] In keeping with her primary orientation, she finds that Celsus and Origen adopt remarkably similar attitudes to the material. They work from the same sources and encounter the same problems in them.[4] Both vacillate between criticism and approval of any given subject, as, for example, with their evaluations of wonder-working activity. That accords with Miura-Stange's general observation that "what is yes today can be no tomorrow, when it furthers the polemic."[5] But, despite his bits of clever sophistry, Miura-Stange finds Origen's defense to be the weakest link in the whole apology. To support her case she adduces a series of his gratuitous interpolations and outright evasions of Celsus' charges. Nor does she find Origen's appeal to the lives of Greek heroes or philosophers to be particularly effective,

especially since he will freely disparage the same evidence when
it suits his purpose.[6]  Ultimately, she traces those weaknesses
to the fact that Celsus and Origen share the same idea of what
a god or son of a god should look like; they even agree closely
on their perception of Jesus.[7]  The similarity of world-view
makes effective apologetics difficult.

Miura-Stange's concern for the similarities between Celsus
and Origen and her subscription to a rather vague and undif-
ferentiated image of the "divine man" hinder her appreciation of
the complexity of the attempts by Celsus and Origen to sort out
the various aspirants to divine status and lead her to minimize
differences in their approaches.  She contends that both Celsus
and Origen subscribed to the same Hellenistic conception of god
or the son of a god.[8]  But Celsus, for example, seems clearly to
have located *his* candidates for divine status in the distant
past, in direct opposition to Origen's espousal of the candidacy
of Jesus.[9]  Thus Celsus and Origen differed at least on the possibility of one of their near contemporaries being a god or son
of a god.  Even if Origen held conceptions of divine men similar
to those of Celsus, that did not preclude his *attempt* to distinguish his own position from that of his opponent.  The outlines
of that attempt and the principles on which it was based can be
made clearer.  Miura-Stange's description of the common Hellenistic conception of the son of god is neither precise enough nor
sufficiently rooted in textual evidence to bear the full weight
of her argument.

When she addresses the topic of divine men, Miura-Stange
falls prey to several familiar problems.  For example, her attempt to distinguish Celsus' and Origen's treatment of divine
men from that of "das Volk" collapses into caricature when she
over-emphasizes both the philosophical approach of Celsus and
Origen and the crude taste for miracles of the masses.[10]  She
makes no further attempt at typology other than that distinction
between philosophical and popular perceptions of divine men.
But that typology itself rests more on generalities than on
analysis of specific texts beyond CC.  Miura-Stange has established the importance of the argument about magic in CC, but
she has not provided a convincing interpretation of its

significance.  Though Beiler allotted less than 4 pages to CC
in the second volume of his ΘΕΙΟΣ ANHP, he also finds that both
Celsus and Origen held the same image of the divine man.  He
details the consequences of that agreement:

> Neither denies the possibility that such men walked
> on the earth:  it is only a question of who was a
> θεῖος and who was a μάγος.  The thought almost
> drags itself out of the reader that the accusation
> of magic against Jesus must have cropped up
> throughout the whole work of Celsus.  Against
> that charge Origen seeks to demonstrate not
> only that the accusation of magic against
> Jesus is unfounded but that the men who Celsus
> introduces as θεῖοι in truth are not.  In
> reality only the Jewish and the true *homines*
> *religiosi*, whose prototype is the θεός become
> man Jesus Christ, deserve the name.[11]

Taken together, the comments of Miura-Stange and Bieler suggest
that accusations that Jesus and others practiced magic may provide a key to the debate between Celsus and Origen.  But to appreciate fully the implications of their positions, it must be
established how, why, and to what extent magic became an important issue for Celsus and Origen.

Although the topic of magic frequently enters the discussion in CC, it is not always met as an *issue* which divides Celsus and Origen.  With few exceptions, Celsus mentions magic in
order to cast suspicion or ridicule on Christians or the founder
of their sect; in his *Alethes Logos* magic usually functions as
the basis for, or the substance of, an accusation.  Not all of
Celsus' charges, however, provoked arguments.  In several instances Origen sidestepped the issue or countered Celsus' accusation with a different one of his own.  For example, Celsus offered his account of the doctrine of the Ophites (in VI.24ff.) so
that the reader of his treatise could compare a mystery of the
Christians with the Mithraic mysteries.  From the outset, however, Origen denies that there is any relationship whatsoever
between the Ophites and the Christians.  He finds the diagram of
their doctrines which Celsus reproduced to be completely unconvincing and he asserts that, despite diligent researches, he has
been unable to find anyone who professed belief in the teachings
of the diagram (VI.24).  Since Origen feels that he has

completely dissociated the Christians from the Ophites, the
magical content of their doctrines does not threaten his position.  Origen does display a detached scholarly interest in the
Ophite formulas--he subjects the names of their archontic demons
to source criticism and concludes that they took some from
magic and some from the Bible, but he says that they muddled
everything together without clear understanding of either
source (VI.32).  Magic does not become an issue there because
Origen consistently denies the relevance of Celsus' remarks to
the Christian religion as he knows it.

Similarly, Celsus' assertion that snakes and eagles are
wiser than men in matters of sorcery (IV.86ff.) elicits from
Origen interesting observations on the use of fennel by snakes
to improve their vision and on the difference between the acquisition of antidotes by nature among certain animals and by
reason, experience, and inference among humans.  Though Origen
does not agree that snakes and eagles are wiser, he rests content with offering a few supplementary observations by way of
clarification.  Curiously, Origen quotes the biblical passage
(Prov. 24:59-63) which he would use were he to join issue with
Celsus and even gives a brief allegorical interpretation of it,
but he does not pursue the matter very far.

In those two instances magic is encountered much less as
an *issue* between Celsus and Origen than as an occasion for each
to demonstrate a range of arcane knowledge and superior erudi-
tion in a series of learned footnotes.  Although interesting
details come to light in the process, none of them seems to have
struck a sensitive nerve.

Origen's attitude towards magical beliefs and practices
was decidedly ambivalent.  At one point (VI.80) he notes that
magic, whose origin and name he traces to the Magi, has spread
to other races to the destruction and ruin of those who use it.
But he claims elsewhere that "so-called magic" is not, as the
followers of Epicurus and Aristotle think, utterly incoherent,
but rather a consistent system whose principles are known only
to a very few (I.24).  When he mentions that system, Origen has
in mind primarily a theory of the inherent power of certain
divine names when they are pronounced in their original languages

and in a sequence "which is natural to them."[12]  He argues "that
it is not the significance of the things which the works describe
that has a certain power to do this or that, but it is the
qualities and characteristics of the sounds" (I.25). Although
Sabaoth, Adonai, and the "name of our Jesus" figure prominently
in Origen's philosophy of the "mysterious significance of names,"
he also admits the effectiveness of certain divine names among
the Egyptians and Persians (I.24). Unfortunately, Origen's account of this "divine science (θεολογία)" of names is truncated.
It was prompted by Celsus' contention that it makes no difference
what one calls the supreme god, and when Origen is satisfied that
it does indeed make a difference, he drops the subject, even
though "much more could be said." But Origen's digression on
the power of names indicates that he was inclined to take at
least some aspects of "magic" very seriously, so long as he could
construct a "philosophical" underpinning for them.

Celsus reveals a similar ambivalence in his own attitude.
He contends, on the basis of the testimony of a certain Egyptian
musician named Dionysius (VI.41) that magic is only effective
with uneducated people and with those of depraved moral character,
while those who have studied philosophy are impervious to its
power since they are careful to lead a healthy life. Celsus'
opinion that magic succeeds only among the immoral and uneducated
may provide a clue as to why Origen was anxious to incorporate
his views on the efficacy of magical names, charms, and spells
into a philosophy which guaranteed their mysterious significance.
By so doing, Origen could clearly separate himself from the immoral and uneducated while retaining a belief in and purchase
on the power of "so-called magic." There again, the great influence of beliefs about magic in the drawing of social and
ideological boundaries becomes evident. Celsus betrays a similar
concern when he offers that certain names and formulas lose power
when they are translated (VIII.37), but it is not clear from the
preserved fragments whether he supported that observation with
the same type of philosophical arguments used by Origen.

Both men had good reasons for their ambivalence. For Origen
magic was explicitly associated with "ruin and destruction of
those who use it" and for Celsus it bore the stigma of illiteracy

and immorality.  Belief in, or practice of "garden variety" magic
tended to provoke doubts about one's character and abilities.
To put it simply, common magicians could not be philosophers.
And, as their comments on magic alone suggest, both Celsus and
Origen prized philosophical ideals.  But since they both acknowledged the power of magic to be very real and very attractive,[13]
it became their task to design an explanation of their appropriation and use of magical beliefs which would preserve their social,
moral, and intellectual status.  Origen, at least, found such an
explanation in his philosophy of names.

The ways in which magic could become an *issue*, rather than
a matter of detached interest, are now clear.  To accuse someone of an unphilosophical use of magic was to impugn simultaneously one's morals and education.  As Celsus relates, belief
in magic could cast doubt on one's entire way of life, whereas
the pursuit of a philosophical mode of life could render one
relatively immune to suspicions of magic--except from other as-
piring philosophers.[14]  In Late Antiquity suspicions and accusations of immorality, illiteracy, and magical activity tended to
cluster together.  The connection worked both ways.  The common
magician was open to those other charges, while his philosophical
counterpart tried to evade their taint.  That Apuleius' apparently
untoward success at love led to the charge that he had won his
lady's hand by magic shows how suspicions of immorality and
magical activity can dovetail.[15]  So by associating the need and
taste for wonder-working solely with "das Volk" Miura-Stange
missed the polemical edge of the ancient authors' statements.
She reports as fact exactly what those who wielded accusations
of magic would have had her believe.

The approach of the French sociological school can do much
to illuminate the attitudes of Celsus and Origen to "magic."
Both are concerned less with specifics than with the systems
into which they fit; as Origen's brief excursus on the mysterious
significance of magical names indicates, it is a particular understanding of those names that renders them either suspect or
harmless.  Hubert's contention that magic in the Roman empire
was perceived as something done by strangers or outsiders, by
*someone else*, is borne out in the remarks of both Celsus and

Origen.  Both demonstrate the accuracy of Mauss' claim that
"magicians possess magical power not through their individual
peculiarities but as a consequence of society's attitude towards them and their kind."[16]  From one point of view whoever
utters magical names is a sorcerer, from another, he is a philosopher participating in a mysterious divine science.  While in
his own eyes the magician's marginal social status may be a
primary source of his power, in the eyes of society at large it
makes him fearful, threatening, and suspicious.  On the other
hand, those who are fearful, threatening, or suspicious are very
susceptible to the accusation that they are magicians.  Celsus
found Jesus and the Christians threatening and suspicious; he
suspected them of practicing magic.  Thus, the accusation that
someone believed in or practiced magic was scarcely the result
of a dispassionate weighing of objective evidence.  Because of
the dominant perception of the magicians, such accusations were
most often the vehicles for social, moral, and intellectual
invective.  Terms like *magia* and γοητεία were used to create,
strengthen, and reassert, social, moral, and intellectual
boundaries, such as those between in- and out-groups, higher and
lower social classes, and true practitioners and charlatans.
Celsus uses similar language to try to separate the magicians
(Jesus and the Christians) from the philosophers (himself and
those he favors).  Origen responds in a similar fashion.

     Magic becomes an issue in CC when Origen responds to Celsus'
attempts to consign Jesus and the Christian religion to inferior
social, moral, and intellectual status.  Origen did not always
accept the challenge, as his remarks on the doctrines of the
Ophites demonstrate.  But it was repeated so frequently that he
could not avoid it totally, particularly if he were to fulfill
his pledge to leave none of Celsus' objections unexamined and
to answer each in detail (cf. CC, II.20).

     That magic is an *important* issue for Origen is suggested
by his comments at the beginning of book I.  Although there is
some question about the place of the fragments preserved in
the first 27 chapters of that book in the original *Alethes
Logos*,[17] it is sufficient here to recognize that they introduce
all of his major themes, as Origen intended (pref. 6).  It

is interesting, then, that Origen takes serious issue with few
of Celsus' points.

In chapter 1 Celsus contends that the Christian groups
constitute illegal secret societies.  Origen concedes that
point but submits that "it is not wrong to form associations
against the laws for the sake of truth."  Similarly, Origen
concedes the barbarian origin of the Christian message in chapter 2 and even praises his antagonist for not criticizing the
gospel solely on those grounds.  In chapter 3 Origen agrees
with Celsus that the Christians risk dangers equal to those
risked on account of philosophy by Socrates.  In the next two
chapters he agrees that there is little new in the Christian
ethical teaching.  It is curious that an ostensibly apologetic
work should open with such an irenic series of major concessions.
Within five chapters of the first book Origen has admitted that
Christianity is treasonous, barbarian in its origin, possibly
foolhardy in its courting of danger, and certainly not novel
in its ethical teaching.

Chapter 6 presents a sharp contrast.  Origen begins by asserting that Celsus is "impelled by some unknown power" to
charge that the "Christians get the power which they seem to
possess by pronouncing the names of certain demons and incantations" (I.6).  As far as Origen is concerned, that charge bla-
tantly misrepresents the gospel.  He contends that Christians
perform exorcisms only by the name of Jesus with the recital
of the histories about him, not by any incantations.  Origen is
adamant in his denial that Jesus performed his own miracles by
magic, as Celsus charged.  Although this passage raises several
interesting questions, it is important here to notice that it
is the charge of magic, not that of treason, secrecy, or any
other in the opening chapters of book I that Origen picks to
refute.  He makes no effort to accomodate Celsus' viewpoint and
he insists on the total separation of Christianity from magic.
Indeed, his charge that Celsus stands under some unknown compulsion, which he elsewhere repeats and amplifies to indicate that
Celsus is beset by demons (VIII.63), reverses the direction of
the charge of magic.  It is clear from I.6 that Origen could be
deeply disturbed by the accusation that Christians practiced
magic.

The decision by Origen to join the issue in 1.6 over the accusation of magic should not be over-emphasized; he may have felt himself in a superior position and attempted to press the advantage. Nevertheless, his choice does set the accusation at center stage; it appears as the leading edge of a cluster of related charges. The association between secrecy (I.1) and suspicions of magic is frequently encountered in Late Antiquity, as is the link between outsiders (I.2) and the same suspicions. According to Celsus (I.3), secret practices entailed risks, one of which was the assumption that what went on in secret was magic. That the argument in I.6 centers on accusations of magic does not mean that it is narrow and one-sided; the social and ideological freight borne by such charges indicates their broad area of influence. Accusations of magic constitute the explicit issue, but they carry with them many implicit undertones. They resonate with many of the individual themes that are at issue between Celsus and Origen.

Although some discussion of magic and related topics is spread throughout the eight books of CC, magic is wielded most powerfully as an accusation in the first two books. Mention of it occurs explicitly in over one-fourth of their 150 chapters, particularly in the charges brought against Jesus and his partisans by the Jewish interlocutor introduced by Celsus in I.28. The speech of the Jew and Origen's response occupy the rest of book I and all of book II. In that discourse Celsus intends to undermine the claims of the Christian religion by discrediting its central figure. He gives no explicit indication, however, why he thought that the Jewish interlocutor would serve his intentions.[18] Despite Origen's indications that the Jew addressed part of his speech to Jesus and part to Jesus' followers, his speech concentrates on the major events of the life of Jesus, reversing the value or questioning the truth of most of them.

In that situation Bieler's observation that the entire treatise of Celsus is animated by the accusation that Jesus practiced magic proves fruitful; it helps focus Miura-Stange's view that the attack on Jesus was the leitmotif of Celsus' treatise. The discourse of the Jew is designed to answer the question of who is a θεός and who is a μάγος. If he can

establish that Jesus was not divine, but rather a magician, the
claims for the Christian religion would be considerably weakened
by the disgrace of its founder.  Through a detailed examination
of the life of Jesus, Celsus attempts to show that he was only
a man (the concluding statement of the second book which summarizes its argument), and a wicked sorcerer at that (the concluding statement of book I).[19]

The basic assumptions of divine man research which were
discussed in the previous chapter prove inadequate for the investigation of CC.  Precisely because they differ, it is premature to decide beforehand that there was a "Hellenistic concept of the divine man" to which both Celsus and Origen could
subscribe.  Though they agree that their argument must depend
on the information available from biographical sources such as
the gospel according to Matthew, their own observations and
conclusions are not set forth in a biographical form.  Open
controversy allows them to state their views more clearly and
forcefully.  Nor is the presumed link between biography and propaganda useful.  Celsus and Origen move almost imperceptibly
from one mode of presentation to the other, sometimes arguing
for one proposition and against another in the same breath.  In
several instances, Origen couches his apologetic response to
the charges of Celsus in terms of a propagandistic appeal.  Although the arguments do focus on claimants to divinity, they do
not take the biographical form which contemporary divine man
studies would cause one to suspect.[20]

Investigation of accusations of magic can prove helpful
because the elucidation of their social and ideological implications has already been undertaken.  But while that focus provides an initial indication of the depth and dimensions of the
argument, in itself it cannot account for either its details or
variety.  Celsus' charges suggest that he worked within a certain
framework, familiar from the Hellenistic "lives" of which some
also served as his sources.  Origen accepted that framework and
made it the basis of his reply.  Within it each advanced his
own criteria, principles of classification, and specific categories in an attempt to assess various claimants to divinity.
Accusations of magic serve as guides to the skeletal arrangements
of that debate, but they do not put flesh on its bones.

The discourse of the Jew covers several incidents in the
life of Jesus, but it concentrates on his birth and early life
in book I, specifically the birth and the flight to Egypt (cf.
I.28-39; 58-61; 66-68). Book I also treats the opening of
Jesus' public career, specifically his baptism by John (I.40-48)
and the gathering of the disciples (I.62-65). The second book
also deals with the public career, but it devotes most of its
space to the arrest, condemnation, and execution of Jesus. The
two books form a unit, loosely arranged as a chronological account of the career of Jesus. But that unity seems more the
result of the inherent logic of chronology, than of reliance on
a single biographical source. In the first book, the Jew appears
to follow the gospel according to Matthew, although Origen reproaches him in I.34 for quoting selectively from that text, and
conjectures in I.40 that he took the story of the appearance of
the dove at Jesus' baptism from other sources as well. It is
difficult to establish firmly whether Celsus was following canonical Matthew or parallel traditions. In a similar vein,
M. Lods has proposed that Celsus used a written Jewish source
which hostilely portrayed the life of Jesus from his birth to
his baptism.[21] But the melange of evidence which he drew upon
(Justin's *Dialogue with Trypho*, the *Acts of Pilate* rabbinic
texts, etc.) can not be used to certify the existence of an
earlier single written source.[22] Nor does Lods account for the
mixture of Greek and Jewish sources in the polemic of the Jew.
Book II provides even less indication that Celsus relied on a
single source. A clearer picture of Celsus' sources might contribute to a better understanding of his intentions and procedure, but none has yet been proposed. Similarly, the now lost
opening chapters of Origen's *Commentary on Matthew* would have
made an instructive comparison of his treatment of the same
events in two different contexts possible. But neither sources
nor writings from Celsus and Origen will do much to clarify the
particular positions which they adopt in CC on the questions of
whether Jesus or any other aspirants could rightfully claim
divinity. Nor does the generally less imaginative use of their
material in later works shed much light on CC. The text itself
is the fundamental source for the nature and purpose of each

man's view on divine men.  It constitutes the most accessible
and clearly defined field for testing the theoretical propositions of my previous chapter.

In what follows I will adopt a loose division of the relevant material into three primary segments:  the birth and youth
of Jesus, his public career, and his final demise and its consequences.  That division merely facilitates the presentation of
the material in manageable sections; it is not an inherent primary characteristic of the material, nor does it presume any
strong links between divine men and biographical literature.  It
assumes merely that arguments that claims to a particular
quality or status were valid appealed to certain incidents in the
claimant's life as evidentiary.  Nor does the division restrict
the enquiry to the arguments about Jesus, since the comparative
method favored by both Celsus and Origen assures an abundance
of parallels in each phase of the argument.  Questions or assertions about one candidate for divine status were usually made
in contrast to assertions made against or on behalf of others.
Comparison is a fundamental strategy of controversy.  That ensures that the criteria, principles of assignment, and categories
are not limited to one or a few special cases.  Both Celsus and
Origen strive to construct widely relevant guidelines for evaluation; that each set would exclude certain candidates' claims
indicates their polemical intent rather than their inherent nar-
rowness.

Detailed investigation of a series of passages can yield
fragments of the systems of classification of would-be divine
men on which the arguments of Celsus and Origen depend.  Neither
spells out in detail such a system, but its outlines can be found
in their own comments.  As far as that investigation yields a
set of principles of assignment ("because" statements), it can
elicit a particular view of the world and of meaningful activity
within it which informed the attempts at classification.  That in
turn will provoke further questions about the historical and
social contexts of the debate over divine men in CC.

Though Celsus' and Origen's comments about the figures themselves are of primary importance, it will be necessary to take
into account their own procedures.  Since they find their

material in story form, they evaluate not only the subjects, but
also the stories and those that told them.  Comments on all
three types of evidence will be in order.

*Birth and Youth:*

A. Birth

The opening shot fired by Celsus' Jew in I.28 provides a
prime example of the style and substance of his argument:

> . . . he [Jesus] fabricated the story of his
> birth from a virgin; . . . he came from a Jewish
> village and from a poor country woman who earned
> her living by spinning . . . she was driven out
> by her husband, who was a carpenter by trade,
> as she was convicted of adultery . . . after she
> had been driven out by her husband and while she
> was wandering about in a disgraceful way she
> secretly gave birth to Jesus . . . because he
> was poor he hired himself out as a workman in
> Egypt, and there tried his hand at certain
> magical powers on which the Egyptians pride
> themselves; he returned full of conceit because
> of these powers, and on account of them gave
> himself the title of God.  (I.28)

In effect, the Jew offers an etiology of Jesus' claim to divinity.  The narrative betrays several points of contact with the
opening chapters of the gospel according to Matthew, but it
hardly concurs with the view of Jesus set forth there.[23]  It
owes a significant debt, it would seem, to Jewish polemic against
Jesus[24] but efforts to demonstrate dependence on a specific text
or texts have not been convincing.  The accuracy of Origen's
quotation of Celsus has not been questioned.

Since the charges grouped together in I.28 elicit a sustained reply from Origen, they merit close scrutiny in themselves.  They function on several levels.  Celsus impugns the
social and economic status of both Jesus and his mother:  they
are poor, common hand-workers and laborers.[25]  Moreover, they
are not *polis*-dwellers; they come from a Jewish village in the
country.  Andresen captures the sting of that portrait:  "What
else can result, when such circles busy themselves with the
highest questions of the knowledge of god?  Nothing other than
philistinism."[26]  Celsus carries over his mean estimate of the
social origins of Jesus and his immediate family to his portrait

of the disciples as characters of similarly marginal and inferior
social status.  For Andresen that tendency to understand the
theology of his opponents as the reflex of their social relations is typical of Celsus.[27]  It forms the first move of the
Jew's opening gambit.

As a corollary of that social inferiority, Celsus stresses
the moral turpitude of the mother of Jesus.  She was an adulter-
ess; he was a bastard.  As their place of origin set them outside
the cultural centers of the network of imperial cities and their
poverty set them at the bottom of the economic ladder, so their
conduct set them outside of the accepted framework of personal
and social relations.  As country folks, as poor people, and as
an adultress and her bastard offspring, Mary and Jesus are portrayed as outsiders *par excellence*.  That status is reinforced
by having them retire to geographically remote Egypt.  It is
further compounded by social invisibility when Mary gives birth
to Jesus in secret.  The stage is being set, quite carefully,
for the accusation that Jesus practiced magic.  Nock's observation that what got the name of *magia* in the Roman empire "was
a varied complex of things, mainly *qua* professional, or *qua*
criminal in intent or *qua* alien,"[28] is apposite here.  Jesus
and his mother are quintessential aliens for Celsus; they are
at the bottom or near the edges of every important social structure of their contemporary world.  The implicit connection between Jesus' tenure as a workman in Egypt and his magical powers
also conveys a faint hint of professional magical activity.
Coming as it does on the heels of a series of charges, the im-
putation of magical activity to Jesus is not surprising; it is
the logical consequence of his multidimensional outsiderhood.
Each specific accusation gains force and credibility in association with the others.  It is their cumulative impact that explains
for Celsus and his Jew, Jesus' wholly unwarranted claim to the
title of God.

In his response, Origen accepts everything but that conclusion.  He concedes the unfavorable circumstances of Jesus'
early life, but asserts that there was nothing particularly
unsavory about them and contends that his success is all the more
to be appreciated in light of the obstacles that he had to

overcome. He appeals to an alternative conception of the life
of a claimant to divine status, and carefully details his reasons for so doing. He begins with a concession:

> Among men of noble birth, honourable and dis-
> tinguished parents, an upbringing at the
> hands of wealthy people who are able to
> spend money on the education of their son,
> and a great and famous native country, are
> things which help to make a man famous and
> distinguished and get his name well known.
> (I.29)

Origen is well aware that Jesus did not take the traditional
route to fame and glory,[29] but he asks whether one who has overcome many and varied hindrances should be denied the fame which
he has achieved, albeit by unconventional means. Origen even
heightens the contrast by admitting that Jesus had no formal education in rhetoric by which he could have learned to become a
persuasive and crowd-pleasing speaker. Social qualifications
and personal abilities are methodically stripped away from Jesus
by both Celsus and Origen. In the end nothing remains for Celsus
but a conceited magician, but for Origen the enormously powerful
message of Jesus, "such noble utterances about the judgement
of God, about the punishments for wickedness, and rewards for
goodness, that not only rustic and illiterate people were converted by his words, but also a considerable number of the more
intelligent" (I.29), remains as well. Origen challenges the
traditional notion that money, class, education, and background
alone warrant claims to great honors. In their stead he advances
a simple criterion: the content and effectiveness of a messenger
and his message.

Origen outlines, in different words, what P. Brown describes
as a conflict between *articulate* and *inarticulate* power:

> On the one hand, there is *articulate* power, power
> defined and agreed upon by everyone (and especially
> by its holders!): authority vested in precise per-
> sons; admiration and success gained by recognized
> channels. Running counter to this there may be
> other forms of influence less easy to pin down--
> *inarticulate* power; the disturbing intangibles of
> social life; the imponderable advantages of certain
> groups; personal skills that succeed in a way that
> is unacceptable or difficult to understand. Where
> these two systems overlap, we may expect to find
> the sorcerer.[30]

In Brown's terms Origen is asserting claims to power through
inarticulate channels, through the peculiar qualities of the
person and message of Jesus that render all considerations of
class, background, education, etc. meaningless.  On the other
hand, Celsus, by exposing Jesus' marginal and inferior status
and by branding him a sorcerer, is upholding articulate channels as the only acceptable routes to power and high status.
Brown's comments could have been made with Celsus in mind:
"in this situation, the accuser is usually the man with the
Single Image.  For him, there is one, single, recognized way of
making one's way in the world.  In rejecting sorcery, such a man
has rejected any additional source of power."[31]

Both Origen's acknowledgement of the traditional articulate
sources of power and his insistence upon the existence of alternative channels are clear from his remarks in I.29.  He supplements those propositions with an anecdote from an unimpeach-
able source, Plato.  He recounts the conversation between the
famous Athenian general Themistocles and a certain Seriphian
(*Republic* 329E), in which the Seriphian traces Themistocles'
fame not to the excellence of his own character but rather to
his good fortune of having come from the most famous city in all
of Greece.  The general mildly reproaches his accuser by saying
that he would never have become so famous had he been a Seriphian, but, Themistocles responds, neither would the Seriphian have
become a Themistocles had he been born in Athens.  In that exchange the contrast between articulate and inarticulate sources
of power is considerably toned down; Themistocles argues for a
combination of personal attributes and the undeniable perquisites
of proper background.  But when Origen uses the anecdote to il-
lustrate the question of the relative influence of πάτρις πόλις
and ἴδιος ἦθος, he heightens the contrast.  Jesus "was a Seriphian of the very lowest class" who triumphed over all obstacles in
his path.  Where the Platonic example argues that the combination
of articulate and inarticulate sources of power leads to fame,
glory, and success, Origen stresses inarticulate channels of
power at the expense of articulate ones.

Origen does not rest content with establishing an alternative, he asserts its superiority, claiming that Jesus had a

more profound effect on human life than Themistocles, Pythagoras,
Plato, or any wise man, emperor, or leader anywhere.  Jesus not
only represents the complete victory of personal character,
ἴδιος ἦθος, over the advantage of privileged background, but his
effects on posterity surpass those of anyone else.  The principle
reason for that claim lies in his combination of a range of
competences which are usually found only in isolation:

> One has been admired and become famous for wisdom,
> another for generalship, and some barbarians for
> miraculous powers in incantations, and some for
> one talent, some for another; they have not been
> admired and become eminent for several abilities
> at the same time.  Yet Jesus, in addition to his
> other abilities, is admired for his wisdom, for
> his miracles, and for his leadership. (I.30)

There Origen furnishes a prime illustration of a synthetic Hellenistic image of the omnicompetent divine man, which he wields
for polemical purposes in the comparisons with wise men, emperors, and generals.

Fixing initially on the channels through which an individual
could claim divine status, Origen opposes Celsus' Single Image
of the articulate sources of power with an alternative image of
personal, inarticulate sources.  He supports his proposition
with anecdotal evidence, and tests it comparatively.  He concludes that, at least in the specific case of Jesus, the influence of ἴδιος ἦθος supersedes that of πάτρις πόλις, which in itself offers telling support for the claims made by and for Jesus.
In his comparison Origen offers three criteria by which the
superiority of Jesus can be evaluated: a) the extent of the effect of a given figure, b) the range of his competence, and
c) the degree to which he overcame obstacles of heredity and en-
vironment.  For Origen, since Jesus' message and actions shook
the entire world, since Jesus combined a range of competences
never before encountered, and since Jesus rose above his simple
and untutored origins, his claims to divinity are patently to be
preferred to those of any others.

The accusations of magic in I.28 open a window on the different perceptions of Celsus and Origen of the ways in which
would-be divine men or their partisans could claim power and
the status that went with it.  Despite Miura-Stange's assertions,

Celsus and Origen are not in agreement. Celsus' appeal to articulate channels of power accords well with the passion he exhibits
for the unity of the empire (especially in book VIII), the suspicion which he had for secret goings-on, and his great reverance
for the lessons and doctrines of the past. Celsus prefers a
world of the Single Image "where power springs from vested
authority, where admiration is gained by conforming to recognized
norms of behavior, where the gods are worshipped in public, and
where wisdom is the exclusive preserve of the traditional educa-
tional machine,"[32] and he views Christianity with apprehension as
the antithesis of such a world. In such situations accusations
of magic often spring up; Celsus is no exception. Origen counters
with an appeal to the Double Image: things are not as they seem.
Jesus' mean origins should not obscure his great accomplishments
and his incomparable character. His qualifications for fame and
distinction are not readily apparent; they are not located in
traditional social structure but in his person and message and
in the influence they have exerted. Those different perceptions
of the appropriate qualifications for a claimant to divine status
determine as well the way Celsus and Origen deal with the stories
about them. The ἦθος of the figure is the crucial indicator of
the truth or falsity of the story.

When he returns to the story of the birth of Jesus in I.31,
Origen adds that Celsus identified Mary's partner in adultery as
a certain Panthera, a Roman soldier.[33] Echoing his opening accusation in I.28, he brands the story a myth (μῦθος), and invention
(πλάσμα), and a lie (ψεῦδος) which was obviously concocted to
do away with the miraculous conception of Jesus through the holy
spirit. Not surprisingly, those who fabricated the story are
called liars. Although in rhetorical usage μῦθος could be used
to describe an account of events which did not take place but
which portrayed truth,[34] in I.31 it echoes the usage of Christian
apologists for whom μῦθος described false tales. Πλάσμα and
ψεῦδος carry similar pejorative force, as does the characterization of the story-tellers as fabricators of myths and lies.[35]
Given that, Origen's claim that the story of Mary and Panthera
is not convincing is to be expected.

To support his judgment, Origen sets out a disparate collection of criteria for evaluating such stories.  On logical grounds,
he contends that the transposition of the virgin birth into an
illegitimate birth indicates that the story-tellers recognized,
and could not deny, that the birth of Jesus was somehow extraordinary.  The remaining traces of extraordinary circumstances
in the Mary and Panthera story indicate the transparency of the
Jew's fiction.  Origen does not stop there.  He makes the following proposition:

> It is therefore probable that this soul, which
> lived a more useful life on earth than many men
> (to avoid appearing to beg the question by saying
> 'all' men), needed a body which was not only
> distinguished among human bodies, but was also
> superior to all others. (I.32)

That "more useful (ὠφελιμωτέραν) life" consisted in urging Greeks
and barbarians alike to turn from evil and to live their lives
in expectation of divine judgment of the Creator, in doing (unspecified) great deeds, in teaching many, and in converting many
from the "flood of evil."  For Origen, the message and actions of
Jesus, coupled with their undeniable effects (the consistent emphasis on the "many" who were reached), indicate that his life
was more useful to humankind than those of many other men.  Thus,
in accordance with the philosophical principle "that there are
certain secret principles by which each soul that enters a body
does so in accordance with its merits and former character"
(I.32), Origen argues that it is probable that the soul of Jesus
should have had a miraculous rather than a disgraceful birth.
Further support is garnered in I.33 from the view of the physiog-
nomists Zopyrus, Loxus, and Polemon.

In his defense of the story of Jesus' birth, Origen combines a philosophical proposition about the conformity between
the characters of bodies and souls with his own specific interpretation of what determines a useful life.  His fundamental contention is that Jesus lived a beneficial life.  Since Jesus lived
such a life, his soul merited a body in conformity with its
character.  The outstanding character of the body is signalled
by the virgin birth; not the body itself, but its mode of delivery
is portrayed as extraordinary.  Thus Origen's defense of the

virgin birth resolves into the assertion that it was an appropriate mode of entry into the world for one who would live such
a useful life.

Origen ranges even farther afield in search for support of
his position.  Using Celsus' fabricated interlocutor to his
own advantage, he asserts that "it would have been appropriate
to the words he [Celsus] has put into the mouth of the Jew to
have quoted the prophecy of Isaiah [Is. 7:10-14] which says that
Emmanuel shall be born of a virgin" (I.34).  The dual nature of
his opponent, both Jew and Greek, allows Origen considerable
leeway in the formulation of his response.  In this instance, he
supplements those remarks more suitable for a Greek audience (the
appeal to philosophical maxims and the views of the physiognom-
ists, e.g.) with those more apt to impress a Jewish audience.
It is not that the earlier arguments would be inappropriate for
Jews, but that, for Origen, the appeal to scripture seems *more*
effective.  Celsus' introduction of the Jew gave Origen the occasion to exploit that character for his own purposes.

For Origen, Celsus' failure to mention the passage from
Isaiah betrays his overall approach, and Origen seizes the opportunity to score polemical points:

> That it was out of wickedness that Celsus did not
> quote the prophecy is made clear to me from the
> fact that although he has quoted several things
> from the gospel according to Matthew, such as the
> star that arose at the birth of Jesus and other miracles,
> yet he has not even mentioned this at all.
> But if a Jew should ingeniously explain it
> away . . . . (I.34)

As he does elsewhere, Origen anticipates and attempts to dispel
objections which have not even been raised by his opponent.  In
response to the Jewish arguments he foresees, Origen adduces
linguistic, logical, and historical evidence to support the prophecy of the virgin birth.  He first reprises the familiar argument about the Septuagint translation of the Hebrew "aalma,"
and decides in favor of rendering it παρθένος, virgin, instead
of νεᾶνις, young woman.[36]  On contextual grounds, he argues
that a young woman giving birth would hardly constitute the
"sign" mentioned in the passage, since it would be a rather
ordinary occurrence.  Finally, he challenges opponents to

identify anyone in the time of Ahaz to whom the prophecy could
be applied.  Origen finds, accordingly, that the evidence overwhelmingly points to the identity of the prophesied Emmanuel
with Jesus, and no other.  Finally, in I.36, a more general defense of prophetic inspiration is addressed to both Jews and
"also to those Greeks who have an open mind" (I.36).

      As it wends its way onward from the Jew's original comments
in I.28, Origen's argument becomes increasingly complex.  It
proceeds on several fronts (the Greeks, the Jews, Celsus, Celsus'
Jew) and picks up a variety of side issues (the veracity of
Jewish prophecy, e.g.).  The styles and strategies of Origen's
apology are clearly laid out.  He envisages a spectrum of possible audiences and devises arguments suitable on each front.
In addressing Greek audiences, Origen fights Celsus toe-to-toe
on his own territory, the common religious and philosophical
heritage of Late Antiquity.  In addressing Jews, Origen confronts
them with his own impressive knowledge of the Hebrew scriptures.
The full array of responses will not be marshalled to meet every
one of Celsus' objections, but it is always there in reserve.
The intricate design of CC cautions against too facile conclusions about either principal's full position on any question.

      In all of Origen's defense of the virgin birth, the evalua-
tion of the story and its authors is secondary to the evaluation
of the character (ἦθος) of its subject.  For Origen, the rejection of the Panthera legend is axiomatic, given his establishment in I.29-31 of the superior character of Jesus.  Celsus,
however, ventured a similar substantiation of the myths about
several Greek heroes:

      The old myths that attributed a divine birth to
      Perseus and Amphion and Aecus and Minos (we do
      not believe even them) are nevertheless evi-
      dence of their great and truly wonderful works
      for mankind, so that they do not appear lacking
      in plausibility (μὴ ἀπίθανοι); but as for you,
      what have you [Jesus] done in word or deed that
      is fine or wonderful?  You showed nothing to us,
      although they challenged you in the temple to
      produce some obvious token that you were the
      son of God.   (I.67)

On the surface, then, it would seem that Celsus and Origen agree
on the criterion by which stories about divine births can be

evaluated:   if the subject can be said to have performed useful,
or great and wonderful, works for humankind, then the story will
not lack plausibility (both use the same rhetorical term).  That
they cannot agree on which stories of divine births are to be
accepted suggests that some difference of opinion exists over
what constitutes a useful or wonderful work.  Again, it is the
evaluation or understanding of certain actions, not the actions
themselves, that animates the criteria.  In his response, Origen
proposes that such acts should be outstanding, important, and
should influence posterity, and he claims that the only evidence
the Greeks can set forth is their stories.  They have no indepen-
dent corroboration.  On the other hand,

> We affirm that the whole human world has
> evidence of the work of Jesus since in it dwell the
> churches of God which consist of people converted
> through Jesus from countless evils.  Moreover,
> the name of Jesus still takes away mental
> distractions from men, and daemons and diseases as
> well, and implants a wonderful meekness and
> tranquility of character, and a love to mankind
> and a kindness and gentleness, in those who . . .
> have genuinely accepted the gospel about God and
> Christ and the Judgment to come.  (I.67)

Origen introduces an historical element:  the ancient heroes who
are truly useful are those whose actions continue to bear pal-
pable fruit throughout history and in the present.  Mighty acts
in the distant past are not sufficient.  Continuing moral reformation, accomplished in the name and through the power of Jesus,
sets him apart from Perseus and other Greek heroes.  That adds
a temporal dimension to Origen's comments in I.32.

Origen also supports the belief in the virgin birth in a
less subtle fashion.  In VI.8, he lumps the story of Plato's
divine birth together with other "incredible tales" such as
those of the ivory [sic] thigh of Pythagoras, the third eye of
Plato, and even the daemon of Socrates.  On the contrary, he
avers that the Christians tell no incredible tales (οὐ
τερατευόμεθα) of that sort about Jesus.  The credibility of
Plato's divine birth is diminished by Origen's associating it with
several more outrageous stories.  Finally, Origen rejects the
suggestion that birth of any sort was unnecessary for Jesus,
since, as Celsus contends, God "already knew how to make men.

He could have formed a body for this one also without having
to thrust his own spirit into such foul pollution" (VI.73).
Miura-Stange accurately relates that mention of pollution
(μίασμα) to the Jew's story of the disgraceful circumstances of
the birth of Jesus.[37]  But Celsus' feeling that the gross details
of the birth could have been avoided is not shared by Origen:
"he said this because he did not realize that the body which was
to minister to the salvation of men had a pure birth from a virgin and was not the result of any immorality" (VI.73).  Origen
takes up the theme of the correspondence in character between
bodies and souls which he had fully outlined in I.32 and 33
and asserts further that the logical possibility of such an
event as the creation of a human being by means other than birth
would have created problems:  "those who saw the body would not
have believed at once that it was not produced by birth" (VI.73).
In general, the discussions of the subject outside of the first
two books repeat themes already sounded and serve only to reinforce the impressions created in the first two books.

     In evaluating stories about divine birth, Celsus and Origen
made a series of implicit decisions like those which underpin
any taxonomic system.  They began with a large and heterogeneous
human population and proceeded to winnow out by a series of
"tests" those to whom a divine birth could rightly be attributed.
The process for Origen is that of reducing the many to the one;
its success depends on the development of principles of assignment which will permit him to reduce the population of each suc-
cessive category until the terminal category has only the desired
number of occupants.  Celsus proceeds in a similar fashion, but
he is less interested in reducing the many to the one than in
establishing the position of Jesus as only one of many candidates
for divine status.

     Their primary categories can be presented diagrammatically:

        humans              candidates for divine status

              performers of non-          performers of
              beneficial actions          beneficial actions

                    transistory or              enduring effects
                    trivial effects             in past and present

Origen affirms each of the propositions on the right-hand side;
Jesus is a candidate for divine status, a performer of beneficial
actions, actions which have provided and continue to provide
enduring benefits.  Celsus, because he is presented with the argument by Christian tradition, concedes that Jesus is a
for divine status, but he attempts to undermine that candidacy
by claiming that Jesus has performed no beneficial actions,
though his trivial and commonplace actions may have had lasting
effect.  The conflict between Celsus and Origen thus centers on
whether actions which each sees as having certain classifying
force are to be understood as beneficial or merely trivial.
Miura-Stange correctly stresses that for Origen (and for Celsus
as well) "the most important thing is . . . the act."[38]

Celsus refuses to see in the action of Jesus the conversion
of many from countless evils.  He prefers to see the works of
a common sorcerer, like those "who are taught by the Egyptians,
who for a few obols make known their sacred lore in the middle
of the market-place and drive daemons out of men and blow away
diseases and invoke the souls of heroes . . ." (I.68).  Jesus
is an unworthy claimant to divine status, and an exclusive claim
is certainly not justified because of his similarity to other
wonder-workers.  Celsus asks:  "Since these men do these wonders,
ought we to think them sons of God?  Or ought we to say that
they are the practices of wicked men possessed by an evil daemon?"  (I.68).  In that passage Celsus stops short of fitting
Jesus into a terminal category by himself; he is merely classed
together with other common magicians whose pretensions are
equally unfounded.  That prompts a clear and quick response
from Origen:

> They might have been comparable if Jesus had done
> his miracles, like magicians, merely to show his
> own powers.  But in fact no sorcerer uses his
> tricks to call the spectators to moral reformation;
> nor does he educate by the fear of God people who
> were astounded by what they saw, nor does he
> attempt to persuade the onlookers to live as
> men who will be judged by God.  (I.68)

There Origen defines the magician by opposition to his criteria
for a useful life.  The magician a) does not work for the benefit of others, b) does not summon his audience to moral reform,

c) does not educate, d) does not proclaim judgement by god, etc.
As a malefactor, the magician is the complete antithesis of the
soul that lives a useful life for all mankind.  What was implicit
in Origen's response to the Jew in I.29 ff. becomes explicit
when Celsus tries to include Jesus among the magicians in I.68.
The same actions which indicate to Celsus that Jesus was a magician lead Origen to conclude that "he was God who had appeared
in a human body for the benefit of our race" (I.68).  The same
actions which lead Celsus to brand the story of Jesus' divine
birth a fiction and its authors liars demonstrate for Origen
its miraculous nature and their essential veracity.

B.  The Visit of the Magi

Though the visit of the Magi is closely related to the
birth of Jesus, the specific questions which it raises for Celsus
and Origen justify its treatment as a separate unit.  In I.58
Celsus offers this interpretation of the visit of the "Chalda-
eans":

> . . . according to the account of Jesus they were
> moved to come to his birth to worship him as God
> although he was still an infant; and they informed
> Herod the tetrarch of this; but he sent men to kill
> those born just at that time, thinking that he
> would destroy him also with them, lest somehow,
> after he had lived for the time sufficient for him
> to grow up, he should become king.  (I.58)

Celsus' comments to Jesus in I.61 specify his problem:  ". . . why
then when you had grown up did you not become king, but, though
son of God, go about begging disgracefully, cowering from fear,
and wander up and down in destitution?" (I.61).  There the social
and economic basis of the polemic against the virgin birth in
I.28 is connected with the visit of the wise men from the east
as well.  Where it was originally used to cast suspicion on
Jesus' pretensions to divinity, it is turned in the second instance on his aspiration to kingship.  Again, Celsus and Origen
differ in their evaluation of the actions and circumstances which
purportedly warrant Jesus' claim to kingship.

To wrest Jesus away from Celsus, Origen uses the same strategy he employed in I.29ff., though in shorter compass.  He appeals
to a treatise of the Stoic Chaeremon for support of the idea
that certain stars have often appeared at crucial junctures in

history such as "significant changes of dynasties, or wars, or
whatever may happen among men which has the effect of shaking
earthly affairs" (I.59). That is, stars like the one at Jesus'
birth frequently accompany major changes in the articulate systems of power. Origen's explanation follows the same lines as
his defense of the virgin birth. He appeals to the character
of his subject:

> If then a comet, as it is called, or some similar
> star appears at new dynasties or other great events
> on earth, why is it amazing (τί θαυμαστὸν) that a
> star should have appeared at the birth of a man who
> was to introduce new ideas among the human race and
> to bring a doctrine not only to Jews but also to
> Greeks and to many barbarian nations as well?
> (I.59)

As in I.29ff., the character of the messenger and the quality of
his message confirm the plausibility of the story. Similarly,
Origen also buttresses his argument with an appeal to prophecy,
quoting Balaam from Num. 24:17 where he says that "a star shall
appear out of Jacob, and a man shall rise up out of Israel."

Origen explicitly addresses both Jews and Greeks (I.59),
charging them both with misunderstanding the kingship of Jesus.
He claims that the angels who appeared at the birth of Jesus
and the divine power in Jesus himself sapped the power of the
daemons upon whom the Magi relied for their magical practices.
In order to discover the reason for their sudden impotence they
followed the sign from Heaven which recalled for them the prophecy of Balaam.

> And they guessed that the man foretold as coming
> with the star had arrived; and as they had already
> found that he was superior to all daemons and the
> beings that usually appeared to them and caused
> certain magical effects, they wanted to worship him.
> They therefore came to Judaea, because they were
> convinced that some king had been born and because
> they knew where he would be born, but without under-
> standing over what kingdom he would rule. (I.60)

The Magi serve as foils for Origen's assertion of the great power
of Jesus and the particularly Christian understanding of the
kingdom of god. Just as Origen appealed to alternative sources
of power for claimants to divinity, he also proposes an alternative understanding of kingship. His conception becomes more

precise in his remarks about Herod:

> He [Jesus] was to be king, not in the way that
> Herod supposed, but because it was fitting that God
> should give him a kingdom for the benefit of those
> under his rule, since he would bestow no moderate
> and indifferent benefit, so to speak, upon his sub-
> jects, but by truly divine laws would educate
> them and lead them on.  (I.61)

Origen accepts the common image of the royal benefactor but
chooses to redefine the nature of the benefits which will accrue
to the subjects.  Instead of through buildings, games, and the
public dole, Jesus will benefit his subjects through education
which is based on divine, not human, laws.  Though the character
of that instruction is not clear in the passage above, it echoes
Origen's emphasis on moral reformation and the conversion from
evil which played a central role in his description of the
character of the deserving claimant to divine status.  Again,
Origen opposes his adversary's emphasis on articulate power; he
values the manifestation of power "not in the way . . . supposed"
more than vested authority and recognized norms of behavior.
Origen's discussion of the visit of the Magi again shows close
agreement with Celsus on the broad outlines of the question.
Both agree that kings should perform certain beneficial actions.
It is in deciding which actions are to be considered beneficial
that they part company.

C.  The Sojourn in Egypt

That process of evaluation also runs through the discussion
of the sojourn in Egypt.  Origen reproaches Celsus for divesting
the narrative of its miraculous character:

> . . . he did not believe all the miracles connected
> with it, not that an angel directed this, not that
> Jesus' departure from Judaea and sojourn in Egypt had
> some hidden meaning.  He made up another tale.  For
> although he somehow accepts the incredible miracles
> which Jesus did, by which he persuaded the multitude
> to follow him as Christ, yet he wants to attack them
> as though they were done by magic and not by divine
> power.  (I.38)

Origen agrees that Celsus got the facts straight, but he vehe-
mently disputes his interpretation.  Celsus' version is an invention (πλάσμα) prompted by his inability to accept miracles as

such.  In this case, Origen does not essay an extensive response.
Instead he proceeds directly to a negative definition of the
magician, similar to the one he proposes in I.68.  He contends
that he does not know why "a magician should have taken the
trouble to teach a doctrine which persuades every man to do
every action as before God who judges each man for all his works,
and to instill this conviction in his disciples" (I.38).  Origen
attempts to remove the taint of Jesus' stay in Egypt by appealing
to the ends to which he used his power.  He makes the distinction
even clearer in I.68, where he claims that magicians perform
miracles solely to show off their own powers.  They do not call
people to moral reform, persuade them to live in fear of god's
judgement, educate them, or present themselves as moral exemplars.  All of which Jesus did do.  Therefore, "if the life of
Jesus was of this character, how could anyone reasonably compare
him with the behavior of sorcerers . . .?" (I.68).  Wherever it
is brought up, the sojourn in Egypt forces the question of
whether or not Jesus practices magic.  In several places Origen
directly confronts the question, defining the magician as the
antithesis of the true claimant to divinity.  The appeal to
power through inarticulate channels which Origen carefully mapped
out and supported with philosophical and prophetic evidence in
I.29ff. also provides the criteria by which Jesus can be distinguished from common magicians.  For Origen, magicians are self-
serving wonder-workers who manifest no concern for the well-
being of others.  Celsus accepted a similar definition, but he
included Jesus among them.

     Celsus also used the flight to Egypt to sharpen his defini-
tion of the θεός, to the exclusion of Jesus.  The Jew asks
Jesus:

> Why when you were still an infant did you have to
> be taken away to Egypt lest you should be murdered?
> It is not likely that a god would be afraid of
> death (Θεὸν γὰρ οὐκ εἰκὸς ἦν περὶ θανάτου δεδιέναι).
> But an angel came from heaven, commanding you and
> your family to escape, lest by being left behind you
> should die.  And could not the great God, who had
> already sent two angels on your account, guard you,
> His own son, at that very place?  (I.66)

Jesus' failure to manifest divine power in a situation which

appeared to call for it clearly puzzled the Jew; he returns to
it frequently in his remarks on Jesus' resurrection. Origen's
response invokes, in typical fashion, the peculiar character of
Jesus as an explanation of the stories about him.  He describes
Jesus as "a sort of composite being (σύνθετόν τι χρῆμά)" whose
actions as a man had to be compatible with his human nature.
Given that, he finds the biblical accounts of the flight neither
incredible (παράδοξον) nor absurd (ἄτοπον).  Moreover, Origen
feels that the manifestation of divine power at that juncture
would have been out of step with the overall plan for Jesus'
life:

> The highly miraculous character and increased pub-
> licity of the help given to him would not have
> helped his object, which was to teach, as a man
> to whom God bore witness, that within the visible
> man he possessed something more divine; this was
> the part to which the title 'son of God' is properly
> applied, the divine Logos, the power and wisdom
> of God, the so-called Christ.  This, however,
> is not the right time to explain the composite
> nature and of what elements the incarnate Jesus
> consisted, since this is, so to speak, a matter
> of private investigation by believers.  (I.66)

Jesus again is cast as an educator, but in that case it is
his own nature, rather than any divine laws, which is progres-
sively revealed.  Moral reformation, divine legislation, and
self-revelation become interrelated aspects of his mission.
The mission is seen to unfold gradually in the life of Jesus,
and to bear fruit gradually in the lives of individual believers.
Origen curtails his discussion of the matter because his apology
is not aimed at convinced philosophical believers like himself,
but rather at those still moving through the process of conversion.  His work is intended for "those entirely without experience of faith in Christ, or those whom the apostle calls 'weak in
faith'" (pref. 6).  Origen's view of the life of Jesus as a
process of gradual education is reflected in the construction of
his reply to Celsus.  He must secure the biblical records
against the objections that they are incredible or absurd, and
he must establish the compatibility between the actions of Jesus
and certain conceptions of divinity such as the idea that a
worthy candidate for divine status will perform beneficial

actions, before he can plumb the depths of meaning they contain.
In CC Origen has to seek the middle ground and to locate areas
of agreement with his adversary.  But at the same time he must
seek to put the characteristic Christian stamp on common material, as with his contention that the benefit granted by Jesus
is moral reform.  That dual nature of his task is evident in his
discussion of Jesus and other claimants to divine status.

D.  Conclusions

     In the first chapter I argued, on methodological grounds,
that the conception of the figure of the divine man was of crucial
importance.  The arguments between Celsus and Origen show that
the figures were a central concern for them as well.  Little
time and less ingenuity is devoted to the analysis of either the
stories about divine men or those who told them.  Both Celsus
and Origen freely adopt critical terms from contemporary rhetoric
for the classification of that material.  They find tales to be
either true or false, credible or incredible.  Authors are liars
or tellers of truths.[39]  The various positive and negative terms
employed divide into two separate classes rather than a fuller
classificatory system.  The stories and their authors are of
only secondary interest.  It is their subjects who claim attention.

     In the process of evaluating the claims of Jesus to divinity,
Celsus and Origen introduce a spectrum of categories ranging
from θεός, the most positive designation, through ἄνθρωπος in the
middle, to μάγος and γόης, the most negative categories.  The
argument about Jesus, like the shorter wrangles about other
figures, can be viewed as a prolonged effort to identify the
proper niche for Jesus within that continuum and to make sure
that he remains there and nowhere else.  A number of supplementary categories enter the discussion for varying periods of
time.  The space between θεός and ἄνθρωπος, for example, quickly
becomes populated by sons of god, divine teachers, composite
beings, daemons, famous men of various stripes, wise men, leaders,
generals, etc.  Those categories are not designed to be air-
tight; the intentions of both Celsus and Origen are not to provide an objective and systematic map of various types of beings
from gods to sorcerers.  They invoke appropriate secondary

categories in order to establish and reinforce the validity of their primary assessments of the major characters. The intervening categories are used to emphasize the nearness of their occupants to one of the three primary categories. They define the web on which a series of close comparisons can be organized. Thus, in the story of the Seriphian and Themistocles in I.29, Origen can use the description of Themistocles as a man of fame and distinction as a fulcrum for his contention that Jesus is *much more* famous and distinguished, and therefore *more* worthy of divine honors. By concentrating on the secondary category, Origen tries to edge his candidate closer to the primary category of θεός. On the other hand, Celsus repeatedly attempts to nudge Jesus closer to the other pole. By lumping him with common magicians, for example, Celsus intends to move Jesus away from the neutral category of ἄνθρωπος and towards the μάγος/ γόης pole. Celsus also proceeds carefully, moving step by step, but with the hope that the cumulative effect of his efforts will be telling. In each case, the force of the individual attempts at classification is centrifugal; each man tries to move his subjects away from the neutral middle toward either the positive or negative pole. The force of the responses, however, is centripetal; each antagonist tries to move his favored subjects back towards the positive pole and to enhance the attraction of his opponent's favorites to the negative pole. The process is the same in the case of Plato, for example, as it is in the case of Jesus. The story of Plato's divine birth might indicate for Celsus that he hovers somewhere between the categories of ἄνθρωπος and θεός. But Origen tries to deflate that fantasy by exposing the divine birth story as teratological, thus subverting, he feels, any claims that Plato was anything more than a mere man. The clash of centrifugal and centripetal forces results from the polemical nature of the discussion. Celsus and Origen describe a dynamic field whose boundaries they commonly acknowledge but whose internal arrangement is constantly disputed. CC displays more the types of arguments which are brought to bear on claimants to divine status than a finished system of classification.

With a partial listing of secondary categories, the field
of debate in CC looks like this:

*Primary Categories*

θεός                          ἄνθρωπος                    μάγος/γόης

*Secondary Categories*

| | |
|---|---|
| son of god | bastard |
| divine man | liar |
| power of god | boaster |
|    composite being | deceiver |
|    divine teacher | brigand |
|    daemon | insurrectionist |
|       wise man |    demoniac |
|       great man |    hawker of spells |
|       famous man |    tricky operator |
|       moral paradigm |    demon |

The diagram attempts only to present graphically an array of
primary and secondary categories which come into play in CC;
the secondary categories are neither paired opposites nor ver-
tical equivalents. The diagram is intended to display only the
relative tendency of secondary categories to move toward one
of the two opposite poles. Celsus and Origen share the polar
opposites and neutral middle as primary categories. It is
through the manipulation of the secondary categories that they
endeavor to decide Bieler's question of "who was a θεῖος and who
was a μάγος."

Many of the principles of assignment to those secondary
categories are also shared by the antagonists. Both proceed by
examining discrete incidents from the lives of their subjects,
on the assumption that those incidents have classifying force.
Certain actions and circumstances are held to separate the wise
man from the ruthless deceiver who spouts false knowledge, the
son of god from the bastard magician, and so on. Celsus puts
the primary criterion succinctly in II.20: "but above all a
god ought to have done good to all men (ὃν εχρην μάλιστα πάντας
ἀνθρώπους εὐεργετεῖν)." Origen subscribes to a similar senti-
ment and gives it this precise formulation in his remarks on
the Pythian Apollo: "if he was a god (θεός), he ought to have

used his foreknowledge as an incentive, so to speak, for the
conversion and healing and moral reformation of men" (VII.6).
Origen is more explicit than Celsus in his opinion of what constitutes doing good; it is doubtful, though, that Celsus would
have accepted the polemical association of εὐεργετεῖν with moral
reformation, conversion, and teaching about the judgement of god
in quite the way Origen proposed it.  Celsus and Origen may
agree that the performance of beneficial actions will support
one's candidacy for divine status, but they do not concur on
which actions are especially beneficial.  Celsus' comments on
oracles suggest that he prized more concrete benefits:

> How many cities have been built by oracles, and have
> got rid of diseases and famines, and how many that
> have neglected or forgotten them have suffered ter-
> rible destruction?  How many have been sent to
> form a colony and have prospered by attending to
> their commands?  How many rulers and common people
> have come off better or worse for this reason?  How
> many that have been distressed at being childless
> have come to possess that for which they prayed
> and escaped the wrath of demons?  How many ailments
> of the body have been healed?  How many, on the
> other hand, have insulted the temples and have at
> once been caught?  For some have been overcome by
> madness on the spot; others have declared what they
> had done; others have made an end of themselves;
> and others have become bound by incurable diseases.
> Some have been destroyed by a deep voice from the
> actual shrines.  (VIII.45)

Thus Celsus' view of benefits as concrete and tangible is
coupled with his Single Image of recognized and sanctioned articulate channels of power, the oracular shrines themselves.  The
strong moral overtones of Origen's conception of beneficial
activity are missing; the channels by which both good and ill
fortune are received are clearly articulated.  Where Celsus at-
tends to the care of the body, Origen aspires to the cure of
souls.  The distinction becomes exaggerated for polemical effect, but is nevertheless crucial for their respective views on
beneficial actions and it eventually determines how each manipulates the range of secondary categories to support his own
position.  The distinctive approach of each will become clearer
as their remarks on the public career and final demise of their
primary subject, Jesus, are considered.

CHAPTER III

CELSUS AND ORIGEN ON DIVINE MEN, II

The discussion in CC of the public career of Jesus is much
more diffuse than that of his birth and youth. Celsus does
single out certain incidents for sustained consideration, but
he also makes a number of general comments which are not tied to
specific events. In addition, he proposes that the careers of
a wide variety of figures were in some ways similar to that of
Jesus. It seems, then, that a detailed examination of the public
career of Jesus was not Celsus' primary objective; he did not
want to write a "life" of Jesus from a negative point of view.
Rather, Celsus was content to comment on those incidents from
Jesus' biography which, in his estimation, had some bearing on
Jesus' claims to divinity. Celsus' isolated criticisms, though
intended to have cumulative effect, were united by their presumed
utility in dissociating Jesus from categories of divinity, not
by their positions in a biographical framework.

*Baptism*

Celsus' comments on I.41 show that Jesus' pretension to
divinity was still the central issue:

> When . . . you were bathing near John, you say that
> you saw what appeared to be a bird fly towards
> you out of the air . . . . What trustworthy wit-
> ness saw this apparition, or who heard a voice from
> heaven adopting you as son of God? There is no proof
> except for your work and the evidence which you
> may produce of one of the men who were punished
> with you. (I.41)

If no trustworthy witnesses can confirm his adoption as son of
God, Jesus' aspiration to that status can again be traced to
arrogant conceit and thus discounted. Though Celsus' tactics
differ from those he used against the birth story, Origen correctly perceives his intention to brand the story of the baptism
a πλάσμα or fiction (I.40). Origen begins his response on the
periphery, by claiming that Celsus, in his typical fashion, has
not followed the order of events in the gospel according to

Matthew.   But he follows that with a more telling admission
in I.42:

> . . . an attempt to substantiate (κατασκευάζειν)
> almost any story as historical fact, even if it is
> true, and to produce complete certainty about it, is
> one of the most difficult tasks and in some cases
> impossible . . . .  We have said this by way of in-
> troduction to the whole question of the narrative
> about Jesus in the gospels, not in order to invite
> people with intelligence to mere irrational faith,
> but with a desire to show that readers need an
> open mind and considerable study, and, if I may say
> so, need to enter into the mind of the writers to
> find out with what spiritual meaning each event was
> recorded.   (I.42)

R.M. Grant has identified the rhetorical context of that passage.
He relates Origen's remarks about the difficulty of confirming
any story as historical fact to Dio Chrysostom's eleventh Oration
in which Dio argues on the basis of refutation (ἀνασκευή) against
the historical accuracy of the Iliad and the Odyssey.   Grant
shows Origen's relation to a different style of Homeric exegesis
according to which the poems were partly true and partly false.[1]
Adopting a similar distinction, Origen sets the reader of the
gospels with the task of deciding what to accept and what to interpret allegorically; the intelligent reader will seek the
"spiritual meaning" behind recorded events.   Though Origen lays
the groundwork for an allegorical interpretation of the baptism
of Jesus, he seems reluctant to build on that foundation.   Apparently, he found such exegesis inappropriate in CC, as he suggests
in I.44:

> A man who has been adorned with the spiritual gift
> called 'the word of wisdom' will also explain the
> reason for the opening of the heavens and the form
> of the dove, and why the Holy Spirit did not appear
> to Jesus in the form of any other living being but
> this.   But the argument does not demand that we ex-
> plain this now.   (I.44)

Origen's hesitancy to venture allegorical interpretation suggests
that his primary audiences in CC are not those readers with "an
open mind and considerable study," but rather those entirely
without faith in Christ or the weak in faith (cf. pref. 6; V.18).
For those audiences certain other arguments are more appropriate,
arguments which could bridge the gap between an author with an

open mind and considerable study and audiences which cannot be presumed to have either. That Origen would frequently[2] defer the type of exegesis which he elsewhere favors suggests that the arguments he *did* use were conceived as commonly recognized strategies for evaluating claimants to divine status. Origen seems to have restricted himself intentionally to categories and modes of argumentation which he could share with his intended audiences. The nature of his task demands that the classificatory field in which he located Jesus not be an idiosyncratic product of his own reflection. For his own argument to succeed it had to be accessible to the intended audiences. Before the spiritual meaning of Jesus' life story could be plumbed, it had to be secured against Celsus' objections.

Origen's defense is again conducted on several fronts. After castigating Celsus for his disorganized approach to the gospels and broaching the possibility of a "spiritual" understanding of the gospel narratives, he turns to the figure of the Jew. Citing the visions of Ezekiel and Isaiah, Origen challenges the Jew to be consistent in the evaluation of such stories. For Origen, the issue resolves into this question: "Should we believe Isaiah and Ezekiel or Jesus?" His answer is hardly surprising, but it reveals an important criterion by which Origen evaluates claimants to superior status:

> No work (ἔργον οὐδὲν) of theirs is to be found of comparable importance; whereas the goodness of Jesus towards men was not confined to the period of the incarnation only, but even to this day the power of Jesus brings about conversion and moral reformation in those who believe in God through him. (I.43; cf. I.47)

The reasoning which enabled Origen to separate Jesus from Themistocles, Plato, and Pythagoras in I.29ff. also allows him to assert the superiority of Jesus to Ezekiel and Isaiah. Once more, the character of the subject determines the plausibility of the story about him. Character is demonstrated by the performance of certain actions; beneficial actions indicate superior character, and beneficial actions of lasting impact (conversion and moral reformation, e.g.) express the surpassing character of the worthy claimant to divine status. That Origen uses the same type of argument against both Greeks (I.29ff.) and Jews (I.43) confirms its central role in his defense of Jesus.

The discussion of Ezekiel and Isaiah next leads Origen to a comparison between Moses and Jesus. As the story of the appearance of the dove at the baptism of Jesus recedes further into the background, Origen concentrates on turning the rhetorical ploy of Celsus to his own advantage. Against the fictitious Jew Origen arrays the same arguments which he claims to have used to great effect in debate with his Jewish contemporaries. His question is simple:

> Is it not absurd (ἀποκλήρωσις: arbitrary) to believe that Moses spoke the truth, in spite of the fact that the Egyptians malign him as a sorcerer who appeared to do his miracles by means of trickery, while disbelieving Jesus, since you accuse him? (I.45)

The style of argument remains *ad hominem*. Celsus' approach to the gospels is confused and disorganized, and his Jew is inconsistent with the presuppositions of his own tradition. Instead of proposing an allegorical interpretation of the appearance of the dove at the baptism of Jesus, Origen attempts to undermine his adversary's right to question the incident at all.

At the beginning of I.46 Origen recapitulates his argument. Specifically against the Jew he argues that "the law and the prophets are filled with accounts as miraculous as that recorded of Jesus at the baptism about the dove and the voice from heaven." More generally, he contends that Jesus' own activities are sufficient to establish the plausibility of the story; "I think that the miracles performed by Jesus are evidence that the Holy Spirit was seen then in the form of a dove." And the attack on the baptism story is linked explicitly to Celsus' overriding characterization of Jesus as a magician: ". . . although Celsus attacks them [the confirming miracles] by saying that he learnt how to do them among the Egyptians." Again, the character and the specific activity of the subject are taken to establish the reliability of the story about him. Origen's two-pronged response is designed to diminish the impact of the accusations and to confirm the plausibility of the story they are directed against.

Origen's reliance on an argument from miracles, and his concomitant avoidance of their allegorical interpretation becomes clearer in the following passage:

> And I will not mention these only, but also, as is reasonable, those which were done by Jesus' apostles. For without miracles and wonders they would not

> have persuaded those who heard new doctrines and new
> teachings to leave their traditional religion and to
> accept the apostles' teachings at the risk of their
> lives. Traces of that Holy Spirit who appeared in the
> form of a dove are still preserved among Christians.
> (I.46)

Miracles, then, are appropriate at a certain phase of the process of conversion. They enable missionaries to accomplish the
difficult task (cf. I.52) of disengaging those entirely without
faith in Christ from their traditional religion; they are not
aimed at those with an open mind and considerable study.
Origen's own position corresponds to his image of the effective
missionary work of both Jesus and the disciples; in CC the appeal
to Jesus' miracles is designed to sway the weak in faith and the
faithless. The performance of miracles dramatizes the contrast
between articulate and inarticulate systems of power and can
hasten the abandonment of traditional religion for an alternative which centers on the particular character of the founder.
Origen's use of the argument from miracles supports his conception of the significance of Jesus in contrast to the traditional
forms of spiritual power in Mediterranean antiquity. Further,
his use of that argument in CC accords with his view of conversion as a process moving from adherence to traditional beliefs
through acquaintance with a new message to mature belief. Miracles were indispensable in helping to loose potential converts
from their traditional moorings. Only later do they become the
subjects of allegorical exegesis.

After his discussion of the evidentiary potential of miracles, Origen continues to circle his subject warily. Admitting
that miracle stories could easily provoke mockery by non-
believers, he resists making them his sole support for the baptism story. But the additional resources which he summons up
do not form a coherent argument. Avenues of thought are opened,
then not pursued, only to be taken up briefly and allusively at
a later point. The discussion of rhetorical criticism and allegorical exegesis in I.42 is reprised quickly in I.44; the *ad
hominem* attack on Celsus in I.40 and 41 gives way to criticism
of the Jew in I.43 and 44, which recurs in I.46 and 47; the argument from miracles in I.46 is interrupted by a return to the
examination of the Hebrew prophets and finds its logical conclusion only at the end of I.47 after an excursus on Josephus'
portrait of John the baptizer. Most of Origen's rhetorical

points are scored at the expense of the Jew, particularly in his
comments on Ezekiel, Isaiah, and Moses.  Though disjointed,
Origen's remarks nevertheless testify to his strong desire to
refute Celsus' view of the baptism of Jesus.

Origen does not neglect his other major audience either,
and in the remarks addressed to "Greeks" he makes a major departure.  Noting that the Jew himself could offer no defense of
the heavenly visions of Ezekiel and Isaiah, Origen sets out in
I.48 to provide one.  Arguing from analogy, Origen finds no inherent reason why the same force which produces dreams by night
could not act during the daytime to produce visions.  He thus
concludes that there is nothing extraordinary (οὐδὲν ἄτοπον) in
the visionary accounts of the prophets.  But then Origen reverses
his field and proposes an allegorical interpretation of the apparition, which he prefaces with some uncomplimentary remarks
about simple believers:

> For I do not imagine that the visible heaven was
> opened, or its physical form divided, for Ezekiel
> to record such an experience.  Perhaps therefore
> the intelligent reader of the gospels ought to
> give a similar interpretation also in respect of
> the Saviour, even if this opinion may cause offense
> to the simple-minded, who in their extreme naiveté
> move the world and rend the vast, solid mass of
> heaven.  (I.48)

Few other passages in CC give as accurate a voice to Origen's
own dilemma.  Origen clearly realized that his treatise against
Celsus had to be directed as well to those entirely without
Christian faith or to those weak in that faith, but his dissatisfaction with their literal readings of the scriptures could not
always be kept in check.  Awareness of the potential weakness
of the argument from miracles and the desire to reach Greeks
as well as Jews drives Origen to introduce the allegory which
he previously declared inappropriate.  But even though Origen
asserts that the prophets, Jesus, and John the baptizer saw the
heavens open by virtue of "a certain divine sense,"[3] which "only
the man who is blessed finds on this earth," he uses that to
cast doubt on the Jew's reading of the gospel.  John, not Jesus,
is said to have spoken about the opening of the heavens:

> . . . he thinks that Jesus himself spoke about the
> opening of the heavens and the descent of the Holy
> Spirit upon him in the form of a dove by the Jordan.
> The Bible does not actually show that he said he
> saw this.  (I.48)

Even with the allegorical interpretation of the apparition,
Origen's purpose is to convict (ἐλέγχειν) Celsus of having attributed inappropriate (οὐκ οἰκείως) remarks to the Jew.

More than the specific treatment of the appearance of the
dove, Origen's estimation of just who his adversaries were warrants attention.  Miura-Stange did notice that Origen frequently
sympathizes with Celsus' complaints against the simple Christian
believers,[4] but Origen at times has to suppress that agreement
in order to tailor his arguments to his intended audiences.
These comments from the preface capture Origen's ambivalence:

> . . . I have no sympathy with anyone who had faith
> in Christ such that it could be shaken by Celsus
> . . ., or by any plausibility of argument.  I do
> not know in what category I ought to reckon one who
> needs written arguments in books to restore and
> confirm him in his faith after it has been shaken
> by the accusations brought by Celsus against the
> Christians.  But nevertheless, since among the
> multitude of people supposed to believe some peo-
> ple of this kind might be found, who may be shaken
> and disturbed by the writings of Celsus, and who
> may be restored by the reply to them if what is
> said is of a character that is destructive of Cel-
> sus' arguments and clarifies the truth, we decided
> to yield to your demand and to compose a treatise
> in reply to that which you [Ambrose, Origen's patron]
> sent us.  (pref. 4)

Origen had to address audiences with whom he was not in deep
sympathy;[5] his dissatisfaction with exoteric doctrine and his
infrequent resort to more esoteric formulations helps further
to situate his remarks in CC.  His comments on the life and
works of Jesus should not be expected to represent his preferred
theological position, rather they represent a compromise position developed to intersect with the interests of varied and
complex audiences, including Greeks, Jews, and Christians of
many different persuasions.  That they represent less what is
peculiar to Origen and more what he shared with his audiences
makes Origen's statements more, not less, important for the
investigation of the diverse attempts to authenticate certain
claimants to divine status.  Although Origen's treatment of the
story of Jesus' baptism adds no new categories or principles of
assignment, it helps to rule out the suspicion that Origen's
position was idiosyncratic.  It was designed, at least, to be
nothing of the sort.

*Collection of Disciples*

Celsus' strategy for dealing with Jesus' initial recruits recalls his treatment of the birth story. He brands the earliest disciples as infamous and most wicked (I.62). For Celsus, Jesus' motley collection of tax collectors, sailors, and wandering beggars barely occupied the lowest rungs of the economic ladder and was marked by its socially marginal or inferior status. At first, Origen reserves his full reply; he is satisfied merely to point out the obvious (φανερόν) inaccuracies in Celsus' version of the story. When the full defense is issued, it follows closely the lines set up in the reply to the charges of the Jew in I.28.

Origen opens with an appeal to the effectiveness of the disciples' teaching: "these men taught Christianity and succeeded in bringing many to obey the word of God by divine power" (I.62). Their success was all the more remarkable because their power did not flow through commonly recognized channels. Like Jesus, they were not steeped in the subtleties of Greek rhetorical and dialectical reasoning. Indeed, such literary sophistication would have obscured the self-evident truth of their message. Origen makes that point sharply in III.39:

> We are convinced that men who had not learnt the technique taught by the pernicious sophistry of the Greeks, which has great plausibility and cleverness, and who knew nothing of the rhetoric prevalent in the law-courts, could not have invented stories in such a way that their writings were capable in themselves of bringing a man to believe and to live a life in conformity with his faith. I think it was for this reason that Jesus chose to employ such men to teach his doctrine, that there might be no possible suspicion of plausible sophisms, but that to those able to understand, the innocence of the writers' purpose, which if I may say so was very naive, might be obviously manifest; and that they might see that the writers were considered worthy to be endowed with divine power, which accomplished far more than seems to be achieved by involved verbosity and stylish constructions, and by a logical argument divided into distinct sections and worked out with Greek technical skill.

Several of Origen's major themes recur in that passage. He cooperates with Celsus in stripping from the disciples all trappings associated with articulate channels of power. By stressing so strongly their independence from contemporary rhetoric, Origen even sets the disciples outside of recognized

channels of inarticulate power.  Origen accepts at face value
the social and economic descriptions which Celsus had intended
to have polemical force, but he attempts to turn them to his
own advantage.  In tabular form the oppositions sketched in
response to Celsus' charges in I.62 are:

| *Articulate* | *Inarticulate* |
|---|---|
| noble birth and background | social inferiority and marginality |
| wealth | poverty |
| wage earners and receivers | beggars |
| education | illiteracy |
| dialectic and rhetoric | arguments without artifice |
| accepted wisdom | wisdom not popularly supposed to be such |
| literary style | plain speech |

Origen agrees with Celsus that the disciples stood outside any
recognized arenas for the exercise of power, but he denies that
they failed to exercise it.  He poses the same question that
the Jew's characterization of Jesus in I.28 provoked:

> If anyone saw fisherfolk and tax-collectors who
> had not had even a primary education . . ., and who
> with great courage not only spoke to Jews about
> faith in Jesus but also preached him among the other
> nations with success, would he not try to find out the
> source of their persuasive power?  For it is not that
> which is popularly supposed to be power.  (I.62)

For Origen, the disciples' status as outsiders merely sharpens
the question of the source of their impressive power; it does
not support the conclusion, as it does for Celsus, that their
power was illusory.  It may not have fit the popular conceptions
of power, but it was power nonetheless.  In the end, the contrast
is drawn between merely human wisdom, which is suspect to Origen,
and wisdom communicated by the power of God, the message of the
disciples.  The proof of the truth of that message is again
found in its effect on the character of individual auditors who
were led to live moral lives in conformity with their faith in
that message.

   Origen invokes the Double Image in his discussion of the
disciples; things are decidedly not as they seem.  The inferior
status of the disciples provokes questions about the source of
their power, not suspicion of it.  Celsus' Single Image is superficial; it does not get at the complexity of events and their
subtle and profound meanings.  Nor does it take account of

change.  Origen cites the story of Paul's conversion as a primary example of the change effected by the power of God.  That
such a staunch enemy of the nascent religion could become its
fierce partisan provides further evidence that social status or
previous disposition did not constitute barriers to the effective work of Jesus.  Just as Jesus' triumph over his own background and the obstacles that confronted him made his accomplishments all the more noteworthy, so also does his ability to
make faithful ministers and true believers out of infamous and
wicked men testify to his immense power.  If an enemy like
Paul could become a Christian,

> Why then is it outrageous (ἄτοπον) if Jesus, wanting
> to show mankind the extent of his ability to heal
> souls chose infamous and most wicked men, and led
> them on so far that they were an example of the purest
> moral character (παράδειγμα . . . ἤθους καθαρωτάτου)
> to those who were converted by them to the gospel of
> Christ?  (I.63)

Jesus' triumph provides a model for the successful mission of
the apostles, and their success makes them models for further
converts.  Origen seems almost to delight in the unorthodox
character of both the Christian movement and its founder.  Its
success could not have been predicted from the perspective of
the Single Image; its history was the antithesis of the recognized route to power, fame, and honor.  From the perspective
of the Double Image the humble origins of the Christian movement are transformed in two distinct ways.  The Christians' lack
of rhetorical skill shows that their message was not invented
but rather inspired by divine power (cf. III.39); their moral
flaws before conversion testify to the immense transformative
power of the gospel (cf. I.63).  For Origen, the very fact that
it survived, let alone prospered, outside of the articulate
system of roles and statuses testifies to the divine inspiration
and guidance of the early Christian movement.  Christianity was
emphatically the "other" way.

     Yet again, Origen had to rein in his enthusiasm for the
alternative Christian system of sources and channels of divine
power, lest he run the risk of having it appear *too* foreign to
his potential audiences.  There was precedent, for example, in
the history of philosophy for the radical conversion of the
dissolute and licentious.  Phaedo was led by Socrates from a

house of ill-repute to the study of philosophy; Polemo, the successor of Xenocrates, similarly changed from a depraved life to philosophy (I.64). That appeal to conversions to philosophy bears the imprint of the apologetic situation. While Origen can portray the Christian religion as an alternative system of access to spiritual power, its attraction to the potential audiences must also be established. That can only be done by describing it in familiar terms. The tension between the portrait of Christianity as something *other* and as something *familiar* is created by the demands of the apologetic enterprise. Were it entirely familiar, its uniqueness would be compromised and its attraction severely diminished. In his response to the charges against Jesus and the disciples which have social and economic bases, Origen tries to demonstrate that there is *an alternative route to familiar goals*. Spiritual power, wisdom, and the moral life can also be gained through inarticulate channels. A creative tension is established between the portraits of the Christian religion as other and the Christian religion as familiar. By appropriating commonly prized goals and asserting alternative ways in which they may be reached Origen tries to provide an image of his own religion which will prove both intelligible to his potential audiences and compatible with his own vision, sufficiently distinctive yet sufficiently familiar.

In his defense of the disciples Origen bridges the gap between the distinctive other and the attractive familiar by making an argument that is both moral and social. In contrast to those few who were converted to the philosophical mode of life:

> among the followers of Jesus there were not only the twelve while he was on earth, but also there continues to be a much larger number who having become a band of self-controlled men say of their past life: "For we also were previously foolish, disobedient, deceived, serving diverse lusts and pleasures, living in malice and envy, hateful, hating one another. But when the kindness of God our Saviour appeared and his love towards man," we became people of such character as we are now (τοιοίδε γεγόναμεν), "through the washing of regeneration and renewing of the Spirit, which he poured out upon us." (I.64, quoting Titus 3:3-6)

Thus adherence to the Christian message and participation in Christian ritual foster moral excellence, not just in a few but in a "much larger number." Origen draws the social implications of that widespread effect explicitly:

> The critics of Christianity do not see in how many
> people the passions are suppressed and in how many
> the flood of evil is restrained, and in how many
> wild habits are tamed by reason of the gospel.
> They ought to have confessed their gratitude to
> the gospel when they observe its services to the
> community[6] and borne testimony to it that, even
> if it may not be true at any rate it is of ad-
> vantage to the human race (τὸ λυσιτελὲς τῷ τῶν
> ἀνθρώπων γένει).   (I.64)

For purposes of argument Origen concedes that the truth of
the Christian message may be immaterial; its effects, plainly
and clearly observable, are sufficient in themselves to certify
its benefit to the world.  On practical grounds alone, the Christians should be welcomed by the communities in which they dwell.
Though their social and economic status marks them as trouble-
some outsiders, they confound all expectations by preaching a
divine message and by leading moral lives in conformity with it.
Things are not as they seem; Christian behavior can only be
viewed from the perspective of the Double Image.  On appearances
alone, Christians were prime suspects for illegal, immoral, and
magical activity, and Celsus tries relentlessly to convert that
suspicion into fact.  Origen, however, attempts to sever the
connection between appearances and actual behavior; he even
manipulates those common expectations to his own advantage by
claiming that the success of Jesus and his followers is all the
more impressive:

> Who, therefore, that does not give merely a cursory
> study to the nature of the facts, would not be
> amazed at a man who overcame and was able to rise
> above all the factors that tended to discredit him,
> and in his reputation to surpass all the distinguished
> men that have ever lived?  (I.30)

Origen's defense of the disciples repeats the major themes of
his defense of Jesus.  He directs his audiences' attention away
from background and toward accomplishment.  Individuals are
proven worthy of honor by their character, which itself is displayed in certain actions; religious messages are proven worthwhile by the effects which they exert on the community.  The
defense of the disciples, like that of Jesus, rests on the assumption that, in the apologetic situation presumed by CC,
Origen's view can best be supported by appeal to concrete, observable actions and events, rather than speculative reasoning.

In his approach to the questions raised by Celsus, Origen repeatedly demonstrates his agreement with Celsus' comments in
II.20 that above all a god ought to do good to men.  Though
Origen shares that definition of a primary category with Celsus, much of the discussion of Jesus is devoted to showing how
"doing good" should be understood.  Origen tries to link the
familiar to the other by introducing a distinctly moral note into the definition of good works.  Celsus' comments in VII.45
show that he viewed good works from the perspective of vested
authority and articulate power; the formation of colonies, healing of sickness, and the provision of children were among the
good works done by gods through oracles.  From the perspective
of insurgent authority and inarticulate power the colonies
formed are those of the people of god, the ills of the soul are
healed, and converts themselves adopt a new family and style of
life.  Throughout his defense of Jesus and his followers Origen
adopts but consistently retools a widespread and powerful image,
that of the civic benefactor.[7]  It becomes the fundamental means
by which he can translate the other, the Christian message, into
terms of the familiar.  It is the linch-pin of his apology.

*The Teaching of Jesus*

In considering Jesus' activity as a teacher Celsus does not
focus on a single incident; he drives instead for the heart of
the matter.  Of converts from Judaism, Celsus' Jew asks:

> What was wrong with you, citizens, that you left
> the law of our fathers (τὸν πάτριον νόμον), and,
> being deluded by that man whom we were addressing
> just now, were quite ludicrously deceived and
> have deserted us for another name and another
> life?  (II.1)

Celsus' reproach to the Jews for leaving their ancestral law
reasserts his overriding concern with the Single Image.  Despite
his earlier doubts in I.14, in book II Celsus chooses to see
the Jewish law as a source of traditional wisdom whose authority
is sanctioned by antiquity; to abandon the law for a message
with none of the trappings of vested authority was vain delusion.
Origen's reply is based on a slightly different application of
the Double Image.  If he is to remain consistent with the presuppositions of his Christian beliefs, Origen cannot take the
approach that he did in his defense of Jesus and the disciples.

Since Christian doctrine posits a continuity with the Jewish
law, he cannot simply propose an alternative to observance of
that law.  The appropriation of the Jewish scriptures assures
that the Christian message will appear familiar to Jewish
audiences, but it leaves Origen with the task of establishing
the difference in the Christian position.  With Jesus and the
disciples Origen described sources and channels of spiritual
power which were different from and superior to those commonly
recognized; in his discussion of the law he must assert both
similarity and superiority.

       After an opening complaint that Celsus failed to recognize
that some misguided Jewish believers in Jesus did not leave the
law of their fathers, Origen makes an essentially historical
argument.  He traces the earliest Christian observance of the
law to the inability to grasp, all at once, its proper spiritual
sense:

> This is my view.  Perhaps because the apostles were
> Jews and had been brought up in the literal inter-
> pretation of the Mosaic law, he had to tell them what
> was the true law, and of what heavenly things the
> Jewish worship was a pattern and shadow, and what
> were the good things to come of which a shadow was
> provided by the law about meat and drink and feasts
> and new moons and sabbaths.  (II.2)

The same scheme of gradually developing awareness of divine
truths which informed Origen's view of the proper role of wonder-working in the Christian mission also determines his treatment of the law.  Jesus' mission was to wean his Jewish followers
from the law a bit at a time.  Origen is again well aware of
the force of traditional assumptions.  His reading of the Jewish
law also relies on an essential weapon of the Double Image, allegory.  The progress of believers is depicted as the movement
from a literal to an allegorical interpretation of the law.
That explanation of the law according to its spiritual sense
was deferred, during Jesus' earthly career, since those disciples
who had been brought up among the Jews were not prepared to grasp
it.  But Jesus provided for the continuing education of his followers with the promise of a paraclete, the spirit of truth who
would continue to guide them after his departure (Jn. 16:12-13,
quoted in II.2).  The vision of progress towards an allegorical
interpretation of the law allows Origen to assert both the continuity between Judaism and Christianity and the superiority of

Christianity.  As a tool of the Double Image, allegory clearly
expresses the conviction that things are not as they seem; it
offers not an alternative system but an alternative *vision* of
the same system.

In his reply to the charge that Jesus led the Jews away
from the law of their fathers Origen has much to say *about* allegory, but he stops short of providing examples of it.  At the
conclusion of II.2 he claims that "another time will be more
suitable for explaining the way to interpret the Mosaic law."
It is less the practice of allegory that interests Origen in
II.1-7 than its theoretical utility in refuting Celsus' assertion that the Jewish believers in Jesus had left the law of their
fathers.  They retain the law but understand it in a different
light.  In passing, Origen gives a clear sketch of the progress
of the individual believer:

> It is true that for Christians the introduction to
> the faith is based on the religion of Moses and the
> prophetic writings.  And after the introduction the
> next stage of progress for beginners consists in the
> interpretation and exegesis of these.  (II.4)

In Origen's view the Jews remain stuck at the initial stage;
they have not looked deeply into their own scriptures, "but read
them superficially and only as stories."[8]  The Christian teaching
is nothing new (καινὸν), as Celsus charges, but rather the perfection and fulfillment of the potential of the Jewish scriptures.  The proof of that is found in the ability of Christian
doctrines "to lift and raise up the soul and mind of a man and
convince him that he has a certain citizenship, not like the
earthly Jews, somewhere down here on earth, but in heaven"
(II.5).  The remaking of Christian believers into a moral community which has its own laws and norms of membership is the
product of an alternative form of spiritual power; the specific
form which its laws develop results from the application of the
interpretative principle of the Double Image, allegory.  Through
allegory Origen can assert that what appears new, or other, is
in reality continuous or familiar.  As in the discussion of
Jesus' baptism, allegory is less important for the interpretations it yields than for the polemical leverage it furnishes.

Celsus' accusation that the "Christians teach nothing new"
(II.5) was designed to bring them back into conformity with the
traditional laws of the Jews, just as his disparagement of

Christian ethics as stale stuff (I.4) was intended to bring them
back into conformity with the ancient philosophical tradition.

That preoccupation with continuity and antiquity, which leads
him to value the Jewish law more highly than the Christian interpretation of it, is the expression of a Single Image of society.
Origen's assertion of both novelty and continuity depends on a
Double Image which asserts the importance of unseen dimensions
of human experience.

Celsus also uses his concern with continuity to undermine
Jesus' claims to divinity.  In II.6 he contends that "Jesus
kept all the Jewish customs, and even took part in their sacri-
fices" and that consequently "we ought not to believe in him as
Son of God."  Where Celsus used the disgrace of socio-economic
origins to discredit Jesus in I.28, in II.6 continuity with
religious origins serves the same purpose.  There is no warrant
in the life of a conventionally pious Jew for pretension to
divinity.  In response Origen simply asserts that "Jesus is the
Son of God who gave the law and the prophets"; the continuity he
sees is not one of practice but of obscure references to Jesus
in the law and the prophets which become clear with Christian
hindsight and the allegorical method.

The sketchy references to Jesus' lying and arrogance which
follow in II.7 may be out of place,[9] and Origen dismisses them
with brief appeals to biblical passages which demonstrate Jesus'
meekness and quibbles about the accuracy of the charges.  Finally, Origen rebuts the charge that Jesus did profane actions
by asserting that the abandonment of the literal injunctions of
the law was in no way profane.

II.1-7 is concerned with the continuity between the practices of Jesus and his followers and those enjoined in the law
of the Jews.  Celsus' concern with continuity stems from his
vision of society as a single set of traditionally sanctioned
roles and statuses.  For him the Christians' apparent abandonment
of the law is a scandal, authored by a deceitful Jesus.  On the
other hand, Jesus' own continuity with Jewish practices lays
bare his scheming pretensions to the status of son of God.  Celsus returns to the theme of Christian discontinuity with Jewish
origins at several points; it is the central issue raised by
the teaching of Jesus.

Celsus' polemical intent shines clearly through in VII.18
when he reveals the purported inconsistencies in the Christian
message. Neither the actual departure from the law, nor the
attempt to cover it over with plausible arguments impresses
Celsus. He finds both to be examples of Christian deceit and
foolishness. In VII.18-26 Origen responds to Celsus' claim that
the Christian exhortations to poverty, meekness, and pacifism
are in direct contradiction to the injunctions of Moses. Celsus
asks "Who is wrong? Moses or Jesus? Or when the Father sent
Jesus had he forgotten what commands he gave to Moses? Or did
he condemn his own laws and change his mind, and send his messenger for quite the opposite purpose?" (VII.18). For Celsus the
claim of the Christians to be in continuity with Judaism, despite
obvious contradiction, creates serious problems with the Christian concept of god. He sees the laws of Moses and those of
Jesus as mutually exclusive, or else as evidence of a curiously
indecisive or forgetful deity. Neither alternative is acceptable. The first denies Christians any hint of antiquity, for
Celsus a precious possession, and the second plays havoc with
the unity and majesty of the deity. Origen eludes that dilemma
by reading the commands of Moses with an eye to their spiritual
sense; promises of wealth and power to the righteous are taken
to be true on the spiritual, not on the literal level. Where
II.1-7 was an assertion of the necessity of allegory, VII.18-26
demonstrates what it can accomplish. The evident moral emphasis
accords with the major thrust of Origen's defense of Jesus, but
the use of allegory is not a common tactic. It may be that the
discussion of Jesus' teaching, rather than of specific incidents
from his life, strikes Origen as more amenable to such exegesis
in the situation presumed by CC.

While allegory could help Origen solve the question of
Christian continuity with Judaism, it could not address Celsus'
other objections. It remained of limited utility in CC. Celsus
felt that the novelty of Jesus' teaching which led Christians
to sever ties with the authoritative past also led them to live
rebelliously outside the recognized social and cultural structures of the present (cf. I.1; II.1; V.37). The refusal of
Christians to participate in imperially sanctioned celebrations

particularly disturbed him.  He views Jesus' saying that it is
impossible to serve two masters as "a rebellious utterance
(στάσεως . . . φωνὴν) of a people who . . . wall themselves off
and break away from the rest of mankind" (VIII.2).  In his answer, Origen returns to a more sociological use of the Double
Image.  He first cites scriptural authority for the superiority
of the one lord over the many gods mentioned in the Bible, but
he admits, alluding to Phil. 3:20, that Christians do pull away
from people who are alien to the "commonwealth of god (τῆς
πολιτείας τοῦ θεοῦ)."  Origen's approach to book VIII is consistent with the principle he introduced at the beginning of book I:
"it is not wrong to form associations against the laws for the
sake of truth."  As the ἴδιος ἦθος of Jesus freed him from the
reproach implied by his lowly origins, so does the ἦθος of the
Christian communities which form the commonwealth of god justify
their withdrawal from the social and cultural structures sanctioned by the imperial government.

For Celsus, the Christian passion for novelty not only
estranges them from the past and present in all their authoritative forms, it leads them to pretentious self-contradictions.
They exalt the author of their sedition (τῆς στάσεως ἀρχηγέτης)
over even his own father.  Celsus wonders whether the command
not to follow two masters should not apply to the Christians
themselves (VIII.15), in which case they should abandon their
unfounded worship of Jesus and return to the worship of the
father.  That would also return them to continuity with their
Jewish origins and pave the way for an accomodation with imperial
power.

Thus Celsus sees the teaching of Jesus as setting Christians
at odds with the tradition from which their movement sprang, the
society in which they lived, and the presuppositions of their
own beliefs.  It is rebellious in every conceivable fashion.
It is set outside all structures of intelligibility.  There is
no way to account for such an aberration from the perspective
of the Single Image.  Origen, in turn, invokes the privileges
of the Double Image.  He expounds the vision of an alternative
society, the commonwealth of god.  He asserts the validity of a
mode of exegesis which is based on the fundamental tenet of the

Double Image, that things are not merely as they seem.  But
since the apologetic task demands that the apologist's argument
be couched in terms well-known to his potential audiences, Origen
carefully founds his alternative system of access to spiritual
power on familiar images and patterns.  The civic benefactor
provides an initial model for the performer of good deeds who
is accorded divine status.  The conversion of the depraved and
the dissolute to the philosophical life is repeated to much
greater effect in the conversion of the simple and lowly to the
Christian mode of life.  Origen consistently strives to show
that the Christian teaching, while apparently aberrant, actually
works for the good of the larger community.  Despite the appearance of Jesus and his followers as the suspicious representatives
of an "other" world, Origen claims that their message can, and
does, do for society what more traditionally sanctioned forms
of religion claim to do, only better.  Another key to Origen's
position is his view of Christianity's superior moral effect.

*The Miracles of Jesus*

     As the discussions of the birth of Jesus and the sojourn in
Egypt showed, Celsus frequently attributed Jesus' purported
miracles to magic.  In response, Origen stressed that magicians
did their works solely to manifest their own powers, not to
call their spectators to moral reformation (cf. I.65).  Again,
the moral dimension of Christian activity proves crucial.  But
since the discussion of wonder-working in CC revolves around
specific incidents in the life of Jesus or in the lives of those
whom Celsus finds similar, further discussion can be postponed
here.

*The Body of Jesus*

     A minor but intriguing theme of Celsus' polemic concerns
the physical appearance and activities of Jesus.  Bader[10] claims
that the attack on the body of Jesus at the end of book I links
the beginning and end of the Jew's speech.  Celsus' doubts that
a god would have a σῶμα like that of Jesus, or that a god's
body would have been born in such an unseemly fashion, or eat,
or speak in the ways that Jesus did, are again designed to move

Jesus away from the positive pole of the spectrum between divinities and magicians and toward at least the neutral middle. No
tactic is left untried in the attempt to deny the divinity of
Jesus; social, historical, and moral complaints are buttressed
by physical ones.

The background of Celsus' brief comments in I.69-70 becomes a bit clearer in VI.75-77. There Celsus contends that if
Jesus' body had housed a divine spirit, it should have differed
in size, beauty, strength, or other characteristics:

> For it is impossible that a body which had some-
> thing more divine than the rest should be no different
> from any other. Yet Jesus' body was no different from
> any other, but, as they say, was little and ugly and
> indistinguished.  (VI.75)

Origen admits at first that Jesus may have been ugly, but he appeals to prophecies to secure for him a certain grandeur, and
even beauty. Celsus' position recalls Origen's remarks in I.32
that the spirit "which lived a more useful life on earth than
many men . . . needed a body which was not only distinguished
among human bodies, but was also superior to all others." But
while Origen used that argument to support the veracity of the
virgin birth, Celsus seems to have taken it in a more literal
fashion. To buttress the argument from prophecy, Origen returns
to his fascinating notion that Jesus' "body differed in accordance with the capacity of those who saw it, and on this account
appeared in such form as was beneficial for the needs of each
individual's vision" (VI.77), a consistent assertion of the
multiple image. But, as he does throughout CC, Origen does not
go into further detail. He fears that Celsus would dismiss any
stories of Jesus' multiple images as πλάσματα, "just like the
stories of Jesus' miracles." The concept of the variability of
Jesus' appearance functions for Origen in the same way as his
use of allegory, and it receives the same fate. It enables him
to disarm momentarily a specific criticism of Celsus, but since
the work is destined for those whose Christian faith is non-
existent or imperfect Origen does not use it in CC to provide a
fully satisfying alternative to the viewpoint of Celsus.

Bader links Celsus' remarks in VI.75 to those in VI.73 which
call the virgin birth of Jesus more directly into question.

For him they are part of an overall scheme of the denial of
Jesus' divinity which denigrates the ideas of incarnation (VI.73)
and of the visit of a god to the remote location of Palestine
(VI.78). It need only be added here, as a supplement to the
earlier remarks on the virgin birth, that Celsus in VI.75 develops
some of the theses from the early part of his treatise as well as
those specific to Origen's book VI. Finally, in VII.13 Celsus
amplifies his concerns with the eating habits of Jesus, with
particular reference to the passover lamb and the vinegar and
gall of the crucifixion. There Origen takes the same tack that
he did in his defense of the flight to Egypt: Jesus' eating is
in full conformity with his having assumed a human form.

Origen's defense of Jesus' physical nature remains in accord
with his basic principle that incarnation imposed certain human
necessities upon Jesus, but he leaves unanswered the question
raised by Celsus' implicit assertion that the superior soul of a
worthy claimant to divine status should have a body that is, in
all respects, a superior vessel. Whether Origen avoided that
side issue intentionally or not can not be discerned. It does
suggest, however, that Origen did not intend to fit all of his
answers to Celsus' charges into a coherent system. As it stands,
the brief debate about the body of Jesus testifies more to the
exhaustive nature of the attack and defense, and to the ability
of both principles to use their familiar tactics on even minor
questions. It does not add any new categories which were used
to interpret claimants to divine status or the criteria of
judgement which underlay them.

*Parallel Careers*

Throughout CC Celsus has occasion to compare the career of
Jesus to those of other candidates for divine status. But he
never makes an extended comparison between Jesus and one other
character. Rather, specific incidents from the careers of a
variety of religious and philosophical figures are adduced as
they contribute to specific points in Celsus' argument. Those
considered by Celsus and Origen can be grouped loosely into four
categories: anonymous wandering holy men, named contemporaries
of Jesus, Greek gods and heroes, Plato and the ancient sages.
Each will be discussed in turn.

Group 1:  Wandering Holy Men

Celsus first introduces the comparison in I.50 in two related statements:

> Why should you be the subject of these prophecies
> rather than the thousands of others who lived after
> the prophecy was uttered . . . . Some people in
> ecstasy and others who go about begging say that
> they are sons of god (υἱον θεοῦ) who have come
> from above.

Clearly, the uniqueness of Jesus is at issue, but the issue is focused on the specificity of the prophecies in the Hebrew scriptures.  In his response, Origen takes Celsus to task for having mentioned only a few of the many prophecies concerning Jesus, but he bases most of his own argument on the passage in Micah 5:2 which discusses a future ruler who shall come out of Bethlehem. Thus Origen attempts to restrict the field of claimants by specifying the birthplace of the son of god.  He also garners indirect support for his reliance on that single passage by noting that "after the advent of Christ people busied themselves with destroying the idea that his birth had been prophesied from early times, and took away such teaching from the people" (I.51). Origen does note that it was difficult for the Jews who were attached strongly to their way of life and religion to abandon them and accept the prophesied Christ; he acknowledges the powerful hold on the Jews of a single, fixed traditional image of life.

In addition to the fulfillment of prophecy, the second major issue raised by Celsus' comparison of Jesus to wandering holy men is that of their effect on posterity.  When, in II.8, Celsus asserts that many others like Jesus have appeared "to people who are willing to be deceived," Origen challenges him to show even one of them who has benefitted the life of mankind and converted men from the flood of sins like Jesus did.  The overwhelmingly beneficial work of Jesus on behalf of mankind becomes the second major theme of Origen's defense against the implications of Celsus' comparison of Jesus with wandering holy men.  While arguments about the specificity of prophecy certify that Jesus alone is the heir to the prophecies of the Hebrew scriptures, arguments about the effects of Jesus' activity certify

that he alone had any lasting impact. One strategy traces the
continuity between the past and the time of Jesus, the other
between the time of Jesus and Origen's present. Origen broadens
the perspective of the argument, moving away from a narrow con-
centration on certain claims to the historical contexts in which
they are to be understood. Again, he offers an alternative
evaluation of the same claims.

Although the appeal to the lasting effects of Jesus' works
for mankind did serve to separate him from the amorphous group
of wandering holy men, it still left open to question the power
which enabled him to perform such works. Celsus articulated his
suspicions in an extended passage in II.49, basing them, it
seems, on Jesus' own words in Matthew 24:23-27:

> O light and truth, with his own voice he explicitly
> confesses, as even you have recorded, that there will
> come among you others also who employ similar
> miracles, wicked men and sorcerers (κακοὶ καὶ γόητες)
> and he names one Satan as devising this: so that not
> even he denies that these wonders have nothing divine
> about them, but are works of wicked men (ὡς ταῦτά γε
> οὐδὲν θεῖον ἀλλὰ πονηρῶν ἐστιν ἔργα). Nevertheless,
> being compelled by the truth, he both reveals the
> deeds of others and proves his own to be wrong. Is
> it not a miserable argument (σχέτλιον) to infer from
> the same works (ἀπὸ τῶν αὐτῶν ἔργων) that he is a god
> (θεὸν) while they are sorcerers (γόητας)? Why should
> we conclude from these works that the others were any
> more wicked than this fellow, taking the witness of
> Jesus himself? In fact, even he admitted that these
> works were not produced by any divine nature (θείας
> θύσεως), but were the signs of certain cheats and
> wicked men (ἀπατεώνων τινῶν καὶ παμπονήρων).

In II.49 it is the particular character of a claimant's ἔργα
which will speak either for or against uniqueness. Since Celsus
finds Jesus himself claiming that certain miracles are not done
by divine power, and since he assumes that the miracles of Jesus
were of the same type, he concludes that there was nothing divine
about the miracles of Jesus. It is clear, then, that there
would be no way of distinguishing Jesus from those he calls sorcerers. In reponse, Origen again broadens the perspective. He
appeals to the τέλος of miracles as their key characteristic.
Just as the wonders of the "Antichrist" bear the fruit of deceit, the wonders of Jesus and his disciples produced the salvation of souls; Origen further denies that one could reasonably

say that the higher life (τὸν κρείττονα βίον) which restricts
evil actions is produced by deceit.  Origen attempts to make
that distinction between divine and counterfeit wonders even
sharper by declaring in the following section that "what is accomplished by God's power is nothing like what is done by sorcery" (II.51).  In Origen's view Celsus has erred by concentrating on the performance of wonders rather than on the effects
that they produce.  He concedes the reality of magic, but argues
from that reality that wonders done by divine power must also
be real, given the "general principle that where something bad
is pretending to be of the same kind as something good, then
there must be something good which is its opposite"[11] (II.51).
Once the reality of wonders done both by magic and by divine
power is granted, it becomes a question of distinguishing one
type from the other.  Origen supplies his distinguishing criterion in a rhetorical question:

> . . . why should we not also examine carefully people
> who profess to do miracles, and see whether their
> lives and moral characters (ἐξετάσομεν ἀπὸ τοῦ βίου
> καὶ τοῦ ἤθους), and the results of their miracles
> (καὶ τῶν ἐπακολουθούντων ταῖς δυνάμεσιν), harm men or
> effect moral reformation (ἤτοι εἰς βλάβην τῶν
> ἀνθρώπων ἢ εἰς ἠθῶν ἐπανόρθωσιν)?  (II.51)

It is both the moral character of the wonder-worker and the moral
character of the results he effects that distinguished miracles
done by divine power from those done by magic.  Again, the benefits which Origen claims have accrued to humanity as a result of
the actions of Jesus are rather different from those which Celsus
attributed to oracles in VII.45:  the building of cities, the
healing of diseases, the averting of famines, the formation of
colonies, etc.  The wonders which Jesus performs "for the benefit of mankind (εἰς ὠφέλειαν ἀνθρώπων)" were of a decidedly
stronger moral and spiritual cast:  the conversion from the
flood of sins, moral reformation, the exhortation to believe in
the true god, etc.

Origen's particular conception of benefits becomes clearer
when the discussion of divine and magical wonders resolves into
a specific comparison between Moses and Jesus in II.52.  (Again,
Origen plays on the dual identity of his interlocutor as both
Jew and Greek.)  At first, in II.50, Origen had used the example

of Moses to show that wonders done by divine power could be
distinguished from those done by magic by their τέλος; in II.52
he argues for the superiority of Jesus over Moses on the basis
of the superiority of his results:

> For if the outcome (τὸ τέλος) which was that a whole
> nation owed its origin to the wonders of Moses,
> shows the indubitable fact that it was God who caused
> the miracles of Moses, why should not this argument
> be even more cogent in the case of Jesus, since he
> did a greater work (μεῖζον . . . ἔργον) than that of
> Moses? . . . Jesus made a greater venture when he
> introduced the life according to the gospel into
> that already existing with its ancestral ethical
> codes and traditional way of life which conformed to
> the established laws.

With those remarks Origen continues to set life (πολιτείαν) according to the gospel in opposition to the accepted traditional
way of life of the Jews; he opposes the ἴδιος ἦθος of the Christians to the πάτριος νόμος of the Jews, just as he had opposed
the alternative route taken by Jesus to fame and glory to the
accepted prerequisites of noble lineage, wealth, and superior
education in I.29. His Double Image leads him to focus on personal accomplishments and morality rather than social status
and tradition, on inarticulate rather than articulate sources
of power.

Origen's remarks in II.49-54 show again that the Jews and
their preeminent leader, Moses, play an ambiguous part in the
defense of Jesus against charges that he practiced magic. On
the one hand, Moses' performance in the court of the Egyptian
pharoah can be used to deflect specific charges away from Jesus
in particular and onto a broader field, thereby confronting
Celsus' Jewish interlocutor with the possibility that the charges
may apply equally as well to Moses. On the other hand, the close
association of Moses and Jesus tends to blur the distinctions
between them. Thus Origen's argument frequently occurs in two
stages. He dissociates Jesus first from the general crowd of
sorcerers and next from those whose wonders might plausibly be
attributed to divine power. Origen can pivot those two stages
around the figure of Moses since Celsus himself introduced the
Jew to make his accusations against Jesus.

Perhaps the most well-known reference to wandering holy
men in CC occurs in VII.9 where Celsus claims to have first-
hand knowledge of prophets in Phoenicia and Palestine:

> There are many . . . who are nameless, who prophesy
> at the slightest excuse for some trivial cause both
> inside and outside temples; and there are some who
> wander about begging and roaming around cities and
> military camps; and they pretend to be moved as if
> giving some oracular utterance. It is an ordinary
> and common custom for each one to say 'I am god (or
> a son of god, or a divine Spirit). And I have
> come. Already the world is being destroyed. And
> you shall see me returning again with heavenly
> power. Blessed is he who has worshipped me now!
> But I will cast everlasting fire upon all the
> rest, both on cities and on country places. And
> men who fail to realize the penalties in store for
> them will in vain repent and groan. But I will pre-
> serve for ever those who have been convinced by
> me.' . . . Having brandished these threats they then
> go on to add incomprehensible, incoherent, and utterly
> obscure utterances, the meaning of which no intelligent
> person could discover; for they are meaningless and
> nonsensical, and give a chance for any fool or sorcerer
> to take the words in whatever sense he likes.

The precise polemical intention behind Celsus' report has been
difficult to ascertain. Reitzenstein acknowledged the similarities between the utterances of Celsus' prophets and those attributed to the Montanist prophetess, Maximilla, by Eusebius
(HE V.16-17), but he did not find sufficient evidence to justify
the conclusion that Celsus was describing Montanists.[12] Elsewhere Reitzenstein suggests that it was Celsus' intent to have
the Phoenician and Palestinian prophets serve as a point of comparison for both the Hebrew prophets and for Jesus.[13] That
suggestion at least accords with Origen's response. In VII.10
he begins a defense of the Hebrew prophets which attributes to
their words effects similar to those accomplished by the words
of Jesus: "the prophets, according to the will of God, said
without any obscurity whatever could be at once understood as
beneficial to their hearers and helpful towards attaining moral
reformation (ἐπανορθώσει)." Origen also refers his readers
to his studies of Isaiah and Ezekiel and the twelve prophets
for a fuller defense (VII.11), and hints at the allegorical interpretations which will be found there. It is striking, however, that Origen mentions neither Jesus or later Christian

prophets as being similar to the figures mentioned by Celsus.
He seems to have construed "prophet" as narrowly referring to
the prophets of the Hebrew scriptures, as when he claims that
"in Celsus' time there were no prophets like the ancients"
(VII.11). Origen dismisses Celsus' claim to have cross-examined
such characters as a lie (φεῦδος) and attempts to expose the
haziness of his information. All in all, Origen denies the relevance of the passage in VII.9 to the first, second, or third
Christian centuries. What might have called forth clear and
full statements about claimants to divine status and their teachings (especially the apocalyptic and messianic statements voiced
by Celsus' prophets) remains a matter for speculation because
Origen did not join the issue. By limiting the relevance of
his adversary's statements, he was able to avoid a potentially
thorny objection. Refusal even to discuss the relative merits
of the Phoenician and Palestinian prophets and Jesus as claimants
to the status of θεός, υἱός θεοῦ, and πνεῦμα θεῖον may indicate
that Origen simply rejected the comparison out of hand. But it
is difficult to argue convincingly from his silence.

Two other passages provide some background for Celsus'
charges against Jesus, but they reveal little of Origen's defense. In III.50 Celsus lumps Christian preachers together with
those who display trickery in the market-place and who go about
begging but would never enter the company of intelligent men.
Jesus himself was charged with the display of trickery and the
practice of begging by Celsus (cf. I.50), but the discussion
following III.50 is limited to Christian preachers, whose philan-
thropic motives are asserted to be superior to those of any
other market-place preachers. Similarly, in VI.39 Origen denies
that any Christians are even suspected of sorcery, the invocation of demons by magical names, or any other magical practices.
The defense is the same that Origen made for Jesus when he was
charged with performing magic. He draws a sharp line between
the moral character of magic and of religion:

> Probably there is no one to whom his objection applies,
> since there are no magicians who practice their art
> under pretence of a religion which is of this moral
> character (τὸν χαρακτῆρα τοῦτον), though perhaps he
> was thinking of some who use such methods to deceive

the gullible so that they may give the impression
of doing some miracle by divine power (θεία δυνάμει
τι).  (VI.39)

Though similar lines were drawn in the discussion of Jesus' wonder-working, Origen's quick assertion that charges of magic are
irrelevant to the Christian situation precludes their consideration in VI.39.

Origen's defense of Jesus from the attack on his unique
status as son of god which Celsus implied by comparing him to
wandering holy men repeats familiar themes.  Origen uses the
imprecision of Celsus' reports and the dual identity of Celsus'
mouthpiece to full advantage.  He attempts to shift the focus
away from the performance of certain acts toward their broader
historical contexts.  In those contexts, he finds, it becomes
clear that only the wonders wrought by Jesus were prophesied and
only Jesus' wonders had any beneficial impact beyond his own
lifetime.  Origen's case seems strong partly because of the lack
of full evidence on the wandering holy men and also because he
carefully avoids some of the more striking parallels (such as
those in VII.9) between them and Jesus.  The discussion becomes
more narrow and more precise with the second group.

Group 2:  Named Contemporaries of Jesus

Contemporaries of Jesus who may have been competing claimants to divine status do not play a large role in the fragments
of Celsus.  Indeed, it seems that Origen introduces them into
the discussion at several points because he possesses convincing
refutations of their claims.  Those mentioned include Simon of
Samaria, Dositheus, Judas the Galilean, and Theudas.  Origen's
treatment of them is most clearly set forth in VI.11.  Celsus
had again attempted to deny the uniqueness of Jesus by claiming
that the "glib slogan (πρόχειρον) 'Believe if you want to be
saved, or away with you'" was shared by many other groups, each
with their own candidate for divine status.  Consequently, he
asks "what will those do who really want to be saved? Are they
to throw dice in order to divine where they may turn, and whom
they are to follow?"  (VI.11).  Origen counters that Jesus was
the only son of god to have visited the human race, and that
others who have aspired to the same status and similar powers
have proved to be of no significance.  He offers several cases

in point.  Simon, the so-called great power of god, absolved his
followers of the risk of death, but there are no Simonians left
anywhere in the world, as far as Origen can tell.  It seems to
Origen that even the evil demon who plots against Jesus and his
teaching found Simon of no use.  Further, the Simonian movement
failed despite having no opposition in its formative period, unlike the Christian movement.  The story is similar for Dositheus.
His movement did not even flourish in its earliest days, and
Origen claims that it numbers less than 30 in the mid-third century.  Judas and Theudas fare no better.  Both, according to
Origen, wanted to be considered a great person (τινα . . .μέγαν),
"but as their teaching was not of god they were killed and all
who believed in them were scattered" (VI.11).  Origen provides
further reason for Simon's failure in V.62.  It seems that he
attributed Jesus' divinity to his performance of wonders, rather
than to the moral reform which they effected.  Thus, "neither
Celsus nor Simon was able to understand how Jesus as a 'good
husbandman' of the Word of God has been able to spread his teaching through most of Greece and barbarians' lands, and to fill
them with doctrines which change the soul from all evil and lead
on to the creator of the universe" (V.62).

Finally, Origen considers Theudas, Judas, Dositheus, and
Simon again in I.57 in response to Celsus' claim that others
will claim that prophecies in the Hebrew scriptures referred to
them and not to Jesus.  Origen arranges his comments around the
statement attributed to Gamaliel in Acts 5:38-39:  ". . . if
this plan or this undertaking is of men, it will fail; but if
it is of God, you will not be able to overthrow them.  You
might even be found opposing God."  Origen recounts the same
sequence in each of the four cases:  the initial appearance of
the leader, the attraction of followers, the death of the leader,
and the dissolution of the movement, in order to show that each
movement was indeed the work of men, not of god.  The tactic of
describing the opposition as fakes with limited appeal who
operated in out-of-the-way areas, though based on a scriptural
passage in I.57, strongly resembles Celsus' own description of
Jesus and his followers.  Origen is able to support his own position, however, by emphasizing the longer duration of Jesus'

effective action.  Like the anonymous wandering holy men, Judas,
Theudas, Dositheus, and Simon are found to have created no
lasting communities and to have performed no works of lasting
moral benefit.  Any claims that they fulfilled the scriptural
prophecies are thus, to Origen, patently false.

Group 3:  Greek Gods and Heroes

     The discussion of Greek gods and heroes is not given a
strong focus by either Celsus or Origen.  Celsus uses them to
provide examples of the widespread occurrence of miracles, of
the fact that many humans were thought to have become gods after
death, and of the performance of many beneficial acts for mankind.  Since much of the discussion concentrates on various candidates for apotheosis, it is difficult to decide under what
heading the material might best be discussed.  Bader suggests
that the material in III.22-33 makes sense in connection with
the resurrection of Jesus,[14] but since Celsus does adduce more
specific parallels to the resurrection elsewhere and since the
discussion of apotheosis is woven into the discussion of wonder-
working and performance of beneficial acts, the material in
III.22-33 will be discussed here under the general heading of
"parallel careers."

     In III.3 Celsus mentions that miracles have occurred in
many places, citing the performance of Asclepius, a certain un-
named Clazomenian, and Cleomedes the Astypalean.  Apparently,
Celsus intended to undermine the uniqueness of Jesus' position
as a wonder-worker.  Origen, however, does not address the issue
of uniqueness directly.  Instead he tries to turn the argument
to his own advantage by criticizing Celsus for having made no
mention of the Jews, whose very history is miraculous.  Origen's
recourse to the Hebrew scriptures is familiar.  Once the claim
that miracles can be found among Jews as well as among Greeks
has been asserted, the way is prepared for claiming the superiority of Jesus and the Christians to the Jews and thus, by im-
plication, to the Greeks originally mentioned by Celsus.  Origen
does, in fact, mention the prophecies of the Hebrew scriptures
about "a certain saviour (τινος . . . σωτῆρος)," but he does not
develop that idea.  The argument which would for Origen distinguish Jesus from Asclepius, the Clazomenian, and Cleomedes remains implicit in III.3; its full ramifications are not pursued.

Celsus raises the issue again in III.22. Concerning the
Dioscuri, Heracles, Asclepius, and Dionysos, he asserts that he
does not tolerate the opinion that they are gods (θεούς), because
they were humans in the first place "even though they performed
many noble acts on behalf of mankind (πολλὰ . . . γενναῖα ὑπὲρ
ἀνθρώπων)." The precise argument of Celsus in that fragment is
difficult to recover. On the one hand, he seems to endorse the
idea that good works for mankind can earn their perpetrators
fame and honor, but, on the other hand, he stops short of accept-
ing the idea that good works can transform humans into gods. The
explicit bearing of those remarks on Jesus is elusive, especially
since the two phrases about Jesus concern his resurrection appearances rather than the bearing of his purported good works
on his status as a divine being. It is clear, though, that
Origen chooses to defend just that link between the performance
of good works and the claim to divine status. He begins by casting doubt on the character of the claimants advanced by Celsus.
After a quick review of several positions on the possibility of
the continued existence of the soul after death, Origen details
the reasons which tell against the acceptance of Celsus' candidates as gods or heroes. In the case of Heracles it is licentiousness (ἀκολασία) which clouds the issue. The death of Asclepius by a thunderbolt of Zeus and the fact that, according to
Homer, the Dioscuri die on alternate days also exclude them from
consideration as θεοί or heroes. That Origen also finds the
conduct of Dionysos licentious (III.23), however, suggests that
a moral judgement is the leading edge of his complaint.

It does not appear that Origen has sharply delimited categories in mind in III.22. He briefly mentions gods, heroes, and
"simple souls" as possibilities, but tends to focus instead on
the ἀκολασία which excludes Celsus' candidates from consideration
as divine. Again, it is the moral qualities evidenced by certain
actions which are crucial in the assignment of candidates to
categories.

That point is made more explicitly in III.25 when Origen
asserts that the power to heal and the gift of foreknowledge are
in themselves "things indifferent" and that they alone do not
prove their possessors to be good. Indeed, Origen doubts that

even an uneducated man would call someone pious (εὐσεβῆ) who
did not have moderation and virtue (μετριότητι καὶ ἀρετῇ). Thus
Origen can accept the attribution of healings to Asclepius and
of divination to Apollo without conceding that those actions in
any way support claims to divinity. Indeed the shameful mode
of Apollo's inspiration of the Pythian prophetess (through her
genitals) contrasts starkly with the pure virgin birth of Jesus,
and the virgin birth strengthens Jesus' dissociation from any
hint of licentiousness.

The moral criterion is even extended to the disciples of
Jesus in III.24, where Origen records Celsus' claim that a great
multitude had seen the miracles of Asclepius but prefers the
testimony of the disciples since "we see their unqualified goodness." Origen's underlying position seems to be that an assessment of the moral character both of claimants to divinity and
their partisans will decide whether the claims are to be honoured.

Origen takes a similar tack in an extended discussion of the
purported parallels between the careers of Aristeas of Procones-
sus and Jesus. Celsus had mentioned Aristeas' wonderous disappearance and reappearance, the amazing tales told about him, and
the fact that Apollo had commanded the Metapontines to regard
him as a god. He added pointedly that "nobody still thinks him
a god" (III.26). In response, Origen first gives the full text
about Aristeas from Herodotus (Hist. IV.14-15); he then voices
his suspicion that Celsus accepted the story about Aristeas as
true, despite his reticence. Proceeding on that assumption,
Origen offers the following guidelines for assessing the relative
truth or falsity of the stories about Aristeas and about Jesus:

> Take an unbiased view of the story about Aristeas,
> and of that related about Jesus, and consider
> whether, in view of the result in the lives of
> those who have been helped to reform their moral
> character (εἰς ἠθῶν ἐπανόρθωσιν) and to become
> devoted to the supreme God, we should not say
> that it is right to believe that the events related
> of Jesus could not have happened apart from divine
> providence, while this cannot be said of Aristeas
> the Proconessian. (III.27)

Origen further upbraids Celsus for providing no explanation of
why providence (πρόνοια) would allow Aristeas to perform such

miracles and of what benefit they might have had for the human
race.  On the other hand, the stories about the miracles of
Jesus have a powerful explanation:

> We argue that God wanted to establish the doctrine
> spoken by Jesus which brought salvation (σωτήριον)
> to men; and it was strengthened by the apostles who were,
> so to speak, foundations of the building of Christianity
> which he was beginning to build, and it is increasing
> even in recent times, when many cures are done in the
> name of Jesus and there are other manifestations of
> considerable significance.  (III.28)

Origen also asks what benefit (ποίαν ὠφέλειαν) has accrued to
the Metapontines for honouring Aristeas as a god, in sharp contrast to the benefit of salvation which accrues to the worship-
pers of Jesus.  In III.29 Origen further amplifies the salvation
wrought by Jesus, describing his destruction of the tyranny of
the demons who enslaved the earth, which in turn began the process of the conversion and reform (ἐπιστροφῆς καὶ διορθώσεως)
of mankind.

With the mention of the conversion and reform of mankind
Origen leaves the comparison of Aristeas and Jesus behind to
linger on the distinguishing features of the members of the
Christian community.  He begins with a rhetorical question:
"Who would not admit that even the less satisfactory members of
the Church and those who are far inferior when compared with
the better members are far superior to the assemblies of the
people?"  (III.29).  The "weak in faith" who elsewhere seem to
frustrate Origen with their imperfect grasp of Christian doctrine
nevertheless are far superior to those outside of the Christian
fold.  Origen even undertakes a brief inventory in the next
section.  He compares the assemblies of the people in Athens,
Corinth, and Alexandria to the churches in the same cities, each
time to the detriment of the popular assemblies.  In general he
finds that

> . . . the councillors in every city do not show in
> their moral character (ἤθεσιν) anything worthy of
> their pre-eminent authority by which they appear to
> be superior to the citizens.  (III.30)

On the other hand, even in the weakest rules of the church,
"there is superior progress towards the virtues surpassing the

character (ἤθη) of those who are councillors and rulers in the
cities." Origen draws the expected conclusion in III.31 that it
is more reasonable (εὔλογον) that the divine element (θειότης)
in Jesus was exceptional and that a similar divine element was
missing in Aristeas, despite the urgings of Apollo to consider
him a god. Thus the moral character of Christians confirms the
truth of the stories they tell, just as the moral character of
Jesus confirms the divine power of his actions, all of which supports his claim to divine status. Since Aristeas himself mani-
fests no superior moral character, and since his wonders effected
no conversion or moral reformation, and since the moral character
of the Greek populace in general is deficient, Aristeas' claims
to divine status are to be denied.

A similar line of reasoning allows Origen to dismiss the
claims made for Abaris in III.31. He can find no reason why the
gift of supernatural flight should be considered a benefit to
the human race; nor is he certain that even Abaris himself derived any benefit from his ability to fly. Perhaps because he
dealt so thoroughly with Aristeas, Origen offers no further
comments on Abaris.

The assertion that the soul of Hermotimus of Clazomenae
frequently left his body and wandered about is treated with similar dispatch in III.32. Origen credits the story to the arrangements of certain demons, denying even that such events ever
actually happened. Similarly, the demons thus intended to cast
the stories about Jesus as inventions (πλάσματα). But Origen
tries to frustrate the design of the demons by citing a string
of scriptural passages which show that the soul of Jesus was
separated from his body not by the compulsion of men but by the
miraculous power (παράδοξον ἐξουσίαν) given to him. In that
instance, Origen's assertion of the differences between Hermotimus and Jesus is clear enough, but the scriptural passages and
his comments on them do not seem to address his initial reason
for that difference.

Origen's treatment of the alleged disappearance of Cleomedes
of Astypalea gives a clear and fuller account of the criteria
he uses to distinguish many types of Greek stories from those
about Jesus:

> Even if this tale is not the invention (πλάσμα)
> which it seems to be, it cannot be compared with the
> stories of Jesus. For in Celsus' examples no evidence
> of the divinity (θειότητος) attributed to them are to
> be found in the life of the men, whereas the evidences
> of Jesus' divinity are the Churches of people who have
> been helped (αἱ τῶν ὠφελουμένων ἐκκλησίαι), the
> prophecies spoken about him, the cures which are done
> in his name, the knowledge and wisdom in Christ, and
> reason which is to be found in those who know how to
> advance beyond mere faith, and how to search out the
> meaning of the divine scriptures.  (III.33)

As they usually do, Origen's criteria attempt to set Jesus in a
broader historical context; they form an "hourglass" pattern
with Jesus at the neck. The prophecies about him distinguish
him from other claimants to divine status because he alone fits
their narrow specifications, as Origen argued in I.50-51.
Similarly, the abundant evidence of Jesus' good work in the present (churches, cures, wisdom, reasoned interpretation of scripture) point back to Jesus as the only candidate for divinity
whose impact was felt beyond his immediate life and surroundings.
That the argument is heavily weighted in favor of evidence from
Origen's own time (four of five criteria) accords with his emphasis on the intention or goal behind the exercise of divine
power.  It is just the lack of such evident intention in the disappearance of Cleomedes which led Origen to suspect that the
story was an invention.

The centrality of the idea of benefaction to Origen's defense of Jesus and the stories about him is expressed clearly in
his summary response to Celsus' remark that he could provide
many more examples of miracles among the Greeks:

> Suppose that this is so, and that there are many other
> such examples; they have done no good to mankind (μηδὲν
> ὠφεληκότας τὸ τῶν ἀνθρώπων γένος); and what action
> done by them could be found comparable with the work
> of Jesus and the miraculous stories about him, of which
> we have spoken at length.  (III.34)

The specifically moral nature of the benefaction which Origen has in mind becomes clearer in his remarks in V.2-3.  Origen
correctly observes that Celsus' objection that no god or child
of god (θεὸς . . . θεοῦ παῖς) has come down to visit mankind
repeats his earlier remarks, but he does take the opportunity

to note that Celsus' general principle, if correct, rules out
the idea that such gods provide oracles to men or heal them.
More telling is his moral argument against oracles:

> Should we regard as divine Jesus who accomplished and
> performed such great miracles, or those who by means
> of oracles and divination fail to reform the morals
> (μὴ ἐπανορθοῦντας μὲν τα ἤθη) of those who are healed
> and, what is more, depart from the pure and holy solemn
> worship of the Creator of the universe, and by means
> of a worship of several gods tear the souls of people
> who pay attention to them away from the one and only
> manifest and genuine God?   (V.3)

Whereas moral reform, conversion from the "flood of sins,"
and the direction of people's attention toward the true god were
evidence in favor of Jesus' candidacy for divinity, the failure
to reform morals, and the substitution of false forms of worship
tell against the claims of the gods of the oracles.

Origen's opposition to Celsus' contention that no god or
son of a god had come down to earth had been anticipated in
III.35 when Origen had asserted that Jesus had been able "to
show a considerable number of men" that such a descent was possible.  Although Origen does not support his claim with specific
evidence at that time, it can be surmised that the performance
of specific moral benefactions such as those mentioned in III.33
was in his mind as unassailable proof.

Finally, since the way in which Origen deals with Celsus'
final example of a claimant to divine status, Hadrian's favorite
Antinous, repeats many of the earlier themes, it can be recounted
in summary.  Origen first mentions the licentiousness (ἀκολασία)
of Antinous which clearly distinguishes him from Jesus.  He proceeds to slander those who tell stories of Antinous' miracles
as liars (III.36) and to attribute his wonders to Egyptian magic
and spells (μαγγαμείας . . . καὶ τελετάς), a tactic which Celsus
had tried against Jesus in I.28.  In general, Origen finds belief
in Antinous to be the result of ill-fortune (ἀτυχής), while belief in Jesus is the result of either good-fortune (εὐτυχής) or
a rigorous examination of the evidence (III.38).  Origen concludes that in the case of Antinous, as in the case of any other
candidates for divinity, Christians will brook no comparisons
with Jesus since they have learned (relying on Psalm 95:5) that

all the gods of the heathens are demons and that the "divine and
holy angels of God are of a nature and character other than that
of all the daemons on earth" (III.37).  The specific place of
Jesus among those divine and holy angels and the full explanation
of that doctrine (λόγος) which, Origen admits, even the Greeks
would find esoteric and mysterious (ἐσωτερικῶν καὶ ἐποπτικῶν) is
deferred for the consideration of a more appropriate audience.[15]

Celsus' and Origen's discussion of various "Greek" claimants
to divine status ranged widely through the mythological and
religious lore of late Antiquity.  More often than not the parti-
cipants merely allude to certain events or personal characteristics which they deem important for their argumentive purposes.
Only in the case of Aristeas of Proconnesus is the evidence sup-
plied in a relatively full form.  But it was neither writer's
intention to provide a survey of ancient religious thought.  They
had more pressing concerns.  Celsus was concerned to choose those
characters and instances which would enable him to cast doubt on
the unique qualifications of Jesus for the status of a θεός or
υἱός θεοῦ.  The crucial element in his characterizations of Greek
gods and heroes is his polemical intent.  The same is true for
Origen.  If their comments on the various gods and heroes seem
disorganized and random, it should be kept in mind that they are
interested not in narrative unity but in the classificatory potential of the events they have chosen.  To return to the vocab-
ulary of the first chapter, they are interested in statements of
the type "X should be considered Y."  The lives of Jesus and the
Greek gods and heroes are ransacked for *reasons why* any candidate
should be considered to manifest a certain quality.  These reasons why are to be found in a random series of events ($Z_1$ . . .
$Z_n$).  Each event, no matter how discrete and unrelated to the
others, is potentially crucial in its classificatory force, but
it is the process of classifying and its ultimate results which
capture the interest of Celsus and Origen, not the discrete incidents which may or may not be useful in that purpose.  They are
merely grist for the mill.

Group 4:  Plato and the Ancient Sages

Discussion here will be limited to those passages which
bear on a comparison of Plato (or the ancient sages of Greece)

and Jesus; a consideration of the underlying philosophical affinities of the treatises of Celsus and Origen would lead too far
afield.[16]   At the outset of his sixth book Origen reports that
Celsus had compared several extracts from the works of Plato with
passages from scripture and had concluded that the common ideas
were better expressed among the Greeks, "who refrained from
making exalted claims and from asserting that they had been an-
nounced by a god or the son of a god" (VI.1).  Celsus returns
to that theme in VI.8 where he denies that Plato orders people
to hold certain beliefs about God, or his son, or about Plato's
own conversations with that son.  Celsus' remarks in VI.10 summarize the differences he intends to sketch between Plato and
Jesus:

> Plato is not arrogant (οὐκ ἀλαζονεύεται) nor does
> he tell lies (ψεύδεται), asserting that he has found
> something new, or that he has come from heaven to
> proclaim it; but he confesses the source from which
> these doctrines come.

The denial of arrogance stands in contrast to the charges made
by Celsus in I.28 that Jesus conceitedly gave himself the title
of θεός after learning magical powers in Egypt.  Similarly, the
denial that Plato tells lies resonates with Celsus' frequently
stated accusation that the disciples of Jesus invented certain
aspects of his biography in order to cover up the awful truths,
such as his illegitimacy.  But the denial that Plato claimed to
have found something new (καινόν τι) strikes closer to the heart
of Celsus' position; it is an assertion of the Single Image in
a different form.  It will be recalled that the innovation of
Jesus, particularly his departure from the πάτριος νόμος of the
Jews, particularly rankled Celsus.  He was unable to account for
the claims of Jesus to divinity by way of the recognized route
to honor and glory; Jesus, and the Christians after him, stood
outside of all recognized channels and structures of power.
They were something *other*; they were something *new*.  By denying
that Plato taught anything new, Celsus indirectly affirms his
entire vision of society and culture.  He will further reinforce
that image by praising the wisdom of "divinely inspired men of
ancient times," the only ones to whom he accords the designation
θεῖος ἀνήρ (cf. VII.28, 49, 58).  They will be depicted as the

source from which Plato derived his doctrine, and they function
for Celsus as the principle of continuity in Greek tradition.
(Celsus' views on the impossibility of a god coming down from
heaven to visit the earth have already been discussed.)

Celsus' comments on Plato set Origen a different task. He
is unwilling simply to dismiss Plato out of hand as he did the
wandering holy men, some of the Greek gods and heroes, and the
named contemporaries of Jesus. Origen like Celsus, owed a great
debt to Plato and the Platonic tradition. He even concedes that
"the great world of mankind has derived help (χρησίμως) from him
also" (VI.2). He thus takes a different tack, or rather several
tacks. To the remarks in VI.10 about arrogance, lying, and the
like Origen offers no direct response. He embarks instead on
proving that the proclamation of future events is a mark of
divinity (τὸ . . . χαρακτηρίζον τὴν θεότητα) which is present in
the utterances of the Hebrew prophets and of the son of god.
Origen attempts to cast doubt on Plato's denial of pretension to
divinity by quoting stories about his divine birth (VI.8) and
by observing that Celsus quotes from his writings as if they
were inspired (ἐνθέως, VI.17). In response to Celsus' claim
that Jesus had borrowed certain teachings from Plato, Origen
denies that Jesus had ever read Plato. When Celsus contends that
Plato was a more effective teacher of θεολογία than Jesus, Origen
admits that the particular passage quoted by Celsus[17] is quite
impressive. Origen does find, however, one recurring theme that
he can use to distance Jesus and Christian teaching from Plato
and Platonic teaching. He introduces it at the outset. In
VI.1, he writes:

> We say that it is the task of those who teach the true
> doctrines to help (ὠφελεῖν) as many people as they
> can, as far as it is in their power to win everyone
> over to the truth by their love to mankind (διὰ
> φιλανθρωπίαν) - not only the intelligent, but also
> the stupid, and again not just the Greeks without in-
> cluding the barbarians as well. . . . all those who
> have abandoned the uneducated confine what should be of
> benefit to the community (τὸ κοινωνικόν) to a very nar-
> row and limited circle.

That passage begins with a dig at the title of Celsus' treatise,
and proceeds to sound several of Origen's favorite themes. He
asserts again that the evidence for divinity is to be found in

good works, and asks that such works should manifestly benefit
the entire community.  From his scattered remarks about the weak
in faith it is clear that Origen is arguing against his own tendencies as well, but because he kept in mind the peculiar nature
of his treatise as addressed to the weak in faith and to those
entirely without faith (cf. pref. 6), he can criticize philosophical exclusiveness without appearing entirely hypocritical.  He
has, after all, frequently refrained from pursuing the allegorical meaning of certain texts; he has often restricted himself
to intimating, but not fully explaining, certain profound doctrines held by "perfect" Christians.  He can point to his appreciation of the function of exorcism and healings performed in
the name of Jesus as crucial in the earlier stages of faith, and
he can refer to his brief outlines of the progress of the individual believer through several stages of faith.  All of those
would serve as evidence that Origen, in CC at least, has taken
pains to avoid the type of exclusiveness which he attributes to
the philosophers in VI.1.  For the Origen of *Peri Archon*, for
example, it might be a different story.  Thus his argument
against the restricted audience of philosophy at least seems
plausible.  He underscores that plausibility in VII.60 by arguing
that the lack of literary style in the Jewish and Christian
scriptures guarantees their broad accessibility.  They have a
style which "gets across to the multitude of men, and which is
not strange to their language, and does not by its strangeness
turn them away from listening to discourses of this kind because
they are in an unfamiliar idiom."  But not only does the style
of the scriptures make them intelligible to the multitude, it
also furnishes a window onto deeper truths:

> For it is obvious even to an ungifted person who
> reads them that many passages can possess a meaning
> deeper than that which appears at first sight, which
> becomes clear to those who devote themselves to Bible
> study, and which is clear in proportion to the time
> they spend on the Bible and to their zeal in putting
> its teaching into practice.  (VII.60)

Just as in his defense of Jesus and his disciples against the implications which Celsus drew from their undistinguished ancestry
and backgrounds, Origen invokes the privileges of the Double
Image to defend the scriptures.  Their poor style turns out to

be a positive attribute, since it enables them to communicate
both simple and complex truths in accordance with the individual
reader's ability to comprehend them.  Things are not only as
they seem; there is a hidden dimension to the scriptures which
Origen, but not Celsus, perceives.  That hidden dimension also
opens the door to allegorical interpretations, but Origen does
not play up that aspect of his conception of the scriptures in
this case.  By stressing their double accessibility, to simple
and "perfect" believers alike, he manages to put sufficient
distance between himself and the philosophers as he sees them.

As mentioned earlier, Celsus finds the source of his Single
Image of society in the utterances of those he calls divine, or
divinely-inspired, men of ancient times.  The antiquity of those
utterances seems to be the key for Celsus; it establishes the
priority of the Greek tradition in general and allows him to
trace lines of continuity and discontinuity from it.  It seems
certain from VII.28 that Celsus numbered Homer among the θείων
παλαιῶν ἀνδρῶν, but the position of Plato as either an origina-
tor, along with Homer, of that tradition or as a continuator of
it seems ambiguous, at least on the evidence of VII.58.  Celsus
does not divulge the identities of any of the others.  It is
their function in his argument rather than their particular identities or doctrines that is important.  His comments on them
constitute one of the clearest expressions of Celsus' Single
Image of society.  He finds truth and inspiration to be located
in a single historical tradition and to be limited to a period
in the distant past.  The utterances of a few men from that
period can then serve as the guidelines by which all other pronouncements can be evaluated.  There is only one canon of judgement in such matters, and Celsus has it.  Things are precisely
as they seem, and cannot be otherwise.  Celsus' distaste for
Christian innovation, which he interprets as arrogance and sheer
folly, stems directly from his conception of the divine men of
ancient times as the sole guarantors of truth.  In such a view,
Jesus and the Christian movement could not but fare poorly.
Celsus also seems to have held a similar disdain for innovations
by any of his contemporaries, not just the Christians.[18]   He
was a traditionalist to the core.

Thus the comparisons between the careers of Jesus and those
of other candidates for divine status in Late Antiquity can be
seen to revolve around the interplay of Celsus' Single Image
of society and Origen's Double Image.  Celsus knows only a single repository of truth, and he judges harshly any departure
from it.  Though he finds other pretensions to the possession of
wisdom, truth, or divinity as absurd as those of Jesus and the
Christians--for example, he was careful to dissociate himself
from the Metapontines in the worship of Aristeas as a god--he
does not hesitate to use any available evidence to deflate the
Christian claims.  In the wide variety of possible parallels to
the public career of Jesus that he does consider, Celsus can be
seen as warily circling his prey, sniping from the edges whenever he finds an opening, and finally arriving at the topic which
concerns him most.  His remarks on Plato and the sages of ancient times, though brief and often allusive, disclose the foundations of his criticism of Jesus and the Christian movement.
Though he attempts to make rhetorical capital from any possible
comparisons, it is only in that last group of figures that Celsus discloses his own preferences.  There he not only makes clear
his approaches to the key categories and the processes by which
certain figures are assigned to them, but he lays bare the conceptions on which his arguments are founded.

CHAPTER IV

CELSUS AND ORIGEN ON DIVINE MEN, III

Celsus' comments on the final days of Jesus center on three
distinct incidents: the arrest, execution, and resurrection.
Though the fragments of Celsus' treatise sometimes treat those
events together, I will discuss each separately. Celsus' analysis of the events surrounding the death of Jesus produces some of
his most explicit classificatory statements, and they provoke
some equally explicit responses from Origen.

*Arrest*

As his opening salvo in II.9 suggests, Celsus' Jew perceived
a discrepancy between the claims made for Jesus and the behavior
reported of him:

> How could we regard him as god (νομίζειν θεόν) when
> in other matters, as people perceived, he did not mani-
> fest anything which he professed to do, and when we
> had convicted him, condemned him, and decided that
> he should be punished, was caught hiding himself and
> escaped most disgracefully (ἐπονειδιστότατα), and
> indeed was betrayed by those whom he called disciples?
> And yet . . . if he was god (θεόν), he could not run
> away nor be led away under arrest, and least of all
> could he, who was regarded as Saviour (σωτῆρα
> νομιζόμενον), and Son of the Greatest God (θεοῦ τοῦ
> μεγίστου παῖδα), and an angel (ἄγγελον), be deserted
> and betrayed by his associates who had privately shared
> everything with him and had been under him as their
> teacher. (II.9)

Clearly, Jesus' candidacy for divine status is under fire, but
the addition of several other categories, such as Saviour, Son
of the greatest God, and angel, suggests that it is not one specific form of the claim to divinity but rather the claim in *all*
its forms that Celsus opposes. Celsus seems to use the various
categories as functional equivalents in II.9. The specific classifying proposition he advances is that Jesus' behavior, in
Gethsemene and at his subsequent arrest, did not demonstrate any
qualities that would be associated with the worthy claimant to
divine status. Though II.9 does not discuss the resurrection,

117

Celsus will bring similar criticisms to bear on that event as
well.

In II.9, however, Celsus' test of a specific category by
appealing to common evidence (the gospel account in Mt. 26:36ff.)
did not provoke an immediate and direct response from Origen.
Instead, Origen chose to expound on the complex nature of Jesus.
He begins by denying that Christians think that the body of Jesus, as perceivable by the senses, was god (θεόν). On the contrary, it was not the body of Jesus that was god but rather the
divine Logos which spoke in him. Origen contends that the same
Logos who uttered statements like "I am the way, the truth, and
the life" (Jn. 14:6) was also addressed in statements like "Let
there be light" (Gen. 1:3). Consequently, Origen upbraids the
Jews and Celsus' Jew for having failed to recognize in the utterances of Jesus the voice of the same Logos that had spoken so
frequently in their own scriptures. That division of the nature
or character of Jesus into different components (in II.9, body
and indwelling Logos) will be the *leitmotiv* of Origen's defense
of the arrest, execution, and resurrection.

The definition of Jesus as a composite being (σύνθετον)
whose body and soul were united with the Logos of God at his
incarnation represents another application of the Double Image.
There is more to Jesus than meets the eye, especially the jaun-
diced eye of Celsus. Certain events which befell him were appropriate to his human aspect, while certain utterances were to
be traced to the Logos with which he was united. That duality
which Origen attributes to Jesus allows him to accept Jesus'
sufferings as both appropriate and noble and to assert that they
in no way compromised his divinity.

In II.10 Origen does reply directly to the charges that
Jesus tried to escape arrest. He first reproaches Celsus for
having misunderstood the gospel accounts or for perhaps having
imported his misunderstandings from Jewish tales about Jesus.
Origen then summons scriptural support to show that Jesus' accu-
sers did not understand his words (Mt. 26:61; Jn. 2:20), that
Jesus was not caught but freely gave himself up to the arresting
party (Jn. 17:4-8), and that Jesus did not resist arrest (Mt.
26:52-54). On that basis Origen argues that it is more likely

that the accusations against the Christians, rather than the
Christian stories about Jesus, are inventions (πλάσματα). Further, he returns, in three separate formulations, to the idea
that the willingness of the Christians to endure any sufferings
ensures the truth of their message about Jesus. Thus, both
scripture and its continuing effects on the faithful testify to
the truth about Jesus.

In II.11 Origen uses Matthew's account of Judas' suicide
(Mt. 27:3-5) to ease the impression that Jesus was wholly be-
trayed by his disciples. In Judas' death, as well as in his
betrayal of Jesus with a kiss, Origen notices a certain ambivalence. Judas' actions show "what effect the teaching of Jesus
could have on even a sinner like Judas, the thief and traitor,
who could not utterly despise what he had learnt from Jesus"
(II.11). Again, Origen asserts that events are not as they
seem; in his mode of betrayal and in his subsequent remorse Judas testified to the power of the teaching of Jesus. Another
positive effect of the events surrounding the arrest of Jesus
is that his willingness to submit to the authorities will teach
his followers "to accept such ill-treatment for the sake of religion without objection" (II.11).[1]

The relations between Jesus and his disciples are of primary
concern to both Celsus and Origen in their discussions of the
arrest. Celsus finds neither the behavior of Jesus nor that of
the disciples to be commendable:

> No good general who led many thousands was ever be-
> trayed, nor was any wicked robber-chieftain, who was
> captain of very bad men, while he appeared to bring
> some advantage to his associates. But he, who was be-
> trayed by those under his authority, neither ruled like
> a good general; nor, when he had deceived his disciples,
> did he even inspire in the men so deceived that good-
> will, if I may call it that, which robbers feel towards
> their chieftain. (II.12)

That passage amplifies the accusations of Celsus in II.9, but
in II.12 Origen appeals to the history of philosophy in his defense. Reviewing Aristotle's desertion of Plato, Chrysippus'
attacks on Cleanthes, and the Pythagorean attitude toward those
who had lapsed out of the philosophical life, Origen concludes
that "from the biographies of the philosophers one might find

many examples of this sort similar to the desertion of Judas
which Celsus makes a ground for accusation against Jesus"
(II.12). Origen made a similar appeal to the history of philosophy in responding to Celsus' accusation that the disciples of
Jesus were "infamous men . . ., the most wicked tax-collectors
and sailors" (I.63); he claimed that there was ample precedent
in philosophy for the conversion of the dissolute to a better
way of life (I.64).

In his defense of the conduct of the disciples at the arrest
of Jesus, Origen supplements the appeal to philosophical precedent with another familiar argument. He accuses Celsus of selectively reading the gospel account:

> Here, so that he may criticize Christianity, he be-
> lieves that the sin recorded in the Gospels took place,
> which was committed when the disciples were still
> beginners and immature. But he is silent about their
> reform after the sin when they were bold in face of the
> Jews and suffered countless distresses at their hands
> and finally died for Jesus' teaching. (II.45)

By asserting that what appeared to be a betrayal of Jesus was
only temporarily so, Origen introduces another variation of the
Double Image: the significance of events changes as the context changes. Far from casting doubt on their character, the
conduct of the disciples subsequent to the arrest of Jesus even
surpasses "many stories told by the Greeks about the courage and
bravery of the philosophers" (II.45) and demonstrates again the
great influence of the teaching of Jesus.

Celsus also objects strongly to the notion that Jesus had
foreknowledge of his arrest:

> If he foretold these events as being a god . . .
> then what he foretold must assuredly have come to
> pass. A god, therefore, led his own disciples and
> prophets with whom he used to eat and drink so far
> astray that they became impious and wicked. But a
> god above all ought to have done good to all men,
> in particular to those who have lived with him. A
> man who had shared meals with another would not further
> a plot against him. Would one who had eaten a banquet
> with a god have become a conspirator against him?
> And what is more outrageous still, God himself con-
> spired against those who ate with him, by making them
> traitors and impious men. (II.20)

Celsus tries to make an issue of Jesus' foreknowledge in several
different ways.  In II.20 he seems to equate foreknowledge with
control and thus argues that Jesus caused his disciples to be-
tray him, an activity hardly in harmony with the principle that
a god ought to do good to men.  But Origen does not join issue in
II.20 on the question of which actions are to be considered
beneficial.  He instead offers a series of technical comments on
foreknowledge and a rhetorical analysis of Celsus' arguments.
To free Jesus of the suspicion that he caused his own betrayal,
Origen claims that "We say that the man who made the prediction
was not the cause of the future event . . . which would have taken
place even if it had not been prophesied . . . " (II.20).  Origen
also makes a technical analysis of Celsus' remarks, accusing him
of making an "idle" and hence invalid argument;[2] and he notes
that Greek and barbarian history is full of examples of people
conspiring against those whose hospitality they had shared
(II.21).  In II.17 Celsus takes a different tack.  He asks "Who,
whether god or daemon, or sensible man, if he foreknew that such
things would happen to him, would not avoid them if at least
he could do so, instead of meeting with just the events which
he had foreseen?" (II.17).  In response, Origen again appeals
to precedent, asking whether Socrates avoided the hemlock, Leo-
nidas avoided Thermopylae, and, extending the argument, whether
Paul avoided Jerusalem, or the Christians avoided persecution.
Finally, Celsus suggests that the disciples invented the notion
of Jesus' foreknowledge in order to excuse him from the embarrassment of his arrest and execution (cf. II.13, 16).

      Though the discussion of foreknowledge tends to wander away
from the specific details of the arrest and execution, it is
clear that Celsus finds something amiss in the story of Jesus'
final days.  The arrest itself was a potential embarrassment,
but Jesus' refusal or inability to avoid being captured and his
disciples' subsequent abandonment of him definitely undermine
Jesus' candidacy for divine status.  Though the discussion of
the arrest does not focus clearly or at any great length on particular classifying statements, Celsus' position that the arrest
and betrayal by the disciples seriously damage Jesus' candidacy
nevertheless clearly comes to light, as does Origen's response

that Jesus suffered those events freely, as predicted, with ample
precedent, and for the benefit of humankind.

*Execution*

Celsus' objections to the death of Jesus center on the mode
of punishment itself, Jesus' own behavior, and the stories told
by Christians about the event.  He finds the mode of execution
shameful, the conduct of Jesus unseemly, and the stories unbe-
lievable.  Again, he asserts that things are exactly as they
seem, if not worse, while Origen contends that there is a different interpretation, a hidden dimension, which reveals the
true meaning of Jesus' death.

For Celsus, crucifixion hardly seems to be the mode of
death appropriate for a candidate for divine status:

> If you think that you provide a true defence by dis-
> covering absurd justifications for those doctrines
> in which you have been ridiculously deceived, why may
> we not think that everyone else as well who has been
> condemned and come to an unfortunate end is an angel
> greater and more divine than Jesus?  . . . anyone
> with similar shamelessness could say even of a robber
> and murderer who had been punished that he, forsooth,
> was not a robber, but a god; for he foretold to his
> robber-gang that he would suffer the sort of things
> that he did in fact suffer.  (II.44)

Crucifixion does not put Jesus in exclusive company; for Celsus
it confirms, as did the facts of his lowly birth, his base
origins and his unworthy character.  One who suffers the fate
of a criminal must perforce be considered one.  As he did in
the discussion of Jesus' birth, Origen again argues that it is
not the external conditions but rather the internal disposition
of the candidate that matters.  Origen admits that it is appropriate for Celsus to have likened Jesus to robbers because "Jesus
in the person of his genuine disciples and witnesses for the
truth is always being crucified with robbers and suffers the
same condemnation among men as they do" (II.44).[3]  However,

> It was not right either for Jesus, who was dying for
> the common good of mankind (κατὰ τὸ κοινωνικὸν
> ἀποθνήσκων), to be put to death, or for these men
> who endure these sufferings for their piety, and who
> of all men are the only people to be treated as crimi-
> nals simply because of the method of worshipping God

> which has seemed right to them. And it was an im-
> pious act that men plotted against Jesus.    (II.44)

Origen has reorganized the elements of Celsus' accusation so
that they serve his own argument.  The crucifixion of Jesus between two robbers was an impious act, implicitly attributed to
the Jews.  Any other association of Jesus with criminals is
turned to his credit.  Like them, he "suffers condemnation among
men," though such a fate is unwarranted for one who died for
the good of mankind.  Nor is it right that his disciples are
persecuted simply because of their piety.  Origen has accepted
Celsus' superficial characterization, but he has changed its
meaning.  Jesus was wrongly condemned and his disciples are
wrongly persecuted; they are not criminals but pious men who
are performing beneficial work.  Jesus only *seems* to be a criminal by virtue of his crucifixion, and the disciples only *seem*
to be criminals because of their faith; in the perspective of
the Double Image Origen finds the truth.

Celsus attributed a strong classifying force to the crucifixion; for him the fact of the crucifixion was sufficient to
overturn the Christian claim that Jesus was the Logos (II.31).
He also advanced others whose noble deaths better supported
claims to divine status, mentioning Heracles, Asclepius, Orpheus,
Anaxarchus, Epictetus, and even the Sibyl, Jonah, and Daniel as
more worthy candidates.  Celsus suggests to his Christian
audience:

> How much better it would have been for you, since
> you conceived a desire to introduce some new doc-
> trine, to have addressed your attentions to some
> other man among those who have died noble deaths
> and are sufficiently distinguished to have a myth
> about them like the gods.   (VII.53)

Celsus' profound distrust of innovation and his belief that
Christian stories are expedient fabrications reinforce his scorn
for the crucifixion.  To him, any new doctrine is suspect, but
the Christians incite further incredulity with the story of the
ignoble death of the founder of their movement.  Origen, in turn,
rejects all of Celsus' alternative candidates.  He adduces
Heracles' theft of cattle as evidence against his candidacy for
divine status, refers to a previous refutation of the claims for

Asclepius,[4] quickly dismisses Orpheus who "said much worse things
about the supposed gods than Homer," admits that although "it
might be right for certain people to reverance a man for his
virtue, it would not be reasonable to call Anaxarchus a god,"
and asserts that Epictetus' calm acceptance of pain is not
"comparable to Jesus' miraculous words and works . . . [which]
when spoken with divine power to this day . . . convert not only
some of the simple people but also many of the more intelligent"
(VII.54). Origen also asserts that by his silence under the
scourge and other tortures Jesus manifested "a courage and pa-
tience superior to that of any of the Greeks" who were subjected
to similar punishments (VII.55). Origen views the candidacy
of the Sibyl as mysterious and unwarranted (VII.56) and he finds
the extent of Jesus' preaching and his power over the demonic
enemy to be vastly superior to Jonah and Daniel, respectively
(VII.57).

Though his comments on Celsus' alternative candidates for
divine status are incomplete, several of Origen's criteria for
the evaluation of candidates for divine status can be partially
recovered. His remarks on Heracles show that any indication of
immorality means a swift disqualification. On the other hand,
his treatment of Anaxarchus shows that mere virtue is not sufficient to support a claim to divine status. "Miraculous words
and works" seem to be required as well, particularly those which
lead to conversion. A limited sphere of activity, as in the
cases of Jonah and Daniel, does not seem to be a sufficient
qualification either. Thus, from Origen's dismissal of unworthy
candidates for divine status, a partial image of the worthy candidate can be reconstructed. Moral activity is a minimal re-
quirement, but it should be supplemented by miraculous words and
works. The candidate's activity should not be limited to a particular location; it should be global in scope, if possible.
The candidate's demonstration of superiority should not be
intermittent but rather perpetual. Indeed, it should continue
after his departure from this life. The picture which thus
emerges from Origen's rejection of unworthy candidates for divine
status is consistent with his remarks in other passages. It suggests that he had in mind a relatively specific, if not totally

fixed, set of criteria which a worthy candidate for divine status
would be expected to fulfill.

That Celsus also had somewhat different criteria for evaluating candidates for divine status is suggested by his remarks
on Jesus' suffering on the cross.  If Jesus had to suffer at
all, apparently Celsus would have preferred that Jesus had suffered in silence, especially if he had foreknowledge of his fate.
He asks, "Why then does he utter loud laments and wailings, and
pray that he may avoid the fear of death, saying something like
this, 'O Father, if this cup could pass by me'?" (II.24).  Again,
Origen accuses Celsus of "exaggerating and quoting the text in-
correctly" and belittles his imperfect understanding of the
scriptures, but he reserves his full explanation of Jesus' utterance on the cross for another audience, "those whom Paul called
perfect" (II.24).  As he has frequently done elsewhere in CC,
Origen invokes the right to apply the tool of the Double Image,
allegory, to the passage at hand, but he does not give any indication of what its application will accomplish.  He also introduces another product of the Double Image, his conception that
some of Jesus' utterances belong to the Logos within him "while
others belong to the supposedly human Jesus" (II.25).  Where
Celsus would attribute all of Jesus' statements to the same
character and would thus take some of them as indicative of his
mere humanity, Origen's concept of Jesus as a "composite being"
allows him to attribute those statements which give evidence of
an anguished and suffering human being to "the supposedly human
Jesus" while attributing others to the Logos.  His Double Image
enables him to unite and hold simultaneously two apparently con-
tradictory views of Jesus.  But for Celsus, Jesus must be man or
god; he cannot be both.

Origen also promises an allegorical interpretation of Jesus'
drinking the vinegar and gall, which for Celsus had demonstrated
Jesus' base humanity, but he again postpones it for a more appropriate audience (II.37).  He rests content to note that it was
predicted in Psalm 68.

Perhaps the most distressing aspect of the crucifixion for
Celsus, the fact which does most to undermine Jesus' candidacy
for divine status, is Jesus' meek acceptance of his fate.  It

provokes several pointed questions.  Celsus asks "what fine action did Jesus do like a god?  Did he despise men's opposition
and laugh and mock at the disaster that befell him?" (II.33),
implying clearly that Jesus' passive acceptance of his death was
*not* an action worthy of a god.  Origen appeals to the earthquake,
the eclipse, and the rending of the temple veil as testimonies to
the "divinity in Jesus" (II.33), but he also states directly that
"the fine action of Jesus consists in this, that to this day people whom God wills are cured by his name" (II.33).  Origen thus
supplements the criterion of miraculous works with the criterion
of lasting impact.[5]  In II.34 Celsus presses the issue by drawing
a specific comparison.  He quotes "the remark of Bacchus in
Euripides:  The god himself will set me free whenever I wish it"
(II.35).  That fragment of Celsus should be read with his criticism of Jesus' wailings and lamentations in II.24; he would thus
be contrasting the calm assurance of Dionysos to the agitated
uncertainty of Jesus.  He obviously sees in the former a more
credible candidate for divine status.  Jesus' relative credibility
is further weakened by his failure to punish his tormentors,
since, as Celsus observes, "the one who condemned him did not
even suffer any such fate as that of Pentheus by going mad or
being torn in pieces" (II.34).  With the benefit of historical
hindsight, Origen does argue that the Jewish people "has been
condemned by God and torn in pieces, and scattered over all the
earth, a fate more terrible than the rending suffered by Pentheus" (II.34), and he notes that the sleep of Pilate's wife was
troubled by the whole affair, but he clearly has a more attenu-
ated notion of revenge than Celsus.  Celsus, who thought revenge
and release appropriate at the moment of arrest, seems exasperated
to find Jesus remaining passive through the execution itself.

For Celsus, the crucifixion represents the final opportunity
for Jesus to demonstrate the worthiness of his candidacy for
divine status.  He asks, "Why, if not before, does he not at any
rate now show forth something divine, and deliver himself from
this shame, and take his revenge on those who insult both him
and his Father?" (II.35).  Origen makes no direct response; instead, he challenges the Greeks "who believe in providence" to
explain why god does not punish those who deny providence.  His

tactics are not completely evasive, however, since he does claim
that there was "a divine sign from heaven in the eclipse of the
sun and other miracles, showing that the crucified man possessed
something divine and was superior to ordinary men" (II.36). But,
to Celsus, such signs were oblique and peripheral. He favored
the direct and traditional route to power and glory; death on a
cross was not part of that route. For Celsus, Jesus' death is
crucial and decisive evidence against his candidacy for divine
status; it even undermines the status of his father:

> You pour abuse on the images of these gods and ridicule
> them, although if you did that to Dionysos himself
> or to Heracles in person, perhaps you would not escape
> lightly. But the men who tortured and punished your
> God in person suffered nothing for doing it, not even
> afterwards as long as they lived. What new thing
> has happened since then which might lead one to be-
> lieve that he was not a sorcerer but son of God? And
> He who sent His son to deliver certain messages over-
> looked him when he was actually so cruelly punished
> so that the messages also were destroyed with him;
> and though such a long time has passed, He has not paid
> any attention. What father is so ruthless? But per-
> haps it was his will, as you say; for this reason he
> submitted to insult. But these gods whom you blaspheme
> could say that this too was their will, and that it
> is why they endure it when they are blasphemed. Where
> the matters are equal, it is best to compare them
> fairly on the same level. The latter, however, actu-
> ally do take severe revenge on anyone who blasphemes
> them; for either he runs away and hides himself on ac-
> count of what he has done, or he is caught and destroyed.
> (VIII.41)

Celsus' position on the debilitating effects of the crucifixion on Jesus' candidacy for divine status is vividly captured in this sentence: "But no one gives a proof of a god or
son of a god by such signs and false stories, nor by such disreputable evidence" (II.30). It is clear from that that Celsus
saw his analysis of the character of Jesus as an essay in classification, and equally clear that he had evaluated the evidence,
and decided to deny the claims made for Jesus by his partisans.
The claim that Jesus' suffering and death were prophesied found
no favor with Celsus. As he had with other prophecies,[6] Celsus
argues that "the prophecies could be applied to thousands of
others far more plausibly than to Jesus" (II.28). Particularly
since "the prophets say that the one who will come will be a

great prince, lord of the whole earth and of all nations and
armies . . . . But they did not proclaim a pestilent fellow
like him" (II.29).  Celsus finds no warrant for the claim that
Jesus' crucifixion had been prophesied.  In general, Celsus
finds any form of the argument from prophecy to be misdirected:

> If the prophets foretold that the great God (to men-
> tion nothing else more offensive) would serve as a
> slave and be sick and die, would it necessarily follow
> from the fact that it was predicted, that God must
> die and serve as a slave and be sick, in order that
> by his death it might be believed that he was God?
> But the prophets could not have foretold this.  For it
> is wicked and impious.  So we should not consider either
> whether they did or whether they did not foretell it,
> but whether the act is worthy of God and is good.  And
> we should disbelieve what is disgraceful and evil,
> even if all men should seem to predict it in a state
> of frenzy.  How, then, is it anything but blasphemy
> to assert that the things done to Jesus were done to
> God?  (VII.14)

Again the strong classifying force of the crucifixion disquali-
fies Jesus from any serious consideration as a candidate for
divine status.  Such an act, in Celsus' eyes, is neither worthy
of a god nor good.  It matters little whether or not it was
prophesied.  Origen's reply has several aspects.  He attacks
Celsus' reasoning as self-contradictory; he asserts that "the
prophets of the great God must necessarily speak the truth"
(VII.15), but most importantly he argues that "the prophecies
did not foretell that God would be crucified" (VII.16).  Origen
again resorts to his concept of the composite nature of Jesus
in defense of the crucifixion, claiming that

> . . . the things that were done to Jesus, in so far
> as they are understood to apply to the divine element
> in him, are pious, and not in conflict with the accepted
> notion of God.  But in so far as he was a man, who
> more than anyone else was adorned by sublime partici-
> pation in the very Logos and wisdom himself, he endured
> as a wise and perfect man what must needs be endured
> by a man who does all in his power on behalf of the
> entire race of men and of rational beings as well.
> There is nothing objectionable in the fact that a
> man died, and in that his death should not only be given
> as an example of the way to die for the sake of reli-
> gion, but also should effect a beginning and an advance
> in the overthrow of the evil one, the devil, who dom-
> inated the whole earth.  (VII.17)

Not only does Origen's Double Image of Jesus as a composite of

human and divine natures enable him to avoid the sting of Celsus'
comments on the crucifixion, it also allows him to assert the
paradigmatic value of Jesus' human suffering for the sake of
religion. Far from being shameful or disgraceful, the crucifixion in Origen's view becomes a noble human act, worthy of imi-
tation, an inspiring model for any who suffer persecution because
of their piety.[7]

Celsus seems also, however, to have anticipated and rejected
the idea that Jesus' death was in any way exemplary or beneficial. His Jew asks the Christians "do you, who are such great
believers, criticize us because we do not regard this man as
a god nor agree with you that he endured these sufferings for
the benefit of mankind, in order that we also may despise punishments?" (II.38). Origen agrees that Christians do criticize
Jews on just those grounds, and reiterates his contention that
the purpose of Jesus' advent among men was to give them "an
example of the life that they ought to live" (II.38). Origen
broadens the discussion to include all the supposed hardships
which Jesus suffered, admitting of the Jews that

> We criticize them because they attack his love to
> man, although he did not overlook either a city or
> even a village of Judaea, that he might proclaim the
> kingdom of God everywhere. For they misrepresent him
> as a vagabond, and they accuse him of being an out-
> cast who roamed about with his body disgracefully un-
> kempt. But it is not disgraceful to endure such hard-
> ships for the benefir of those in all places who are
> able to understand him. (II.38)

Origen again counters the image of Jesus as the disgraceful, suffering outsider who can bring no good to anyone with an image of
the benefactor whose good works may not take the expected or
even a tangible form ("the kingdom of God") but who nevertheless
endured such hardships "for the benefit of those in all places."
His Double Image enables him to see through the external conditions of Jesus' career to his internal disposition and its lasting benefits. Origen criticizes Celsus sharply for claiming
"that Jesus' message of salvation and moral purity was not sufficient to prove his superiority among men" (II.40).[8] He rejects Celsus' contention that a certain type of behaviour should
have accompanied the message:

> He supposes that he [Jesus] should have acted in a
> way contrary to the character of the role which he
> had assumed, and although he had assumed mortality,
> should not have died; or, if he had to die, at least
> he should have not died a death which could become
> an example to men:  for they would know even from that
> very deed now to die for the sake of religion, and
> to be bold in maintaining it in face of those who have
> been perverted in their ideas of piety and impiety,
> and who think that pious people are the most impious.
> (II.40)

That Celsus thought Jesus should not have died, at least in such
a shameful fashion, is clear from his remarks in other fragments
quoted by Origen (cf. II.33, 44, 47, 55).  In his paraphrase of
Celsus in II.40 Origen also attributes to Celsus the opinion that
Jesus should not have died an exemplary death.[9]

Celsus' consideration of the crucifixion thus seems to have
reinforced his rejection of Jesus' candidacy for divine status.
He found the mode of execution itself disgraceful and shameful,
more suitable for robbers and murderers than for a god or a son
of a god.  Moreover, Jesus' behaviour at his execution did nothing
to evince his purported divinity; his piteous wailings and his
desire to escape punishment, coupled with his failure to revenge
himself on his torturers, show him to be a mere man.  Finally,
the stories told by Christians about the crucifixion were patently
untrue; as the Jew tells his Christian audience:  "although you
lied you were not able to conceal plausibly your fictitious
tales" (II.26).  The criticisms of the event, Jesus' behaviour,
and the partisan reports about it combine to support Celsus'
position that Jesus was an unworthy pretender to divine status.

In many respects, Origen's defense of the crucifixion resembles his defense of Jesus' lowly birth.  He frequently asserts
that things are not as they seem.  His Double Image allows him
to find and trace the workings of inarticulate sources of power.
In the case of the crucifixion, Origen relies heavily on his
concept of Jesus as a composite being, which allows him to deem
certain utterances and experiences totally appropriate for either
the human aspect or the indwelling Logos.  Further, Origen again
asserts the utility, but reserves the use, of the major weapon of
the Double Image, allegory.  Though he does not produce it, he
claims the existence of an alternative explanation for the events

that trouble Celsus.  The other major element of Origen's defense
of the crucifixion is his contention that Jesus died for the
good of mankind.  That statement represents a transformation of
the widespread image of the civic benefactor by the application
of a Double Image which prizes spiritual and moral benefits more
highly than those in the realms of economics or prestige.  In so
doing, Origen both subscribes to and subtly alters Celsus' dictum that "above all a god ought to have done good to all men"
(II.20).  Viewed in the proper light, the crucifixion is neither
shameful nor disgraceful; it is the ultimate beneficial act of
god for mankind.

## Resurrection

Celsus' criticisms of Jesus' resurrection concern the fundamental plausibility of the event itself, the purported uniqueness of a return from the dead, the validity and appropriateness
of the resurrection appearances, and a number of finer points in
the Christian accounts of the resurrection.  He again finds no
warrant for Jesus' candidacy for divine status.  Origen disputes
his conclusions at every turn.

Perhaps Celsus' bluntest and most succinct objection to the
resurrection comes in a single question:  "How can a dead man
be immortal?" (II.16).  Origen's reply is again based on the image of Jesus as a composite being:

> Anyone who is interested may realize that it is not
> the dead man that is immortal, but he who rose from
> the dead.  Not only was the dead man not immortal,
> but even Jesus, who was a composite being (σύνθετος),
> was not immortal before his death since he was going
> to die.  No one who is going to die at some future
> date is immortal, but he becomes immortal when he
> will no longer die.  (II.16)

Such a passage might be read against the background of a
"mythology of the immortals,"[10] but it is also necessary to take
account of how that mythology is used in the arguments of each
adversary.  Celsus' question in II.16 does fit well with Talbert's
synthetic portrait of the "mythology of the immortals," and it
encapsulates many of Celsus' objections to the resurrection.
Talbert claims that

> . . . whenever Mediterranean peoples spoke about the
> immortals, constant in their description was the
> explicit or implicit idea that "he was taken up into
> heaven." Some evidence of this ascent is usually given.
> Either his ascent to heaven was witnessed or there was
> no trace of his physical remains. That the absence
> of the hero's physical remains points properly to an
> ascent to heaven is known because of a) predictions/
> oracles during the hero's life that he would be taken
> up; b) a heavenly announcement at the end of his earthly
> career stating or implying that he had been taken
> up; and c) appearances of the hero to friends or dis-
> ciples confirming his new status.[11]

Celsus' question, "How can a dead man be immortal?", might
well indicate his doubts about an ascension, his distrust of
any predictions of one, of any purported heavenly announcement,
or of any purported appearances. Indeed, his criticism of the
resurrection does sound most of those themes; he does not go so
far, however, as to claim actual possession or knowledge of the
whereabouts of the physical remains.

Origen's reply does not deny the death of Jesus, but rather
affirms the resurrection, and subsequent immortality, of at least
a portion of that composite being. Origen's particular affinities to and departures from a general mythology of the immortals
are difficult to assess on the basis of a single passage, but it
is clear that he wants to affirm *both* the death *and* the resurrection of Jesus, because as he claims "if he really died, then if
he did rise again, his resurrection was real; but if he only appeared to die, then he did not really rise again" (II.16). It
is in his simultaneous affirmation of both the death and the
resurrection of Jesus that Origen departs from Celsus' version
of a mythology of the immortals; the device which facilitates
that departure is his Double Image of Jesus as a composite being, which enables him to assert that Jesus was both mortal and
immortal, both man and god. Origen's response to Celsus' question in II.16 shows that a static conception of a "mythology of
the immortals," such as that developed by Talbert, can minimize
the variety of ways in which a candidate for divine status can
be accorded the status of an "immortal."

As he had with the arrest and crucifixion, Celsus also disputes the contention that Jesus had predicted his resurrection;
even if such a prediction is granted, Celsus finds nothing

extraordinary in it:

> Come now, let us believe your view that he actually
> said this. How many others produce wonders like this
> to convince simple hearers whom they exploit by de-
> ceit? They say that Zalmoxis, the slave of Pythagoras,
> also did this among the Scythians, and Pythagoras him-
> self in Italy, and Rhampsinitus in Egypt. The last-
> named played dice with Demeter in Hades and returned
> bearing a gift from her, a golden napkin. Moreover,
> they say that Orpheus did this among the Odrysians,
> and Protesilaus in Thessaly, and Heracles at Taenarum,
> and Theseus. But we must examine this question
> whether anyone who really died ever rose again with
> the same body. Or do you think that the stories of
> these others really are the legends which they appear
> to be, and yet the ending of your tragedy (καταστροφὴν)
> is to be regarded as noble and convincing--his cry
> from the cross when he expired, and the earthquake and
> the darkness? (II.55)

Origen first criticizes the Jew for lapsing out of character; he
would find reference to Moses more appropriate than reliance on
"prodigious stories" about Zalmoxis, Pythagoras, and the others.
Origen also claims that "Jesus' resurrection from the dead cannot be compared with such tales" as Celsus' Jew has quoted, since
Jesus was crucified in full public view so "that no one may be
able to say that he deliberately retired out of sight of men, and
that although he appeared to die he did not really do so, but,
when he wanted to, again reappeared and told the portentous tale
that he had risen from the dead" (II.56). In passing, Origen
seems to agree with the judgement of Celsus that the stories
told of Zalmoxis and the others were fictions and that their alleged descents and returns were elaborate ruses. He further
castigates the Jew for apparently denying the possibility of
resurrection with the same body, in open disagreement with the
scriptural evidence attributing resurrections or resuscitations
to Elijah (I Kings 17:21-22) and Elisha (II Kings 4:34-35). In
the remarks directed to the Jew, Origen combines an appeal to
scripture with the argument from prophecy in order to convince
the Jew first of the plausibility of the resurrection and second
of the superiority of the resurrection of Jesus to those effected
by Elijah and Elisha:

> The myths which you have quoted we regard as such;
> but we certainly do not consider as legends the stories
> in our Bible which we and you share in common, which

> not only you but we also hold in reverence.  For this
> reason we believe that the authors who wrote in scrip-
> ture about people who rose from the dead were not
> telling cock-and-bull stories, and we believe that
> Jesus actually rose again as he foretold and as the
> prophets predicted.  But Jesus' resurrection from the
> dead was more remarkable than the former instances.
> . . . For what important benefit has come to the world
> from the fact that the boys were raised up by Elijah
> and Elisha comparable to that brought about by the
> preaching of the resurrection of Jesus when it is be-
> lieved by divine power?  (II.58)

Celsus had attempted to diminish the importance of the resurrection by denying its uniqueness.  In his response, Origen attempts
to turn his own comparative method against Celsus.  He seizes on
the character of the Jew first as a way of lessening the impact
of the parallels from Greek literature and second as an entry
into discussion of the Jewish scriptures.  In those scriptures,
which Origen recognizes as the common possession of Jews and
Christians, he finds ample confirmation of both the plausibility
and superior benefits of the resurrection of Jesus.  In II.55-58
Origen does not venture a detailed refutation of the candidacies
for divine status of Zalmoxis, Pythagoras, and the others, such
as he had attempted in evaluating those who Celsus had claimed
had died noble deaths.[12]  Nevertheless, he does allude to several
positive criteria which frequently occur in Origen's defense of
Jesus.

The importance, and particular character, of Jesus' beneficial actions in substantiating his candidacy for divine status
becomes clearer in a later remark of Origen.  When Celsus asks
"But when he had put off this flesh, perhaps he became a god?
Then why rather not Asclepius, Dionysus, and Heracles?", Origen
answers as follows:

> What work as great as his has been done by Asclepius,
> Dionysus, and Heracles?  Can they support their claim
> to be gods by proving that there are people who have
> been reformed in morals and have become better as a re-
> sult of their life and teaching?  (III.43)

The great works of Jesus, which continue to be done in his name
and through his divine power, are sufficient to substantiate the
story of his resurrection.  Origen again relies on historical
hindsight to distinguish his candidate from the others.  It is

not the resurrection in itself, so much as the effects which it wrought, which supports the candidacy of Jesus for divine status.

Celsus finds the Christian stories of resurrection appearances of Jesus to be suspect on two counts. On one hand, he does not find the evidence produced convincing in the least; on the other, he finds that appearances were not granted to those on whom they would have made the most significant impression. Celsus' low estimation of the evidence for resurrection appearances is evident:

> While he was alive he did not help himself, but after death he rose again and showed the marks of his punishment and how his hands had been pierced. But who saw this? A hysterical female, as you say, and perhaps some other one of those who were deluded by the same sorcery, who either dreamt in a certain state of mind and through wishful thinking had a hallucination due to some mistaken notion (an experience that has happened to thousands), or, which is more likely, wanted to impress the others by telling this fantastic tale, and so by this cock-and-bull story to provide a chance for other beggars. (II.55)

Origen rejects all of Celsus' criticisms. He observes that more than one person is reported to have seen the resurrected Jesus (II.59); he disputes Celsus' idea of an hallucination and finds no evidence of hysteria in the texts (II.60). He uses John's story of Thomas' touching the wounds of Jesus (Jn. 20:26-27) to refute the suggestion that "Jesus used to produce only a mental impression of the wounds he received on the cross, and did not really appear wounded in this way" (II.61), again appealing to the notion of Jesus' composite being. Thomas could touch Jesus' wounds because Jesus was in transition between two states:

> . . . at the time of his resurrection he was, as it were, in a sort of intermediate state between the solidity of the body as it was before his passion and the condition of a soul uncovered by any body. (II.62)

Thus Origen manipulates his Double Image of Jesus as both man and god, as a composite being, to support the resurrection against Celsus' objections that it was all a phantasm or hallucination; the tangible post-resurrection flesh proves the reality of the resurrection itself in a fashion accessible even to those weak in faith or entirely without faith in Christ.[13]

Celsus may have in mind the incident with Thomas or perhaps a broader rejection when he asks, "What God that comes among men is disbelieved, and that when he appears to those who were waiting for him? Or why ever is he not recognized by people who had long been expecting him?" (II.75). Origen's reply is more rhetorical than substantive as he challenges the Jew to explain why Jews disbelieve the miracles attributed to Moses. It is thus difficult to determine the specific incident which sparked Celsus' criticism. But it is clear that Celsus thinks that any disbelief weakens the candidacy of Jesus for divine status.

As with his remarks on the arrest and crucifixion, Celsus discovers in Jesus' post-resurrection behaviour towards those who accused and executed him no warrant at all for his candidacy for divine status. Celsus asserts that "if Jesus really wanted to show forth divine power, he ought to have appeared to the very men who treated him despitefully and to the man who condemned him and to everyone everywhere" (II.63). Celsus also offers another alternative: ". . . if he really was so great he ought, in order to display his divinity, to have disappeared suddenly from the cross" (II.68). He views the limiting of resurrection appearances to the inner circle of believers with open suspicion: "At the time when he was disbelieved while in the body, he preached without restraint to all; but when he would establish a strong faith after rising from the dead, he appeared secretly to just one woman and to those of his own confraternity" (II.70). Again: "When he was punished he was seen by all, but by only one person after he rose again; whereas the opposite ought to have happened" (II.70). Finally: "after his resurrection from the dead he ought to have called all men clearly to the light and taught them why he came down" (II.73). Those passages demonstrate that Celsus clearly had a fixed concept of the appropriate behaviour for Jesus, or for any other individual who might claim divine status by virtue of resurrection, after the resurrection. Jesus should not have limited his appearances to his own confraternity, above all to an hysterical woman. Rather, he should have appeared to everyone, but especially to those who had condemned and executed him. Celsus again compares Jesus'

career to his Single Image of the life of the worthy claimant
to divine status; again he finds that Jesus does not measure up.

Origen's response demonstrates the full range of defensive
strategies made possible by the Double Image.  After quoting
Paul's passage on the resurrection appearances in I Cor. 15,
Origen intimates, but does not divulge, its deeper significance:
"I suspect that this passage contains certain great and wonderful
truths, the understanding of which is beyond the merit not only
of the multitude of believers but even of those quite advanced"
(II.63).  He repeats the idea that "although Jesus was one, he
had several aspects" as a way of explaining the selectivity of
the resurrection appearances.

> Accordingly, as we hold that Jesus was such a wonder-
> ful person, not only as to the divinity within him
> which was hidden from the multitude, but also as to
> his body which was transfigured when he wished and be-
> fore whom he wished we affirm that everyone had the
> capacity to see Jesus only when he had not 'put off
> the principalities and powers' [Col. 2:15] and had not
> yet died to sin; but after he had put off principal-
> ities and powers, all those who formerly saw him could
> not look upon him, as he no longer had anything about
> him that could be seen by the multitude.  For this
> reason it was out of consideration for them that he
> did not appear to all after rising from the dead.
> (II.64)

A clearer statement of the same idea is that

> Jesus, then, wanted to show forth his divine power
> to each of those able to see it, and according to the
> measure of his individual capacity.  In fact, perhaps
> he avoided appearing simply because he was considering
> the mean abilities of people who had not the capacity
> to see him.  (II.67)

Both of those statements are buttressed by the theological assertion that when Jesus "was sent into the world he did not merely
make himself known; he also concealed himself" (II.67).  Thus
Origen's defense of the resurrection appearances is fit into his
over-arching theological perspective, a perspective which is
governed by the Double, or even Multiple, Image.  Just as Origen
sees a progression from lack of faith, through simple faith, to
mature faith, so he sees the beholder's perception of Jesus
changing accordingly.  There are some events of Jesus' career
which are easily grasped by the "multitude," while others may be

imperfectly grasped even by the perfect.  Even simple events may
contain deeper meanings.  In such a perspective no hard and fast
meaning, no Single Image, can be applied to the "facts"; the
Double Image sanctions open-ended and inventive interpretation.
For every objection there are several explanations.  Celsus'
central objection that Jesus should have staged a public confrontation with those who condemned him is opposed by Origen's much
more complex and nuanced view of the relations between Jesus and
those who beheld him.  The relative veracity of each view is not
in question; what impresses, rather, is the extreme fidelity with
which they give expression to the dominant perspectives of the
two adversaries:  Celsus' Single Image of the career of the
worthy candidate for divine status, and Origen's Double Image.

The rhetorically heightened literal-mindedness of Celsus'
Single Image surfaces again when he inquires about the whereabouts of the resurrected Jesus:  "Where is he then, that we may
see and believe?" (II.77).  For Origen, Jesus' absence is only
apparent; the evidence of Jesus' work and his resurrection is
the preaching of his disciples; the Double Image converts physical absence into metaphorical presence.

The discussion of several of the finer points of the resurrection narratives, such as the gospels' disagreement on the number of angels that appeared at the tomb (cf. V.56-58), adds no
new criteria or arguments.  Both Celsus and Origen are relentless
in the application of their particular perspectives; where one
sees only the surface and reads it in the worst possible light,
the other seeks hidden depths of meaning which cast on the subject the best possible light.  As much as any other topic, the
discussion of the arrest, execution, and resurrection reveals the
deep divisions between Celsus' and Origen's views of the world.
Where Celsus sees and advocates rigid hierarchy and orderly process, Origen sees and prizes flux and unexpected change.  For
Celsus a man who dies a criminal can be nothing more; for Origen
he can be a god.

Celsus' and Origen's extensive consideration of candidates
for divine status comes to no univocal conclusion.  As they had
from the start, Celsus and Origen continue to disagree on the
proper evaluation of nearly every candidate, especially Jesus.

In the course of the argument, the grounds for that disagreement
are fully disclosed. Celsus and Origen differ fundamentally in
their views of human behaviour and society. Celsus has a Single
Image; society is an organized, articulate system of roles and
statuses, and access to them is gained through recognized channels. As Peter Brown writes of the man with the Single Image:
"for him, there is one single, recognized way of making one's
way in the world."[14] Origen, on the other hand, has a Double
Image; he realizes that there are "personal skills that succeed
in a way that is unacceptable or difficult to understand."[15]
Origen repeatedly emphasizes *inarticulate* over against *articulate*
sources of power; he grasps the subtle meaning, sees the hidden
dimension. Celsus and Origen may share many categories and
strategies for the evaluation of candidates for divine status,
but their governing perspectives dictate that their specific
evaluation of individual candidates will eventually differ.
Even the fundamental proposition accepted by both Celsus and
Origen, that a worthy candidate for divine status should perform
beneficial actions for humankind, receives widely disparate interpretations. Nevertheless, that basic concept, whatever its
particular form in the arguments of Celsus and Origen, might
represent the crucial point of contact between the currents of
thought in CC and broader trends in the Hellenistic world.

The fundamental criterion of evaluation for Celsus and
Origen receives clearest expression in Celsus' assertion that
"above all a god ought to have done good to all men" (II.20),
and it is supplemented in his remarks on the benefits conferred
by traditional oracles:

> How many cities have been built by oracles, and have
> got rid of diseases and famines, and how many that
> have neglected or forgotten them have suffered terrible
> destruction? How many have been sent to form a colony
> and have prospered by attending to their commands?
> How many rulers and common people have come off better
> or worse for this reason? How many that have been dis-
> tressed at being childless have come to possess that
> for which they prayed and escaped the wrath of demons?
> How many ailments of the body have been healed? How
> many, on the other hand, have insulted the temples and
> have at once been caught? (VIII.45)

The benefits (and punishments) Celsus envisages are direct, immediate, and tangible: they concern the physical and social

welfare of individuals and the corporate group.  Origen's remarks
on the Pythian Apollo indicate that he gave a somewhat different
emphasis to the basic criterion of evaluation:  "if he was a
god, he ought to have used his foreknowledge as an incentive, so
to speak, for the conversion and healing and moral reformation
of men" (VII.6).  In Origen's view the important benefits, those
with the greatest classifying force, are less direct, immediate,
and tangible; they concern more the inner transformation of an
individual's character.  Moreover, the benefits which he ascribes
specifically to the activity of Jesus were longer-lasting since
"the goodness of Jesus towards men was not confined to the
period of the incarnation only, but even to this day the power
of Jesus brings about conversion and moral reformation in those
who believe in God through him" (I.43).  Evidence of Jesus'
beneficial action is not to be found primarily in healthy individuals or cities nor in prosperous colonies, but rather in the
"great numbers of churches, which consist of men converted from
the flood of sins and who are dependent on the Creator and refer
every decision to His pleasure" (I.47).  The proof of Jesus'
divinity is that he "benefited the life of mankind and converted
men from the flood of sins" (II.8).  Thus, although both Celsus
and Origen seem to subscribe to the idea that "above all a god
ought to have done good to all men," they invest different actions with primary classifying force.  In each case the author's
dominant perspective determines his view of beneficial actions.
Celsus' Single Image leads him to favor the clear exercise of
articulate power and traditional routes to its acquisition;
Origen's Double Image enables him to discover inarticulate sources
of power and extraordinary ways in which it was acquired.

*Benefactors and Honors in Late Antiquity*

It remains to inquire after the background of the conception
that a god ought to do good for men.  In so doing, the discussion
will return to one of the major unsolved questions in the contemporary study of divine men:  whether there was a "Hellenistic
conception of the divine man."  I will contend from the outset
that the question, when put in that fashion, cannot yet be
answered.  Instead, I will try to locate Celsus' and Origen's

primary criterion of evaluation within its broader context by
reviewing some other comments on candidates for divine status
which seem to be based on the same criterion. That attempt will
yield neither definitive sources for the actual arguments employed
by Celsus and Origen nor the full outline of a native Hellenistic
conception of the divine man. Rather, it should demonstrate
that there was at least one fairly widespread criterion for the
evaluation of candidates for divine status in Late Antiquity.
Whether there were other criteria and whether they indicate the
existence of a "Hellenistic conception of the divine man" await
further discussion. But this preliminary step towards answering
those questions should demonstrate that there is an alternative
approach to the unsubstantiated assertion of the existence of
such a "Hellenistic conception of the divine man" and also to
the ideal-type analysis pursued by Bieler and so often misunderstood by his critics.

It is not possible here to provide a full inventory of texts
which disclose a link between the performance of beneficial actions and the benefactor's reception of divine honors. Inscriptions alone span a period of several hundred years and are found
throughout the Mediterranean area. I can only hope, through the
analysis of a few examples, to strengthen the possibility that
the proposition that a god ought to do good to men was not idiosyncratic in the works of Celsus and Origen but was rather a
recognizable element of thought about divine and human action in
Late Antiquity. To establish that possibility is to move beyond
unquestioning acceptance of the existence of a "Hellenistic conception of the divine man" and towards a preliminary analysis of
the elements that may have comprised it.

Despite the wide temporal and geographical variations of
the evidence, the language used to describe the work of benefactors and to bestow on them the honors they earned remains relatively consistent. That consistency stems in part from the rigid
form of the inscriptions[16] and also from the tendency of many of
the groups which received benefits to manifest similar structures
and organizations. Samuel Dill describes that patterning of a
smaller social group after a larger one: "As the municipal town
was modelled on the constitution of the State, so we may say that

the college was modelled on the municipal town.  The college, indeed, became a city for the brotherhood, at once a city and a
home."[17]  More specifically, of the relationship between a patron
or benefactor and a *collegium*, Jean Gagé writes that "in everything that concerns the general mechanism of its functioning, it
is obvious that it copies that of municipal bodies."[18]  In general, according to Ramsey MacMullen, "associations thus resembled
the whole social context they found themselves in and imitated
it as best they could."[19]  It should not be surprising, then,
that the language used to accord honors to patrons of *collegia*
or associations should mirror that used in praise of benefactors
of cities, just as that used of civic benefactors replicates the
praise of emperors.  The difference is one of degree rather than
of kind.  The conservatism of the literary form of the inscriptions and the replication of social forms combine to promote
uniformity in the praise of benefactors on all levels.  More
than the recurrence of similar titles, like εὐεργέτης, there is
the repetition of a common logical structure which expresses
the basic notion that those who perform beneficial actions are
to be honored accordingly.

Texts honoring patrons of *collegia* are perhaps the most
modest in their praise of benefactors.  This late second century
A. D. text from central Italy nevertheless clearly displays
the relation between the performance of direct, immediate, and
tangible beneficial actions and the reception of certain honors:

> To Marcus Aurelius Marcellus, son of Elainus, priest
> with right of jurisdiction of the Sorrinenses Novenses,
> *quaestor* of the public funds, patron of the associa-
> tion of smiths and quiltmakers.  To this man, first
> of all, the distinguished council, from the gifts which
> they had received, voted that a statue should be set
> up on account of his services.  For the dedication
> of this statue he gave to the councillors bread and
> wine and forty sesterces, and moreover on account of
> the honour conferred upon him he gave 5,000 sesterces
> to the people for the corn supply in perpetuity.[20]

The provision of victuals and money earned Marcus Aurelius
Marcellus both an inscription and a statue in his honor; beneficial actions were rewarded by an increase in status.

The larger the stage on which the benefactor played, the
more expansive was the praise he received.  This late first

century A. D. inscription from the Greek mainland is notable
for connecting the benefactor's munificence to his moral character, a theme which recurs in both Celsus' and Origen's comments
on candidates for divine status:

> Resolution of the Antigoneans:  since Euphrosynus,
> son of Titus, our citizen, inheriting the goodwill
> displayed by his fathers towards the fatherland, so
> far from detracting anything from his family's worth,
> had enhanced it, always and everyday contriving to
> provide some advantage for the city, being a man who,
> although possessed from birth of excellent moral qual-
> ities, has surpassed these in developing a character
> excelling his natural disposition, a man lavish in
> his gifts . . . . He directed by statute that the
> income from the land should be used for the support of
> the corn purchase fund, providing for the unfailing
> supply of food in perpetuity.
> [the decree goes on to praise Euphrosynus' wife,
> Epigone]:  For they were linked together in a union
> of body and mind in their lives and they shared a com-
> mon and undivided concern in always seeking to go
> beyond the other in devoting themselves to the per-
> formance of good deeds; thus, they rebuilt the temples
> which had been in utter ruins and they added dining-
> rooms to those existing and they provided the [reli-
> gious] societies with treasuries, extending their piety
> not only to the gods but to the places themselves.
> Epigone, indeed, a woman of saintly dignity and devoted
> to her husband, imitated his example herself by taking
> up the priesthood ordained for every goddess, worship-
> ping the gods reverently at sacrificial expense, in
> providing all men alike with a festive banquet.[21]

Though the particular honors which Euphrosynus and Epigone were
accorded are not specified, the means by which they earned
them are.  The opening lines recall the dispute between Celsus
and Origen in CC I.28-31 about the relative merits of noble and
ignoble birth for a candidate for divine status.  Origen had
admitted earlier that

> Among men of noble birth, honourable and distinguished
> parents, an upbringing at the hands of wealthy people
> who are able to spend money on the education of their
> son, and a great and famous native country, are things
> which help to make a man famous and distinguished and
> get his name well known.  (I.29)

But Origen also argued that the success of Jesus was all the
more wonderful, since he had triumphed over so many obstacles.
Euphrosynus seems to have encountered no such obstacles; his
career is portrayed as the epitome of the Single Image of the

traditional route to the acquisition of articulate power.  He
inherited a tradition of doing good for the fatherland and both
his family's reputation and his own character were enhanced by
his untiring benefactions for the city.  Significant also, in
light of the arguments in CC, is the implicit assumption that
Euphrosynus' and Epigone's lavish giving of gifts reflects directly
on their moral character.  Euphrosynus is not portrayed as merely
competently discharging an inherited responsibility, but rather
as "developing a character excelling his natural disposition"
by virtue of his generosity.  Origen also argues that Jesus'
beneficial actions reflect his moral character.  The nature of
his benefactions, however, still makes Euphrosynus very much fit
for Celsus' Single Image.  From the provision of food, to the
rebuilding of temples, to the replenishment of their treasuries,
his benefits are direct, immediate, and tangible.  Though they
reflect on his ἴδιος ἦθος, they are still of a different order
than the moral reformation and conversion from the flood of sins
with which Origen credits Jesus.  A moral dimension is present
in the praise of Euphrosynus and Epigone, but it supplements
rather than supplants the praise of their primary benefactions,
which were direct, immediate, and tangible.

The resolutions in honor of Marcus Aurelius Marcellus and
Euphrosynus and Epigone reveal more about the types of actions
which were considered beneficial and praiseworthy than about the
specific honors which were accorded.  Both inscriptions seem to
depend on the same criterion which was fundamental for Celsus'
and Origen's evaluation of candidates for divine status, but it
is not at all certain that either Marcus Aurelius Marcellus or
Euphrosynus and Epigone were considered candidates for full divine status.  What is more likely is that their benefactions
prompted their partisans to situate them on the continuum between
gods and ordinary humans somewhat closer to the gods than were
the majority of their fellows.  By honoring them with statues and
inscriptions, their partisans singled them out as extra-ordinary,
as in some ways superior to the bulk of humanity.  In so doing,
those who praised them followed some of the same procedures, relied on some of the same criteria, and used some of the same
categories that Celsus and Origen employed in their evaluation of

candidates for divine status.  They differ only in that their
continuum of possible evaluations is more restricted, a narrow
band of positive secondary categories between the ordinary mortals and the gods.

With the granting of honors to emperors, a fuller range of
categories comes into play.  A.R. Hands traces that directly to
the enormity of the favors they could bestow:

> When, therefore, an individual conferred a gift of al-
> most superhuman proportions--and it was the monarch of
> a great kingdom who was best placed to do so--there
> seemed in a world where no clear distinction was made
> between the human and the divine, little alternative
> but to accord the donor the status of a god and to
> hold commemorative ceremonies in his honor.  In the
> acquisition of "divine" status the struggle for honour
> via giving and benevolence had reached its logical
> conclusion . . . this development provided Hellenistic
> kings--and, later, Roman emperors--with a convenient
> moral basis for their rule.  They claimed precedence
> in the state by virtue of their outstripping all
> others in terms of benefits conferred.  The Hellenistic
> king was Euergetes (benefactor par excellence), or even
> Soter (Saviour)--so dependent were his subjects on
> his beneficence.[22]

Of the numerous texts on imperial beneficence, I will take two
well-known ones as exemplary.  The first is a decree of a provincial synod of Asia in honor of the Roman emperor Augustus,
dating to 9 B. C.  The prefatory letter raises the question of
whether the birthday of Augustus "is to be observed most for the
joy of it or for the profit of it" and contends that that day
might be regarded as equivalent "to the beginning of all things
. . . if not in reality, at any rate in the benefits he has
brought."  Augustus is described as "a blessing to the whole of
mankind."  The actual resolution makes clear the connection between Augustus' beneficial actions and the divine status which
he was granted in appreciative response:

> Resolved by the Greeks of the province of Asia, on
> the proposal of the high-priest Apollonius, the son
> of Menophilus, of Azani:  Whereas the Providence
> which orders the whole of human life has shown special
> concern and zeal and conferred upon life its most per-
> fect ornament, by bestowing Augustus, whom it fitted
> for his beneficent work among mankind by filling Him
> with virtue, sending Him as a Saviour, for us and for
> those who come after us, one who should cause wars to
> cease, who should set all things in fair order, and

> whereas Caesar, when He appeared, made the hopes of
> those who forecast a better future [look poor compared
> with the reality], in that He not only surpassed all
> previous benefactors, but left no chance for future
> ones to go beyond Him, and the glad tidings which
> by His means went forth into the world took its rise
> in the birthday of the God; . . . .[23]

The resolution concludes that a fitting recognition of the emperor's (the god's) birthday would be to reckon time from his
birthday, and that the first day of the month should thenceforth
be the birthday of Augustus.  The repeated emphasis on Augustus'
beneficent activities leads directly to the explicit granting of
divine status to him, although the list of beneficial actions itself is somewhat wanting in specifics.  A slightly later inscription, found at Halicarnassus and dated near the turn of the eras,
also makes the explicit connection between Augustus' benefactions
and his divine status, and in addition provides more specific
examples:

> Whereas the eternal and immortal Nature of the Uni-
> verse has granted to men the things of greatest good
> for extraordinary benefits, in bringing forth Caesar
> Augustus, who in this our happy age is Father of his
> own country, the goddess Rome, and is Zeus Patroös,
> Saviour of mankind, whose providence has not only ful-
> filled the prayers of all men, but gone far beyond
> them, seeing that there is peace over land and sea,
> and the cities flourish with law and concord and pros-
> perity, and there is a rich yield of all good, and
> men are filled with bright hopes for the future and
> joy regarding the present . . . .[24]

The specific benefits with which Augustus is credited center on the effects of the Augustan peace.  Both inscriptions
mention the cessation of wars and the ensuing "peace over land
and sea."  The second notes further the concord and prosperity of
the cities of the empire.  The first mentions Augustus as the
guarantor of universal order, while the second attributes to him
a "rich yield of all good."  Both note that he has instilled in
the citizens of the empire significant hopes for the future.
Aside from the cessation of war, however, those benefits, at
least as described in the texts, are hardly as direct, immediate,
and tangible as those mentioned in praise of Marcus Aurelius
Marcellus or Euphrosynus and Epigone.  It may be that the enor-
mous impact of the Augustan restoration could only have been

adequately described by chronicling its psychological impact,
the sense of calm, hope, and joy that it infused in the inhabi-
tants of the empire.  A mere list of concrete benefactions or a
simple statue honoring the emperor would not have sufficed if,
as Hands suggests, the magnitude of Augustus' benefactions drove
his subjects to hyperbolic praise.  At any rate, the benefits
attributed to Augustus resemble more closely those which Origen
attributes to the activity of Jesus, particularly moral reformation and the salvation of many from the flood of sins.  In both
cases the benefactors are credited with instilling an attitude,
a frame of mind, and a disposition towards action in their audiences.  In both cases, the beneficial effects are thought to extend to all mankind and to continue after the time of the benefactor himself; the provincial decree claims that Augustus was
sent as a Saviour "for us and for those who come after us."  In
similar fashion Origen repeatedly mentions that the divine power
of Jesus can be seen at work throughout the world, even in the
third century.  Thus, while there is a sharp distinction between
such concrete benefactions as the provision of grain, the repair
of a temple, or underwriting of the cost of a statue and the
moral and spiritual benefactions which Origen attributes to Jesus, the inscriptions in honor of Augustus show that a non-
Christian view of beneficial actions was not strictly limited to
such concrete benefactions.  Origen's emphasis on the moral and
spiritual dimension of the beneficial action of Jesus is consistent and fully developed, but it is not entirely without precedent.

In addition to benefactors of collegia, cities, and the empire as a whole, certain deities were also credited with beneficial actions which warranted their being accorded divine status.[25]  Two brief examples will show that their benefits were
thought to have taken both the more concrete form of the provision of necessary material goods and also the more intangible
form of the establishment of universal order.  Diodorus Siculus,
Charles Talbert's principle source for a Hellenistic "mythology
of the immortals," repeatedly makes the causal connection between
the performance of good works and the elevation of the benefactor
to divine status.[26]  In the first book alone of his *Library of*

*History* he mentions Heracles (I.2.4; I.24.7f.), unspecified
"other gods" (I.13.1), Hermes (I.15.9), Osiris, (I.17.1), Isis
(I.25.4), and Horus (I.25.7) as deities whose primary qualifications were to be found in their performance of beneficent acts
for humankind.  Though Talbert does not stress it, it should be
recognized that the conception of a benefactor who receives divine status in recognition of philanthropy is an important element of Diodorus' treatise.  The link between benefaction and
the attainment of the status of an immortal is clearly described
in Diodorus' comments on Osiris:

> Of Osiris they say that, being of a beneficent turn
> of mind (εὐργετικὸν ὄντα) and eager for glory, he
> gathered together a great army, with the intention
> of visiting all the inhabited earth and teaching the
> race of men how to cultivate the vine and sow wheat
> and barley; for he supposed that if he made men give
> up their savagery and adopt a gentle manner of life
> he would receive immortal honours because of the mag-
> nitude of his benefactions (διὰ τὸ μέγεθος τῆς
> εὐεργεσίας).  And this did in fact take place, since
> not only the men of his time who received this gift,
> but all succeeding generations as well, because of
> the delight which they take in the foods which were
> discovered, have honoured those who introduced them
> as gods most illustrious (ὡς ἐπιφανεστάτους θεούς).[27]

Osiris' primary benefaction was direct, immediate, tangible, and
also long-lasting; the enduring importance of the food-stuffs
which he first discovered, continually reinforces his divine
status.  Similarly, Origen takes the continuing success of the
Christian movement in his own time to reinforce the divine status of Jesus.[28]  Diodorus echoes Origen's emphasis on the duration of the beneficial act, but the difference between them still
hinges on their respective views of just which acts are to be
considered beneficial.

In his praise of Sarapis, however, Aelius Aristides ventures
beyond the realm of strictly tangible benefits towards a conception of the deity as the guarantor of universal order.  At the
outset of his eighth oration Aristides claims to prescind from
any theological investigation of the nature of Sarapis in favor
of an enumeration of his many beneficial actions for humankind.
Nevertheless, Aristides does imply that the enumeration of benefits *will* reflect on the character or nature of his subject:

> Who the God is and what His nature is, it may
> be left to the priests and learned men of Egypt
> to declare and to know:  we shall praise Him
> sufficiently at the present time, if we state
> how many good things and what manner of good
> things come from Him to men, and at the same
> time from these things some insight may be got
> into His nature . . . .[29]

Aristides' claim that the beneficial actions performed by
Sarapis will furnish clues about his nature accords well with
the procedures of both Celsus and Origen who made that premise
the basis for their evaluations of candidates for divine status.
Among the specific benefactions which Aristides attributes to
Sarapis are his presiding over the birth of every individual,
exercising providence throughout the course of each life, preserving the health of the body, and providing the soul with wisdom, not to mention lining the wallet with money.  Aristides
goes on to describe Sarapis as the benefactor of all things:

> Indeed he holds together for men all the framework of
> life and deals out each of life's constituents and
> in this way may be rightly thought of as embracing
> all things, as governing the whole of our life's
> course . . . in regard to nothing does He come short
> in power, but goes through everything and has filled
> the universe.[30]

So many and various are the good works of which Sarapis is the
author that "the sacred depositories of sacred books contain in-
numerable examples . . . .  The marketplaces are full, and the
harbours, and the broad places of the cities, with those who tell
the manifold things He has done."[31]  Like those of Augustus,
Osiris, and Jesus, "His mighty works have not come to a stand-
still; they are more today than yesterday; each day, each night,
adds new ones to the tale."[32]  Finally, Aristides concludes by
begging acceptance of his hymn, again alluding to his governing
conception of Sarapis as the benefactor *par excellence*; he asks
"do Thou accept graciously, a thankoffering for past benefits,
a supplication and entreaty concerning future things, that they
may be better and happier than the things which now are."[33]  Although the conception that benefactions reveal the character of
their perpetrator and the focus on intangible benefits, such as
the establishment of universal order, come closer to Origen's

position than an emphasis on strictly material good works,
Aristides still has not duplicated Origen's relentless insistence
on the moral and spiritual nature of the most important benefits
that a god could bestow on men.

That review of some remarks about deities, recipients of
divine honors, and those who were accorded lesser, if still extraordinary, honors cannot in itself establish the existence of
a "Hellenistic conception of the divine man" or even a clear
delineation of the native conceptions about the worthiness of
various types of benefactor for divine honors. It can, however,
contribute to the lessening of the suspicion that the primary
criterion used by Celsus and Origen in their evaluations of candidates for divine status was an idiosyncratic conception removed
from the mainstream of religious and philosophical thought in
Late Antiquity. Others do seem to have affirmed the proposition
that a god ought to do good to men, and there is evidence of
their affirmation in formal decrees, orations of praise,
historical narratives, and philosophical arguments and exhortations. It would be premature to suggest that such varied evidence
can be traced to a single, unitary conception which admitted little variation over a long period of time. Rather, it seems likely
that the root conception was subject to several variations, de-
pending on the context, author, and subject to which it was applied. Celsus' and Origen's different applications of their
central criterion of evaluation furnish evidence enough of possible variations. More work needs to be done on tracing the
history and subsequent variations of the conception of the benefactor as worthy of divine status.[34] But this brief survey
should suffice to suggest that the conception has a wider currency beyond Celsus' and Origen's treatises and that, consequently, if the outlines of a *native Hellenistic* conception of
the divine man are to be sought, the contribution of the conception of the benefactor as worthy of divine status needs to be
considered. Celsus was hardly alone in his insistence that
"above all a god ought to have done good to all men" (II.20).

In the following chapter I will try to establish at greater
length that that conception can also be seen at work in a series
of texts which are closely related to both Celsus' *Alethes Logos*
and Origen's *Contra Celsum*.

CHAPTER V

DIVINE MEN IN LUCIAN, PHILOSTRATUS, AND EUSEBIUS

*Introduction*

At the end of the first chapter I offered brief justification of the choice of CC as a focus for the investigation of
indigenous categories and criteria for the evaluation of candidates for divine status.  I suggested that CC preserves the most
detailed and influential presentation of claims made for and
against Jesus' candidacy in the early centuries of the Christian
era.  In particular, the presentation in CC is much fuller than
the brief considerations of any of the second-century apologists,
and it exercised a decisive impact on Eusebius in his refutation
of the attack upon Jesus by Hierocles.[1]  Similarly, Celsus' *True
Doctrine* is certainly the most detailed and possibly the most
influential attack upon Jesus and the Christian religion during
the same period.[2]  It remains to be considered whether the specific categories, criteria, and arguments employed by Celsus and
Origen had a broader currency.  I will limit the discussion to
three texts.  Two of them, Lucian's *Alexander the False Prophet*
and Philostratus' *Life of Apollonius*, have played significant
roles in contemporary studies of divine men.  The third, Eusebius'
*Against Hierocles*, has not received much attention, perhaps because it is not biographical but rather apologetic in form.  Its
inclusion is dictated, however, by the principles proposed in
chapter I.[3]  Each of those texts presents a scheme of classification of candidates for divine status; they are important for
their structural and thematic resemblances to CC rather than for
any alleged historical connections with either Celsus or Origen.[4]

*Lucian*

Lucian's vigorous attack on the character of Alexander of
Abonuteichos most closely resembles the work of Celsus.  Like
Celsus, he aims not to defend and rehabilitate but rather to expose and debilitate his subject's candidacy.  Lucian's feelings
about Alexander are evident from the outset; he is a charlatan

and a crook who preys on the superstitious and fleeces the rich
(cf. Alex. 1).  Greed for riches becomes a dominant theme of
Lucian's case against Alexander, perhaps because he is asserting
his negative view of Alexander in the face of the evident success
of the cult that he founded.[5]  The readily apparent success of
the cult exerts a profound influence on Lucian's characterization
of Alexander.  He cannot, as Origen did with the followers of
Simon Magus in CC I.57, dismiss the cult as an overnight success
with no lasting impact.  Instead, Lucian focused on the *reasons
behind* Alexander's success.  He turns his attention to Alexander's motives and moral character, the relative mental and spiritual capacities of his clients, and, most extensively, to the
details of the foundation and daily management of the oracular
shrine.  His strategy resembles Origen's use of the Double Image.
To Lucian, things are certainly *not* as they seem.  Behind the
outward success of Alexander's enterprise lurk shocking facts
and scandalous revelations.  Lucian aims to bring each to light,
often in lurid detail.

For Lucian, Alexander himself is a potentially good man gone
wrong.  He readily acknowledges that Alexander "was tall and
handsome in appearance, and really godlike (θεοπρηπῆς)" (Alex.3).
But in this case appearances are definitely deceptive, as Lucian's summary comments indicate:

> In sum, imagine, please, and mentally configure a
> highly diversified soul-blend, made up of lying,
> trickery, perjury, and malice; facile, audacious, ven-
> turesome, diligent in the execution of its schemes,
> plausible, convincing, masking as good, and wearing
> an appearance absolutely opposite to its purpose.
> (Alex. 4)

Nor did Alexander appear to Lucian to have put his considerable
abilities to proper use:

> In understanding, quick-wittedness, and penetration
> he was far beyond everyone else; and activity of
> mind, readiness to learn, retentiveness, natural apti-
> tude for studies--all these qualities were his, in
> every case to the full.  But he made the worst possible
> use of them, and with these noble instruments at his
> service soon became the most perfect rascal of all
> those who have been notorious far and wide for vil-
> lainy. . . .  (Alex.4)

Thus, eminently qualified for a good and virtuous life, Alexander
set off instead in the opposite direction.  Where Origen's use
of the Double Image allowed him to dismiss Jesus' humble origins
as irrelevant to his candidacy for divine status, Lucian's use
of *his* Double Image produces the opposite effect, by demonstrating that Alexander's external qualifications in no way support
his candidacy.

Lucian attempts to show that Alexander's abuse of his natural abilities was reinforced by his choice of associates, including a Tyanan magician (Alex. 5) and a songwriter given to
swindles (Alex. 6).  The tactic of casting doubt on a candidate
for divine status by exposing his association with questionable
characters was also used by Celsus.[6]  Motivated by greed and
spurred on by his songwriter associate, Alexander hatched the
plan that earned him fame, fortune, and, eventually, Lucian's
relentless opposition.

Lucian's invective focuses on the oracular shrine founded
by Alexander in Abonuteichos.  He attacks the patrons of the
shrine as easily-fooled, ignorant, and bereft of sense (cf. Alex.
9, 30), recalling Celsus' accusation that Christian preachers
concentrated their efforts on easy marks in the market-place
(cf. CC I.68, III.50).  In each case the success of the venture
is undermined by the easy credulity of the audience.  But Lucian
did not stop there; he took it upon himself to expose for all
interested the clever devices by which Alexander accomplished
his impressive effects.  Lucian's basic method is *mechanistic*;
he intends to show how the structure and processes of the shrine
are dependent on human artifice rather than divine activity.
Lucian discounts from the start the possibility of divine activity, as his comments in chapter 17 show:

> Really the trick (τὸ μηχάνημα) stood in need of a
> Democritus, or even Epicurus himself or Metrodorus,
> or someone else with a mind as firm as adamant toward
> such matters, so as to disbelieve and guess the truth
> --one who, if he could not discover how it went, would
> at all events be convinced beforehand that though the
> method of the fraud (ὁ τρόπος τῆς μαγγανείας) escaped
> him, it was nevertheless all sham (ψευδός) and could
> not possibly happen (γενέσθαι ἀδυνατον).  (Alex. 17)

Lucian painstakingly compiles an elaborate inventory of the
ruses employed by Alexander.  He begins with Alexander and the

songwriter Cocconas[7] burying in the temple of Apollo in Chalce-
don bronze tablets which predicted that Asclepius and his father
Apollo would very soon take up residence in Abonuteichus.[8] He
exposes Alexander's attempt to acquire for himself a divine genealogy of the house of Perseus.[9] Lucian also details the steal-
thy preparations for the advent of the god, noting how Alexander
constructed a large lifelike serpent which would become the
mouthpiece of the god (Alex. 12), and how he buried one night in
the foundations of the temple that was being prepared for Asclepius a goose egg in which he had secreted a small snake (Alex.
13). Then, in a scene of high theatre which Lucian laces with
low comedy, Alexander appears in the market place in a maniacal
frenzy. He exhorts the people to receive the visible presence
of the god and conducts them to the site of the future temple.
Once there, with appropriate ceremony, he fishes out the egg and
presents the god to the people, to their complete amazement
(Alex. 14).

Lucian's presentation of the founding of the shrine in
Abonuteichos resembles a drama; it divides easily into acts,
scenes, and striking tableaux. But it is a drama with a difference. Lucian, the narrator, not only includes the stage directions in the performance, but he makes certain to include as much
technical information as necessary to explain to the audience
exactly how certain striking effects are achieved. It is a
drama utterly shorn of its dramatic impact; it is demystified,
trivialized, and reduced to the level of play-acting. Lucian
depends on the assumption that an audience apprised of how certain effects are achieved will not be taken in by them.

Lucian's reduction of art to artifice continues in his depiction of the rubes' initial visits to the god. The citizens
of Paphlagonia were duped by Alexander's clever arrangement of
a large, real, tame serpent and a constructed serpent mask to
represent the god. In case they might suspect something amiss,
they were hustled in and out so quickly that they didn't notice.
In order to unmask Alexander's pretensions to prophecy, Lucian
also lavishes particular attention on the means by which Alexander ascertained the queries to which he was to reply. He mentions explicitly three different procedures for removing the seal

and replacing it undisturbed, after reading the query.[10]  Yet
even though he was thus furnished with the exact questions put
to the oracle, Alexander's responses were less than crystalline
in their clarity.  Lucian traces that to his conception of the
proper procedure for an oracle:  "He gave responses that were
sometimes obscure and ambiguous, sometimes downright unintelli-
gible, for this seemed to him in the oracular manner" (Alex. 22).
Lucian's other attempts at demystification concern the organiza-
tion, payment, and duties of the staff of the shrine, and the
eventual establishment of cultic mysteries there (Alex. 23, 24,
36, 39).

In all his efforts Lucian presupposes that his providing
detailed information about the functioning of the oracle will
dissipate the mists of spirituality that enshroud it.[11]  The
accumulated evidence of deceitful practices will reflect on
Alexander's character.  The operation of the shrine is the fullest
indication that Alexander "made the worst possible use" of his
native abilities.  If the performance of certain actions has
classifying force, Alexander's show him to be a fraud, villain,
and liar.  Lucian's treatise does present a full range of negative categories, though a shorter range of positive ones.  Sche-
matically, they look like this:

| god | human | wizard/magician |
|-----|-------|-----------------|
| prophet | brigand | |
| wise man | rascal | |
| celestial | villain | |
| godlike | knave | |
| divine son | liar | |
| | perjurer | |
| | prostitute | |
| | fraud | |
| | trickster | |
| | pederast | |
| | adulterer | |

Lucian's strict attention to the operation of the oracular
shrine, and his assertion that Alexander made the worst possible
use of his abilities also indicate that certain actions were
presumed to have classifying force.  In addition, Lucian portrays
Alexander as working on similar presuppositions.  In response
to the Paphlagonians' questions about whether or not Alexander
had the soul of Pythagoras, the oracle declared that Alexander

had been "sent by the Father to aid good men in the stress of
the conflict" (Alex. 40). Later, Alexander claims that on leaving Abonuteichus he will travel "to Bactra and that region, for
the barbarians too must profit by my presence among men" (Alex.
43). Each of those statements presumes that Alexander's aid and
profitable activity support his candidacy for divine status.

Perhaps the clearest statement of the principle that a
candidate for divinity ought to do good for men is made by the
citizens of Abonuteichos themselves, though it is also satirized
by Lucian in the process. On first hearing of the imminent arrival of the god in their town, the citizens of Abonuteichus
"immediately voted to build a temple and began at once to dig for
the foundations" (Alex. 10). When Alexander made his first
speech in the city, "he congratulated the city because it was at
once to receive the god in visible presence" (Alex. 13). What
that presence would mean was clear enough to the assembled
Paphlagonians, who, on seeing the snake-god retreived from the
temple foundations "at once raised a shout, welcomed the god,
congratulated their city, and began each of them to sate himself
greedily with prayers, craving treasures, riches, health, and
every other blessing from him" (Alex. 14). In their minds, at
least, there seems to have been a clear connection between the
arrival of the god and their own reception of benefits which he
could bestow. The expectations of the Paphlagonians show that
they viewed the benefits bestowed by oracles much as Celsus did:

> How many cities have been built by oracles, and have
> got rid of disease and famines, and how many that have
> neglected or forgotten them have suffered terrible
> destruction? How many have been sent to form a colony
> and have prospered by attending to their commands?
> How many rulers and common people have come off better
> or worse for this reason? How many that have been
> distressed at being childless have come to possess
> that for which they prayed and escaped the wrath of
> daemons? How many ailments of the body have been
> healed? How many, on the other hand, have insulted
> the temples and have at once been caught? For some have
> been overcome by madness on the spot; others have de-
> clared what they had done; others have made an end of
> themselves; and others have become bound by incurable
> diseases. Some have even been destroyed by a deep
> voice from the actual shrines. (CC VIII.45)

If the Paphlagonians shared those sentiments, it is no wonder
that they welcomed Alexander so gratefully. Such benefits would

provide good reasons for congratulating the city, and such potential dangers would provide ample caution against disregarding
the newcomer.

Lucian, clearly, did not share the enthusiasm of the Paphlagonians. He exercised his version of the Double Image to
show that what were considered benefits were in reality the result of an elaborate ruse, a complex *trompe d'oeil*. The god
was no god but a mere snake; the prophet was a fraud; the oracular responses were gibberish. The only benefits to be had were
monetary, and they all accrued to Alexander and his coterie.
Alexander is a virtual parody of the civic benefactor; he only
*seems* to deliver what the city so fervently expects. Since he
does not deliver, since he does not perform beneficial actions,
Lucian discounts his candidacy for divine status. But though he
arrives at a negative conclusion, the criteria and categories
he uses have much in common with those employed by Celsus and
Origen.

## *Philostratus*

Like Origen in CC I and II, Philostratus is engaged in the
rehabilitation of a subject who had fallen under attack as a
magician and *poseur*. The apologetic dimension of VA is evident
at the outset when Philostratus denies any connection between
his subject and the magical arts, noting that "we might as well
accuse Socrates of the same . . ." (VA I.2).[12] He claims to
write "a true account of the man, detailing the exact times at
which he said or did this or that, as also the habits and temper
of wisdom by means of which he succeeded in being considered a
supernatural and divine being (τοῦ δαιμόνιός τε καὶ θεῖος
νομισθῆναι)" (VA I.2). Although Philostratus' loosely-knit tale
does not focus exclusively on Apollonius' candidacy for divine
status, there are several instances in which evaluations are
essayed, and his opening comments show that Philostratus was
clearly concerned with the *correct* classification of Apollonius.

Philostratus frequently mentions that Apollonius was received as a divine being (θεῖος) by those he encountered in his
travels. Frontier satraps (VA I.21), the king of India (II.17),
the Brahmans (III.50), and many others welcomed the sage as

someone out of the ordinary.  Many were converted to Apollonius'
way of life and modelled their actions after his.  Philostratus
reports that in the subjects of the gods, customs, moral principles, and laws "He corrected the errors into which men had
fallen" (VA I.2).  Among those who benefitted from Apollonius'
care were his elder brother (VA I.13); the citizens of Antioch
(I.17); a young debauchee who after his encounter with Apollonius
"gave up his dainty dress and summery garments and the rest of
his sybaritic way of life, and he fell in love with the austerity
of philosophers, and donned their cloak, and stripping off his
old self modelled his life in future upon that of Apollonius"
(IV.20); the philosopher Demetrius of Corinth who adopted his
doctrines "and converted to the side of Apollonius the more
esteemed of his own pupils" (IV.25); Apollonius' own followers
for whom "it was an essential part of their philosophic discipline to imitate his every word and action" (V.21); and a youth
who had previously spent most of his time trying to educate birds
to speak with human voices (VI.36).  Apollonius also took great
interest in the reform of traditional cultic practics; in many
Greek cities "he would call the priests together and talk wisely
about the gods, and would correct them, supposing they had de-
parted from the traditional forms" (VA I.16).  All of those works
which directly benefitted individuals, groups, and institutions
earned Apollonius praise and spread his fame.  When he went to
Egypt he was greeted as if he were a god (VA V.24), and Vespasian
addressed him as if in prayer (V.28, cf. V.33).

On the other hand, Apollonius was refused initiation into
the Eleusinian mysteries on the suspicion that he was a wizard
(VA IV.18), a suspicion which flared anew when he visited the
oracle of Trophonius (VIII.19).  At the opening of his work
Philostratus acknowledges that

> some, because he had interviews with the wizards of
> Babylon and with the Brahmans of India, and with the
> nude ascetics of Egypt, put him down as a wizard
> (μάγον), and spread the calumny that he was a sage
> of an illegitimate kind (ὡς βιαίως σοφόν), judging him
> ill.  (VA I.2)

Philostratus, of course, denies the truth of those accusations.
He notes that Empedocles, Pythagoras, and Democritus associated

with wizards but never themselves stooped to practice the "black art," and that Plato also went to Egypt and learned much from the priests and prophets there, and concludes that if Apollonius' foreknowledge is to be imputed to wizardry then the same might just as well be said of Socrates.  Just as Lucian had attempted to undermine the candidacy of Alexander by pointing to the unsavory nature of his associates, so also Philostratus tries to absolve Apollonius of any suspicion of wizardry by linking him with Socrates, Plato, Pythagoras, Empedocles, and Democritus.[13] But, as the incidents at Eleusis and the oracle of Trophonius indicate, such suspicions would not just fade away.  They crop up again when Apollonius is accused of impiety in Rome for having made an offhand remark about the behaviour of the populace in temples during an outbreak of influenza (VA IV.44).  They are also woven throughout the running quarrel which Apollonius had with the philosopher Euphrates (cf. VA I.13; VI.28).  Apollonius himself claimed that Euphrates had slandered him among the sages of Egypt as "a boaster and a miracle-monger (τερατώδη)" (VA VII. 14), and it seems that Euphrates may have also been behind the accusations at Apollonius' trial that he was a wizard (VIII.3).

His contemporaries' strong interest in classifying Apollonius dominates a series of short episodes in book VII.  As Apollonius goes through the judicial process leading to his trial before Domitian, his character is subjected to a battery of tests.  Aelian, the consul of Domitian and the arresting-officer, was sympathetically disposed to Apollonius, since in an earlier meeting the sage had foretold his success in the imperial service.  After Apollonius had been arrested, the prosecutor immediately began to abuse him as a wizard and a magician, but Aelian interceded and warned him to withhold the charges until the trial proper.  In the meantime he will make his own investigation:

> Leave me the time that will elapse until his trial
> begins; for I intend to examine the sophist's char
> acter privately (ἔλεγχον γὰρ ποιήσομαι τῆς τοῦ σοφιστοῦ
> γνώμης ἰδίᾳ), and not before yourselves; and if he ad
> mits his guilt, then the pleadings in the court can
> be cut short, and you can depart in peace, but if he
> denies his guilt, the emperor will try him.
> (VA VII.17)

Aelian takes the opportunity to apprise Apollonius of the

emperor's intentions and mode of procedure and to explain the role which he, as consul, is constrained to play in the proceeding. Apollonius commends his philosophical spirit, but asserts that he must make a defense lest he be branded a traitor. Though Aelian professes admiration for the sage's steadfastness and courage, his test produces no clearcut verdict on Apollonius' character, but rather the vague impression that Aelian did not think him guilty as charged.

A skeptical Roman tribune proposes a more decisive test. He informs Apollonius that "it is allowing yourself to be worshipped by your fellow-men that has led you to be accused of setting yourself on a level with the gods" (VA VII.21). The tribune sees a simple way of determining the validity of such aspirations:

> I have prepared a method of defence for yourself, which will rid you of the charge against you. For let us go outside the gates, and if I cut off your head with my sword the accusation will have defeated itself and you will go scot free; but it you terrify me to such an extent that I drop my sword, you must needs be thought a divine being (θεῖόν), and then it will be seen that there is a basis of truth in the charges made against you. (VA VII.21)

Apollonius ignored him.

Finally, an officer of the court informs Apollonius that the emperor wants to speak to him before the trial, "for he wants to see you and find out who you are (ὅστις ὢν τυγχάνεις), and to talk with you alone" (VA VII.29). When Domitian meets Apollonius, he renders an immediate verdict. He "was so much struck by Apollonius' appearance, that he said: 'O Aelian, it is a demon (δαίμονά) that you have introduced to me'" (VA VII.32). Though that is the clearest decision to have come from any of the three encounters between Apollonius and the representatives of the Roman order, it is not allowed to stand for long. Apollonius quickly reproaches the emperor for his inability to distinguish mere men from demons, and the emperor in turn proceeds to question Apollonius' motives and loyalty in his association with Nerva.

With the possible exception of the last, those three tests of Apollonius' character are notable for their lack of

decisiveness and even their lack of criteria on which a decision
could be based. What impresses most is the elusiveness of the
figure to be tested. Aelian's conversation is more a set of
strategic suggestions for the trial than a test of Apollonius'
character; the tribune's proposed test is never undertaken, and
that of the emperor is abortive. As such, they appear as virtual
parodies of the form. Apollonius emerges as figure whose character is not to be tested. He is, simply, Apollonius.[14]

The evaluations of those who encountered Apollonius, though
divided into fierce partisans (the Brahmans, Egyptian sages, et
al.) and equally fierce detractors (Euphrates, the Eleusinian
hierophant, the representative of the oracle of Trophonius, et
al.) are clear. But Philostratus himself takes a position somewhere in between those extremes. He stresses Apollonius' inces-
sant pursuit of the ideal Pythagorean life (VA I.2, 7), the
esteem in which he was held by the gods (I.9), his activity as a
reformer (IV.22, VI.40, 43; esp. VIII.7), his purification and
rectification of ritual procedures (IV.40, 42; V.25), and his
general championing of right and justice (V.20, 27; VI.41; VII.
3). Nevertheless, Philostratus seems to equivocate in his final
judgement. He links Apollonius' disappearance from the courtroom
to a demonstration of his "true nature" (VIII.5), but he is notably hesitant to detail just what that nature might be. Though
he seems to affirm Apollonius' claim to immortality (VIII.5),
he accords comparatively little space to the exposition of that
statement.

In Philostratus' characterization, Apollonius himself is
more adept at describing what he is *not* than at giving a full
delineation of his own character. He is not prophet (VA IV.44),
though he does have foreknowledge as a revelation from the
gods (V.12). He has been granted, by the ineffable form of wisdom, the ability as a philosopher to distinguish a god, recognize
a hero, and detect phantoms (VA VI.11), but he uses it sparingly.
He is apprehensive about being branded a traitor (VII.19).
Above all, he is not a γόης. In his final speech before Domitian
he confronts the issue directly, claiming that his meeting with
Domitian's father Vespasian in Egypt shows that 1) he was not
asked to compel the fates, 2) he held his conversation in public

in a temple, 3) there were even witnesses to his more private
conversations, both sympathetic and hostile, 4) he never asked
for money for consultations; moreover, 5) the exercise of foreknowledge is not sufficient grounds for such an accusation, and
6) such a person would not dedicate his achievement to a god,
nor 7) offer prayers to Hercules (VA VIII.7.ii). Apollonius
does claim to be a good man (VII.36) and for that reason to be
worthy of being called a god, according to the usage of the sages
of India (VIII.5, 7). Beyond that, his self-testimonies are
ambiguous. His claim, on disappearing from Domitian's courtroom,
to be immortal (a quotation from Iliad 22.13) seems to indicate
aspirations to divine status, but they are not fully developed
in the course of the narrative. The assertion remains opaque.

But if Apollonius' own statements tend toward the inscru-
table, those of his close associates are more definite. When
Apollonius extricates himself from his fetters in prison, Damis
belatedly realizes, unlike the simple-minded who attribute such
feats to wizardry, that his nature was truly divine and super-
human (VA VII.38, 39). Demetrius claims that he had always
thought that Apollonius had been providentially cared for by
god (VIII.12). Their evaluations, however, remain only two of
many. They are opposed, for example, by that of an anonymous
court secretary who agrees that Apollonius was a wizard (VIII.3).
In the context of the entire narrative that clash of evaluations
is never wholly resolved. It is thus with some justification
that a view of the "divine man" as a quicksilver personality, a
*sui generis* being, an object of misunderstanding by friend and
foe alike, has been based on Philostratus' text.[15]

Philostratus does not entertain an unlimited range of possible evaluations of Apollonius' character. He clearly intends
to absolve his candidate of all charges of venery (VA I.13),
lying (V.37), boasting (VII.14), miracle-mongering (VII.14),
treason (VII.19), and magic and wizardry (I.2; IV.18; V.12; VII.
17; e.g.). But his work is marked more by the apologetic attempt
to move Apollonius *away* from the negative pole of evaluation than
by the desire to situate him precisely within the continuum of
positive evaluations.[16] Apparently believing that he has dis-
pelled any possibility of a convincing hostile evaluation of

his subject, Philostratus seems content to allow his readers to
draw their own conclusions about what sort of "true nature"
Apollonius may have possessed. He furnishes suggestions, to be
sure, but he does not impose a single solution. He leaves room
for diversity of opinion, but only within the positive spectrum
of evaluations.

Part of the difficulty in determining the firm and final
evaluation of the character of Apollonius in Philostratus' text
stems from the variety of evaluators. Apollonius, Philostratus,
Damis, Euphrates, and a host of others give voice to evaluations
of Apollonius. Thus, though the field of possible evaluations
can be sketched with some accuracy, a predominant trend of
evaluation is more difficult to isolate. That lack of final definition, however, may have served Philostratus well in the propagandistic dimension of his endeavor by making Apollonius potentially susceptible to a wider range of positive evaluations.
No positive evaluation is definitely excluded; a diffuse positive
image is projected to potential partisans.

A partial schema of the classifying statements in Philostratus' text looks like this:

| god | human | wizard/magician |
|---|---|---|
| philosopher | | liar |
| daimon | | boaster |
| divine being | | addict of venery |
| son of Zeus | | miracle-monger |
| man esteemed by the gods | | traitor |
| divine man | | demon |
| wise man | | imposter |
| master of the elements | | illegitimate sage |
| immortal | | |

Again, because of the diversity of evaluators it is difficult to determine a common set of criteria which a candidate had
to fulfill to warrant being included in any of the categories
outlined above. It is nonetheless clear that Philostratus also
presumes that the performance of certain actions has classifying
force. Indeed, in his remarks on those actions which would tend
to strengthen the candidacy of individual aspirants to divine
status, he replicates in some detail the principles articulated
by Origen in response to Celsus and later followed by Eusebius
in response to Hierocles.

Philostratus offers this description of the dual duties of the sage:

> For, hard as it is to know oneself, I myself consider
> it still harder for the sage to remain always himself;
> for he cannot ever reform evil natures and improve them,
> unless he has first trained himself never to alter
> in his own person.   (VA VI.35)

It is clear from that that Philostratus considers it the task of the sage not only to perfect himself but also to work actively for the betterment of others.  In Apollonius' own mission, that active work consisted of the reform of cities (e.g. VA I.16; IV.4, 10; VIII.7.viii), temples (I.16, 31; II.40; IV.41; VI.40; VIII.7), and numerous individuals (I.13; IV.20, 25, 32; V.21; VI.36).  His work in Antioch is illustrated in his response to a question about how the sage should converse:

> "like a law-giver," he replies, "for it is the duty
> of the law-giver to deliver to the many the instruc-
> tions of whose truth he has persuaded himself."   This
> was the line he pursued during his stay in Antioch,
> and he converted to himself the most unrefined people.
> (VA I.17)

In accordance with Philostratus' views in VA VI.35 Apollonius is portrayed in I.17 as first having trained himself and then having passed on the benefits of that training to the people. Apollonius also reformed the traditional worship in Rome during his stay there:

> The result of his discourses about religion was that
> the gods were worshipped with more zeal, and that men
> flocked to the temples where he was, in the belief
> that by doing so they would obtain an increase of divine
> blessings.   And our sage's conversations were so far
> not objected to, because he held them in public and
> addressed himself to all men alike; for he did not
> hover about rich men's doors, nor hang about the mighty,
> though he welcomed them if they resorted to him, and
> he talked with them just as much as he did to the com-
> mon people.   (VA IV.41)

Apollonius' impact on the personal level is evident in his conversion of his elder brother (VA I.13) and a young debauchee
(IV.20) from their lives of indolent pleasure to lives motivated
by a philosophic ideal.  The specific virtues which Apollonius
inculcated in his mission of moral reform are detailed in a
witty exchange with a toll-keeper:

And as they fared on into Mesopotamia, the tax-
gatherer who presided over the Bridge (Zeugma) led
them into the registry and asked them what they were
taking out of the country with them. And Apollonius
replied: "I am taking with me temperance, justice,
virtue, continence, valour, discipline." And in this
way he strung together a number of feminine nouns of
names. The other, already scenting his own perquisites,
said: "You must then write down in the register these
female slaves." Apollonius answered: "Impossible,
for they are not female slaves that I am taking out
with me, but ladies of quality." (VA I.20)

Such lists of qualities, when coupled to the specific instances
of Apollonius' performance of beneficial actions, give substance
to his subscription to the dictum of the sages of India that
"every man who is thought to be good, is honoured by the title
of god" (VA VIII.5). That suggests further that the expectation
that a candidate for divine status would perform good works of
some sort, particularly of moral reform, does animate VA to a
certain extent. Unlike Lucian's Alexander, Philostratus' Apollonius is a civic benefactor who lives up to expectations. His
reform of the traditional cultic practices as well as his reform
of individual lives supports his candidacy for divine status.
That Philostratus does not settle on a specific aspect of that
status as most appropriate for his candidate diffuses, but does
not diminish, the classifying force of Apollonius' beneficial
actions.

*Eusebius*

The situation in Eusebius' treatise against Hierocles most
closely resembles that of CC. Eusebius is responding to a comparison between Jesus and Apollonius which was intended to de-
stroy the candidacy of Jesus for divine status while promoting
that of Apollonius. In *Against Hierocles* the clash of evaluations of Apollonius' candidacy is captured vividly in chapter
36. There Eusebius appeals to an incident in the career of
Apollonius as a "fresh test of his character (φύσεως)."[17] He
relates how one of the Tyanan's jailers had informed Apollonius
that he would be moved to a jail where prisoners were not bound
by chains and that Apollonius was so pleased by that news "that
he suddenly drops out of his gift of foreknowledge, and asks

outright, 'Who then will get me out of this place?' and the
messenger replied: 'I myself, so follow me'" (AH 36). Eusebius
quotes that exchange in order to cast doubt on the claim that
Apollonius was "superior to mankind" and that he had foreknowledge of what was to occur. One who did not even know how he
would be transferred from one cell to another could scarcely
be expected to foretell more momentous events. The test of
Apollonius' character produces negative results. The claims for
Apollonius' superiority are, for Eusebius, confuted by the events
of his own life. The test is simple, but effective.

That brief test reveals the dynamics of the entire treatise
in microcosm. AH can be viewed as a series of tests whose cumulative effect will determine the appropriate evaluation of Apollonius. To a great extent, the whole work is an essay in classification; between them Eusebius and Hierocles (who seems to
rely totally on Philostratus)[18] propose a full range of possible
categorizations, and each argues fervently for the accuracy of
his own position. Hierocles, for example, reckons Apollonius
"not a god, but only a man pleasing to the gods" and attacks the
easy credulity of the Christians who on the strength of a few
miracles consider Jesus a god (AH 2). On his part, Eusebius
is willing to grant (AH 5) that the man of Tyana may have been
"a kind of sage" and he even declares himself willing to number
Apollonius among the philosophers, but Eusebius draws the line
at anyone who would "overleap the bounds of humanity and tran-
scend philosophy" (AH 5). If such claims are made for Apollonius,

> . . . in that case his reputation for us as a phi-
> losopher will be gone, and we shall have an ass in-
> stead concealed in a lion's skin; and we shall detect
> in him a sophist in the truest sense, cadging for alms
> among the cities, and a wizard, if ever there was
> one, instead of a philosopher.  (AH 5)

Thus, the possible evaluations of Apollonius form the familiar
continuum between the gods and the wizards; intermediate categories include "those pleasing to the gods," sages, philosophers,
sophists, liars, flatterers, and magicians. AH, like the works
of Celsus, Lucian, Philostratus, and Origen, is an attempt to
locate specific candidates for divine status somewhere along
that continuum.

The purpose of the treatise is clearly expressed in this passage:

> One may learn then from the whole treatise and from the particular episodes set forth therein, whether we ought to rank (κατατακτέον) him [Apollonius] among the divine and philosophic men or among wizards. (AH 38)

Further indication that Eusebius conceives his task to be the development of a proper classification of Apollonius occurs in AH 8 when he reviews the curious events associated with Apollonius' birth and death and ironically concludes that "for these reasons we must surely class the man among the gods" (AH 8). Eusebius also alludes to the enterprise of classification when he acknowledges that he would see no objection to including Apollonius in the ranks of temperate men. As his summary comment in AH 38 suggests, Eusebius' evaluation of Apollonius is based on the examination of a series of discrete incidents which are presumed to have classifying force.

One such incident is examined in AH 23. There Eusebius subjects to ironic scrutiny the report of Philostratus (cf. VA IV.4, 10) that Apollonius had averted a plague in Ephesus by detecting its demonic cause. He finds neither the narrative nor the incident it relates worthy of credence:

> For if anybody feels the shadow of doubt about the matter, the very manner in which the story is told will convince him that fraud and make-believe (τὸ πλάσμα καὶ ἀπατηλὸν) was in this case everything, and that if anything ever reeked of wizardry (γοητείας) this did. (AH 23)

In the process Eusebius employs a series of terms which frequently are used to express the negative evaluation of candidates for divine status. Terms for the invention of fanciful stories, the deception of the credulous, wizardry or magic, and the performance of false wonders have been found clustered together in CC, for example, quite frequently. They constitute part of the arsenal of polemic. In this instance they represent *Eusebius'* evaluation of the character of Apollonius, a judgement which is supported by the fact that none of the derogatory terms occur in Philostratus' account of the incident. Indeed, the incident assumes almost heroic proportions in Apollonius' final speech in his own defence, when he acquires virtue by association:

> And do you think that there is any wise man (σοφός)
> who would decline to do his best on behalf of such
> a city, when he reflects that Democritus once liberated
> the people of Abdera from pestilence, and when he
> bears in mind the story of Sophocles of Athens, who
> is said to have charmed the winds when they were blowing
> unseasonably, and who has heard how Empedocles stayed
> a cloud in its course when it would have burst over
> the heads of the people of Acragas?   (VA VIII.7.viii)

That one author can conclude that Apollonius was a γόης and
another that he was a σοφός, from the same evidence, suggests
that the mere act of evaluation in isolation was not sufficient
to settle the identification crisis.   Further criteria had to
be introduced.

    Those criteria come to light when one candidate is compared
to another; the resulting clash of evaluations elicits clearer
statements of the criteria on which they are based.   Eusebius'
comparison of his own preferred candidate for divine status,
Jesus of Nazareth, with Apollonius demonstrates the full range
of his arguments.

    Although Eusebius asserts that any comparison of Jesus and
Apollonius is absurd, he offers rather full support of the candidacy of Jesus before reaching that conclusion.   His argument
is constructed as a series of rhetorical denials, ("we will not
stress that Jesus was the only man whose advent among mankind
was prophesied," e.g.), but the following points nevertheless
come to light:

1.   Jesus is more divine
2.   Jesus worked more miracles
3.   Only about Jesus was it prophesied that he would come
     to mankind
4.   Jesus converted many to his divine teaching
5.   Jesus formed a group of sincere disciples who would die
     for his teaching
6.   Jesus established a school of sober and chaste living
     which survives him
7.   By his divinity Jesus saved the entire world and still
     gains converts
8.   Jesus triumphed over bitter opposition and persecution
     everywhere
9.   Even now the invocation of the name of Jesus expels
     demons (AH 4)

The first two phrases are in a slightly different rhetorical form
than the others, but that does not alter the cumulative effect.
The emphasis on the *extent* of Jesus' influence, both temporal

(# 6, 7, 9) and numerical (# 4, 7, 8), is clear.  In Eusebius'
view, it is not only Jesus' character but also the movement
which he founded which is without parallel.  In effect, the success of the movement confirms the uniqueness of Jesus' character
and the validity of the candidacy for divine status, just as
Origen used the failure of the Simonian movement to disparage
the character of its founder and to deny his candidacy for divine
status (cf. CC I.57).

Eusebius summarizes his position when he claims that anyone
who is truly divine (θεῖος ἀληθῶς) "will leave the effects
(τοὖργον) of his eternal divinity for the contemplation of future ages" (AH 6).  In the following chapter Eusebius discloses
a series of criteria which Apollonius should meet if he is to
be reckoned à divine being.  He asks Hierocles "to point . . .
out effects wrought by his divinity enduring to this day," and
claims that it would be absurd if "a human character claimed to
be divine should, after shedding its glory upon mankind, finish
in darkness its short-lived career, instead of displaying for
ever its power and excellence" (AH 7).  The performance of good
works again appears to be the central criterion, and Eusebius
subjects it to several clarifications.  The benefits should not
be limited to an individual (like Apollonius' companion Damis)
or a group of admirers; nor should they be limited to the contemporaries of the candidate.  Rather, they should continue forever
(ἐἰς αἰῶνα).  A divine being "should surely make its coming
among us the occasion of blessings (ὠφελείας), conferred on myri-
ads not only of his contemporaries, but also of his posterity"
(AH 7).  Moreover, those benefits should be of a certain order;
the worthy candidate would imitate "the sages of old [who] raised
up earnest bands of disciples, who continued their tradition of
moral excellence, sowing in men's hearts a spirit truly immortal
of progress and reform" (AH 7).  Eusebius applies those criteria
consistently to both Jesus (AH 4) and Apollonius (AH 7, passim.);
that he finds the former's candidacy acceptable and the latter's
unacceptable is not surprising.

The field of category statements within which Eusebius attempts to situate both Jesus and Apollonius looks like this:

| god | human | wizard/magician |
|-----|-------|-----------------|
| friend of the gods | | sophist |
| saviour | | possessed |
| sage | | liar |
| noble man | | madman |
| good man | | boaster |
| divine man | | flatterer |
| superior nature | | |

Like Celsus and Origin, Hierocles and Eusebius are concerned to
move their respective candidates towards the positive and away
from the negative poles of that field. In addition, they attempt
to move the other's candidate(s) away from the positive and towards the negative pole. They do so, as Eusebius clearly states
in AH 38, by examining particular episodes in the life of each
candidate. Those episodes are important insofar as they do, or
do not, give evidence of the candidate's possession of a particular faculty or quality, such as foreknowledge in AH 36, which
would warrant the candidate's being included in a particular
category. Thus, in AH 36, Eusebius interpreted Apollonius'
dialogue with his jailor to indicate that Apollonius did not possess the faculty of foreknowledge, and that consequently his
candidacy for divine status was undermined by the testimony of
his own life. Such individual tests of character are intended
to have cumulative impact. Though they often focus on the intermediate categories, they do so with the intention of gradually
moving the candidate closer to one of the two poles. No test presents in full the criteria on which a final evaluation can be
based; the full set has to be pieced together from the fragments.
Criteria which recur can be assumed to be relatively important.

One such criterion, which has appeared in Celsus, Lucian,
Philostratus, Origen, and Eusebius, is the performance of good
works. The assertion, in Celsus' words, that "above all a god
ought to do good for all men" (CC II.20) is the fundamental pre-
supposition shared by those who would evaluate candidates for
divine status. It is the basis for Eusebius' attribution to
Jesus of a series of good works in AH 4 and the basis for his
challenge to Hierocles to produce similar evidence in AH 7.
Those passages show again that it is not an abstract quality of
character but its concrete embodiment in action that is decisive
in the process of evaluation. Eusebius returns to that idea in
his discussion of Apollonius' view of destiny. Imputing to

Apollonius a strict position on predestination, Eusebius poses
this rhetorical question: "Why then do you go wandering about,
preaching the virtues to those who are incapable of reform
(διορθώσεως)?" (AH 41). He wonders further why Apollonius does
not do away with the gods and

> sacrifice to Necessity alone and to the Fates, and pay
> your respects rather to Destiny than to Zeus himself.
> In that case no doubt you would have no gods left;
> and rightly, too, seeing that they are not even able
> to help (ὠφελεῖν) mankind. (AH 41)

That passage gives clear expression to Eusebius' conviction that
gods, or worthy candidates for divine status, ought to benefit
mankind through their actions. His earlier statements suggest
that good works are to be conceived of as leading to moral reform
and the virtuous life; in that he does not differ from Philostratus. But as their respective comments on Apollonius show, they
differ on which candidate fulfills those criteria.

One further element of Eusebius' argument should be noted.
By stressing the enduring historical impact of his candidate
(cf. AH 4), he can diminish the significance of the purported
similarities in the earthly careers of Jesus and Apollonius.
Like Origen in his argument against the candidacy of Simon Magus
(cf. CC I.57), he solves the identification crisis in retrospect.
Time is on his side. Presumably, such a strategy would not have
been available to a contemporary of Simon. The fluctuating
utility of the argument from historical impact suggests that the
evaluation of candidates for divine status in the first few
centuries of the Christian era was not a static enterprise.
Though many of the same figures, such as Jesus or Apollonius,
enter the discussion at different points, the process of evaluation appears at least slightly different each time. The historical context of the controversy, the author's intention, the
genre of the text, and the specific challenges posed and ac-
cepted--all influence the form which the process of evaluation
takes. But the broadening of this investigation to include
Lucian, Philostratus, and Eusebius should strengthen the proposition that, within those shifting boundaries, the evaluation of
candidates for divine status was carried on with a remarkably
consistent set of categories, criteria, and arguments. The

categories describe an arc between the positive pole of the gods
and the negative pole of the magicians.  The criteria ultimately
rest on the shared assumption that "a god ought to do good for
men."  And the arguments incessantly strive to prove that one
candidate meets, or does not meet, that fundamental criterion
and thus deserves, or does not deserve, to be reckoned among the
gods and their congeners.

# CHAPTER VI

## CONCLUSIONS

In the first chapter I argued that the current scholarly investigation of divine men in Late Antiquity would profit if three questions were posed and answered. They were:

1) Was there a Hellenistic concept of the divine man? If so, what were its contours, variations, etc.?

2) Was that concept expressed solely, or primarily, in biographical texts? That is, is there a necessary connection between divine men and certain types of literature, such as the "aretalogy"?

3) In what contexts were such texts produced, circulated, and received? Is there a necessary connection between divine men, aretalogies, and religious propaganda?

The third question can be decisively answered in the negative. No necessary connection can be made between divine men, aretalogies, and religious propaganda. Not only were texts produced in a variety of contexts for various purposes, but it has also been shown that a simplistic view of religious propaganda has governed contemporary discussions of divine men. Propaganda cannot be treated in isolation. Propaganda and apologetics are virtually inseparable; one implies or responds to the other. Accounts of the activity of divine men may well have served purposes of religious propaganda, but they also played a larger role in the complex missionary scenario that was a crucial element in the religious life of Late Antiquity. When the connection between propaganda and apologetics is severed, when the contexts in which images of the worthy candidate for divine status are formed and altered are obscured, it becomes easier to maintain that the divine man was a pre-existent pattern, a ready-made unchanging "device" (Koester) which could be easily appropriated and used for the purposes of religious propaganda. Such a static image of the divine man not only risks granting historical existence to an ideal type but can also diminish the crucial elements of controversy and change which surrounded candidates for divine status in Late Antiquity.

173

The second question can also be answered decisively in the
negative.  The evidence of Celsus, Origen, Diodorus, Hierocles,
Eusebius, and the inscriptions, among others, supports the hy-
potheses advanced in the two basic propositions of chapter one[1]
and clearly demonstrates that neither praise nor disparagement
of candidates for divine status was limited to a single literary
form.  The presumed link between "aretalogies" and "divine
men" has artificially limited the choice of texts for examination; it is not only in aretalogies that the θεῖοι ἄνδρες are
to be found.[2]  Rather they are to be found in biographies, apologetic texts, historical narratives, formal decrees, orations of
praise, philosophical arguments, and exhortations to virtue--in
a wide range of texts not specifically biographical in form.
When that other source material is taken fully into account, it
becomes increasingly difficult to preserve the static image of
a "Hellenistic concept of the divine man" that predominates in
the current scholarly literature.  Rather, such a concept was
always in the process or being created, altered, attacked, and
defended.

Indeed, there was no native *Hellenistic* conception of the
divine man--at least in the sense in which that term has recently
been used.  Ideal types and unsupported assumptions can not be
taken as accurate representations of the empirical phenomena.
The answer to the first question is thus more complex than the
answers to the other two.  It does seem clear, however, that
there was considerable interest in the world of Late Antiquity
in answering the question of who was a θεός and who was μάγος,
especially since both epithets were likely to be applied to the
same individual.  The records of attempts to decide who was a
θεός and who was a μάγος yield a range of categories and a set
of criteria of evaluation which constitute *not* the Hellenistic
conception of the divine man, but rather the basic building
blocks from which a variety of native conceptions could be, and
were, formed.  The typical phenomenon in Hellenistic accounts
of divine men is not the adoption of a pre-existent device or
pattern, but rather the attempt to situate, for whatever purposes, a specific candidate within a spectrum of possible
evaluations.  Though the particular categories employed may vary,
as they do from Celsus to Lucian to Origen to Philostratus, for

example, the drive to attain a proper and satisfactory classification of the candidate at hand remains constant.  The criteria
of evaluation may also vary, but the proposition that a god or
worthy candidate for divine status ought to do good for humankind seems to have enjoyed a wide currency.  There thus seems
to be at least one central concern which animates discussions of
candidates for divine status in Late Antiquity; there is no
fixed image that could rightfully be described as a device or
pattern, but rather at least one basic criterion which all candidates were measured against.  Though that criterion is subject
to divergent interpretations, as Celsus and Origen continually
demonstrate, its fundamental importance does not seem to have
been challenged.

Thus, while the search for a native Hellenistic conception
of the divine man yields no single image and simple answer, it
can lead to a fuller appreciation of the roles of literary accounts of candidates for divine status in the religious life of
Late Antiquity.  Especially during a period of intense missionary
activity, the general populace was frequently challenged to
evaluate a welter of conflicting messages.  Often those messages
concerned specific individuals whose deeds and pronouncements
were asserted by their partisans to be of crucial importance.
When such messages about specific individuals conflicted with
either rival claims or with traditional assumptions, decisions
had to be made.  In the case of candidates for divine status
those decisions were reached by measuring the candidates against
a set of criteria which were judged capable of effectively lo-
cating the candidate within a spectrum of possible evaluations.
For example, the Christian message about Jesus challenged both
Celsus' traditional assumptions, his Single Image of power and
authoritative teaching being rooted in the distant past and in
a distinctly articulated hierarchical social system, and also
rival claims of which Celsus was aware even if he did not per-
sonally approve of them, such as those made for Asclepius, Dionysos, Heracles, and Simon and Menander.  That clash between the
Christian message about Jesus on one hand and his traditional
assumptions and familiar, albeit suspect, claims made for other
candidates for divine status on the other hand, sparked Celsus'

attempt to make a prolonged evaluation of the claims made for
Jesus. The fragmentary remains of that evaluation are now found
primarily in the first two books of Origen's CC. Celsus' evaluation of Jesus took the form of an examination of a series of
events in the career of Jesus which Celsus presumed to have
classifying force. Those events were presumed to demonstrate in
action certain qualities which would, or would not, be appropriate for a candidate for divine status. Celsus measures the
qualities he finds in specific events against a set of largely
implicit criteria which he thinks should be fulfilled by a worthy
candidate for divine status. The story of Jesus' birth, for
example, demonstrates for Celsus that the candidate was poor, a
common laborer, not a *polis*-dweller, and a bastard to boot.
When Celsus finds none of those attributes appropriate for a
candidate for divine status, the outlines of an implicit criterion of evaluation begin to emerge. For Celsus, noble birth, a
wealthy family, good education, and a distinguished homeland
appear to be more fitting qualifications for divine status.
Other criteria, notably the statement that a god ought to do
good for humankind, are expressed more explicitly. In either
case the criteria are wielded for the purpose of situating the
candidate somewhere on the continuum between the gods and the
wizards. The cumulative effect of a series of discrete tests or
evaluations is designed to fix firmly the final evaluation of
the candidate. Thus Celsus concludes that Jesus was merely a
man (II.79) and a sorcerer as well (I.71).

     That Origen follows a similar procedure of adducing specific
incidents as having classifying force, isolating the qualities
which those incidents demonstrate, evaluating the demonstrated
qualities according to largely implicit criteria, and assigning
the candidates to specific categories in accordance with their
fulfillment or nonfulfillment of the criteria, suggests that
Celsus' approach to candidates for divine status was not idiosyncratic. That the outlines of a similar process of evaluation
can be found, for example, in the works of Diodorus, Lucian,
Philostratus, Hierocles, and Eusebius as well further suggests
that such a process of evaluation was an important component
of native Hellenistic thinking about "divine men." The contemporaries of Jesus of Nazareth, Apollonius of Tyana, Alexander of

Abonuteichos, and other candidates for divine status in Late
Antiquity were involved in an enterprise of classification by
their encounters with the claims made for and against the various
candidates for divine status.  They used not a single, rigid
"Hellenistic concept of the divine man" as their guideline for
evaluation, but rather a shifting and flexible collection of
categories and criteria which could be adapted to fit the demands
of particular situations.  If it can be said at all, and that is
doubtful, that there was a *native Hellenistic* conception of the
divine man, it was certainly a more fluid conception than is
portrayed in much contemporary scholarship.

Far from being a purely abstract undertaking, the attempt
to evaluate candidates for divine status was firmly rooted in
social experience.  Categories and criteria themselves constitute
social facts as they are passed from one generation to another,[3]
Eusebius' explicit reliance on Origen being a case in point.
Furthermore, specific categories such as the μάγος[4] and specific
criteria such as the proposition that a god ought to do good
for humankind[5] can be traced to specific types of social experience in the Late Antique world.  Such a reflection of social
experience in the categories and criteria used for the evaluation
of candidates for divine status supports the generalization of
Mary Douglas that "human thought . . . carries in itself at any
given moment the social configurations of that time and place."[6]

Further, the very fact that individual candidates for divine
status become objects of controversy also promises to reveal
aspects of the social and ideological background of their partisans and detractors.  As Lewis Coser writes of social conflict,
"the very outbreak of conflict usually denotes that there exists
a common object of contention.  If there were no common interest
in some object, there could scarcely be conflict since there
would be nothing to fight about."[7]  At stake for both Celsus
and Origen are not simply allegiances to one or another candidate
for divine status, but rather fundamental visions of society,
human activity, and the nature of divinity.  As it is the impos-
ition of order on "an inherently untidy experience"[8] that creates
meaning for that experience, Celsus and Origen, in their attempts
at classification of candidates for divine status, are ultimately
arguing about alternative views of the meaning of experience.

Little could be more fundamental.  For either to accept the
other's "Image" would be to deny the validity and accuracy of
the meaning formerly ascribed to one's own experience and view
of the world.  For Celsus, if Jesus were actually a θεός, the
world would drastically alter its meaning.  For Origen, if Jesus
were a μάγος or γόης, it would do the same.  It is the connection between the enterprise of classification on one hand and
social experience and world-view on the other which gives the
altercation between Celsus and Origen about Jesus its particular
urgency and import; for each adversary the validity and accuracy
of a comprehensive view of the world and human experience, an
"Image" of reality, rests on the proper evaluation of Jesus'
candidacy for divine status.

      Thus, a fundamental reason why there can have been no
"Hellenistic conception of the divine man" is that there was no
unanimous assent to a single "Image" of society, human activity,
and the nature of divinity.  While a fundamental proposition
such as Celsus' "above all a god ought to have done good to all
men" (II.20) might appear to have gained widespread acceptance,
a closer examination of its use in specific arguments leads to
an appreciation of both the similarities and differences among
those who adopted it as a criterion for the evaluation of candidates for divine status.  The figure of the divine man might
therefore still prove useful for the purposes for which it was
originally introduced, the investigation of the relations between
early Christianity and the other religions of Late Antiquity.
It cannot be presumed, however, that assumptions about the dis-
tinctiveness of early Christianity will thereby be reinforced.

      The proposition that there exist connections between systems
of classification, social experience, and world-view has been
advocated most forcefully by several contemporary anthropologists.  Though the data from Late Antiquity will not allow their
theoretical proposals to be checked by the methods developed to
test them, their conclusions nevertheless remain suggestive.
It remains for the reader of this work to determine whether they
have indeed proved fruitful.  But it should be noted that the
study of divine men has from its inception remained within the
province of the comparative study of religions.  From the ancient

attempts of Celsus and Origen to wield comparisons to deleterious
effect to the strong reliance on evolutionary theory and the
concept of mana at the beginning of this century, the study of
divine men has remained strongly wedded to the concepts and
methods of the comparative study of religions.  If outmoded or
barren concepts and methods are to be abandoned, they must be
replaced.  I suggest that the contemporary anthropological thought
about systems of order and the enterprise of classification can
aid in the identification of important topics in the contemporary
study of divine men.

A complementary perspective is also furnished by recent
theoretical investigations of charismatic leadership which treat
charisma less as a vague quality inherent in some persons and
more as the result of a social relationship between a leader and
followers.  As Michael Hill puts it:

> . . . no leader can be labelled charismatic unless
> he is accredited with the possession of such a quality
> by his followers; his claim must be evaluated by the
> 'population' which constitutes his potential followers
> in the light of those characteristics that may be
> registered as having a source in revelation or inspira-
> tion, and if this claim is validated, then obedience
> to the leader . . . is a matter of obligation.[9]

Such a definition of charisma, with its emphasis on the evaluation of a would-be leader by a "population" or audience according to a set of implicit criteria, provides further theoretical
support for the approach favored here.  Taken together with the
more sophisticated analysis of classification and evaluation in
the anthropological literature, it offers a solid theoretical
background for the investigation and analysis of native Hellenistic conceptions of divine men.

One advantage of the adoption of such a theoretical framework is that it will facilitate the analysis of particular phenomena of Hellenistic religious life as representative both of
the specific traditions to which they belong and as exemplars of
more general problems and themes in the study of religions.  A
higher degree of mutual intelligibility between culture-specific
analyses and broad theoretical formulations is a primary desid-
eratum.  In the words of Mary Douglas:

A silence lies between anthropology and the history
of religion.  The first asserts that religious systems sustain social structures and that social structures sustain beliefs.  Historians, if they want to
apply these notions, ask what kind of social structures go with what kinds of religious ideas.  The
anthropologist can start to answer in terms of local
and esoteric typologies.  There are classifications
of ancestor cults, nativistic movements or witchcraft
beliefs.  But so far we lack a way of relating our
materials to the European experience.  Unless we can
think of tribes as secular, or given to mystery cults,
dualist philosophies, or heterodoxies about the nature
of grace and godhead, the questions that have unleashed
historic wars and mass executions, we have hardly begun the anthropology of religion.[10]

On the other hand, unless we can think of our more familiar
"European experience" as being in many respects similar to the
experience of those more esoteric groups which are the traditional province of the anthropologists of religion--similar,
for example, in their possession of elaborate and intricate
systems of classification which reflect social experience and
mirror views of the world--we have not yet begun the history of
religions.

NOTES

CHAPTER I

[1]See H.D. Betz, "Jesus as Divine Man" in F. Thomas Trotter, ed., *Jesus and the Historian* (Philadelphia: Westminster Press, 1968), pp. 114-133; idem, *Lukian von Samosata und das Neue Testament* (Berlin: Akademie-Verlag, 1961), pp. 100-143; Helmut Koester, "One Jesus and Four Primitive Gospels," in James M. Robinson and Helmut Koester, *Trajectories Through Early Christianity* (Philadelphia: Fortress Press, 1971), pp. 158-204; idem, "The Structure and Criteria of Early Christian Beliefs," in *Trajectories*, pp. 205-231; Theodore J. Weeden, *Mark--Traditions in Conflict* (Philadelphia: Fortress Press, 1971); Dieter Georgi, *Die Gegner des Paulus im 2. Korintherbrief* (Neukirchen-Vluyn: Neukirchener Verlag, 1964). For a survey of much of the relevant literature see Morton Smith, "Prologomena to a Discussion of Aretalogies, Divine Men, the Gospels and Jesus," *JBL* 90 (1971): 174-199.

[2]I will use the phrases "Ancient Mediterranean Religions," "Religions of Late Antiquity," and "Hellenistic Religions" as rough equivalents. See Jonathan Z. Smith, "Native Cults in the Hellenistic Period," *HR* 11 (1971): 236-249, and *Encyclopedia Britannica*, 15th ed. (1975), s.v. "Hellenistic Religions," by Jonathan Z. Smith.

[3]See Smith, "Prologomena."

[4]Richard Rietzenstein, *Hellenistic Mystery-Religions: Their Basic Ideas and Significance*, trans. John E. Steeley, (Pittsburgh: The Pickwick Press, 1978), pp. 143-144. See Reitzenstein, *Hellenistische Mysterienreligionen* (Stuttgart: B.G. Teubner, 1973); rpr. of the 1927 3rd ed., p. 94.

[5]Cf. Reitzenstein, *HMR*, Steeley trans., p. 26f. (*HMR*[3], p. 26f.).

[6]Ibid., p. 18 (*HMR*[3], p. 17).

[7]Ibid., p. 25 (*HMR*[3], p. 25).

[8]G.P. Wetter, *Der Sohn Gottes: Eine Untersuchung über den Charakter und die Tendenz des Johannes-Evangeliums* (Göttingen: Vandenhoeck & Ruprecht, 1916), pp. 186-187.

[9]Ibid., p. 188.

[10]Cf. R.R. Marett, *The Threshold of Religion* (London: Metheun & Co., 1929, 4th ed.), esp. pp. 99-121; for a review of the early theoretical statements about mana see Raymond Firth, "An Analysis of Mana: An Empirical Approach" in Firth, *Tikopia Ritual and Belief* (Boston: Beacon Press, 1967), pp. 174-194,

and also E.E. Evans-Pritchard, *Theories of Primitive Religion* (Oxford:  Oxford University Press, 1965), pp. 31-35.

[11]Otto Weinreich, "Antikes Gottmenschentum," *Neue Jahrbücher für Wissenschaft und Jugendbildung* 2 (1926):  633-651; passage cited from p. 634.

[12]Ibid., p. 635.

[13]Ibid., p. 637.

[14]Hans Windisch, *Paulus und Christus:  Ein Biblischreligionsgeschichtlicher Vergleich* (Leipzig:  J.C. Hinrichs'sche Buchhandlung, 1934), p. 25 n.1.

[15]Ibid., p. 37.

[16]Ludwig Bieler, ΘΕΙΟΣ ANHP:  *Das Bild des "göttlichen Menschen" im Spätantike und Frühchristentum* (Darmstadt:  Wissenschaftliche Buchgesellschaft, 1976, rpr. of 1935 and 1936 edition, two volumes in one, separate pagination), 1:  4.

[17]Ibid., 1:  5.

[18]Ibid., 1:  9.  Bieler's notes and parenthetical references show an acquaintance with a wide variety of folk literature, but here, as elsewhere, he makes no explicit statement about the theoretical underpinnings of his assertions.

[19]Ibid., 1:  21.

[20]Ibid., 1:  144.

[21]Max Weber, "Religious Rejections of the World and their Directions" in H.H. Gerth & C. Wright Mills, trans. and eds., *From Max Weber* (New York:  Oxford University Press, 1946), pp. 323-359; passage quoted from p. 324.

[22]Cf. Michael Hill, *A Sociology of Religion* (New York:  Basic Books, Inc., 1973), pp. 149-150.

[23]Cf. Axel Olrik, "Epic Laws of Folk Narrative" in Alan Dundes, ed., *The Study of Folklore* (Englewood Cliffs, New Jersey:  Prentice-Hall, Inc., 1965), pp. 129-141; passage quoted from p. 138.

[24]Cf. Bieler, ΘΕΙΟΣ ANHP, 1:  145.

[25]Ibid., 1:  148.

[26]Ibid.

[27]Weber, "Religious Rejections" in *From Max Weber*, p. 324.

[28]Cf. Bieler, ΘΕΙΟΣ ANHP, 2:  1.

[29]W. Von Martitz, "υἱός (Classical Greek)" *TDNT* 8:  335-340; passage quoted from p. 338 n.23.

[30]Paul Achtemeier, review of David Lenz Tiede, *The Charismatic Figure as Miracle Worker* in *CBQ* 35(1973):   560.

[31]Cf. Bieler, ΘΕΙΟΣ ΑΝΗΡ, 1:   1-20.

[32]Betz, "Jesus as Divine Man," p. 116.

[33]Ibid., p. 117.

[34]Koester, "One Jesus," p. 188.

[35]Koester, "Structure and Criteria," p. 217.

[36]On the common problem of the reification of types, see John C. McKinney, *Constructive Typology and Social Theory* (New York:   Appleton-Century-Crofts, 1960), p. 17.

[37]*International Encyclopedia of the Social Sciences* (1968), s.v. "Typologies," by E. Tiryakian.

[38]Thomas Burger, *Max Weber's Theory of Concept Formation: History, Laws, and Ideal Types* (Durham:   Duke University Press, 1976), p. 164.

[39]Cf. Bieler, ΘΕΙΟΣ ΑΝΗΡ, 1:   146, 148; 2:   i.

[40]Cf. Hill, *A Sociology of Religion*, p. 47.

[41]David Lenz Tiede, *The Charismatic Figure as Miracle Worker* (Missoula, Montana:   Scholars Press, 1972), p. 238.

[42]Ibid., p. 243.

[43]Ibid., p. 246.

[44]Ibid., p. 289.

[45]Ibid., p. 5.

[46]Cf. Bieler, ΘΕΙΟΣ ΑΝΗΡ, 1:   4, 21, 22f.

[47]Tiede, *Charismatic Figure*, p. 98.

[48]Ibid., p. 59.

[49]Ibid., p. 15.

[50]Ibid., p. 28.

[51]See Morton Smith, review of D.L. Tiede, *The Charismatic Figure as Miracle Worker* in *Interpretation* 28 (1974):   238-240; idem, "On the History of the 'Divine Man'" in A. Benoit et al., eds., *Paganisme, Judaisme, Christianisme:   Mélanges offert à Marcel Simon* (Paris:   de Boccard, 1978), pp. 335-345.

[52]In *Jesus the Magician* (New York:   Harper & Row, 1978) Morton Smith refers to that phenomenon as an "identification crisis," cf. pp. 19-20.

[53]See VA I.2, for example.

[54]Tiede, *Charismatic Figure*, p. 153.

[55]Charles Talbert, "The Concept of Immortals in Mediterranean Antiquity," *JBL* 94(1975):  419-436; passages quoted
from pp. 419 and 420 respectively.

[56]Diodorus 6.1, as quoted in Talbert, "Concept of Immortals," p. 421.

[57]Ibid., p. 429.

[58]Ibid., p. 430.

[59]Ibid., p. 431.

[60]For a brief account of Euhemerism and Diodorus' role in
preserving Euhemerus see J. Geffcken, "Euhemerism" in *Encyclopedia of Religion and Ethics*, vol. V, James Hastings, ed.,
(New York:  Charles Scribner's Sons, 1912), pp. 572-573.

[61]Diodorus I.20.5-6.  Greek text and English translation of
Diodorus are taken from C.H. Oldfather, trans., *Diodorus*, vol.
I (Cambridge:  Harvard University Press, 1933).

[62]Ibid., I.24.7-8; I.25.4, respectively.

[63]Plutarch, *Isis and Osiris*, 360 A.  Greek text and English
translation are taken from F.C. Babbit, trans., *Plutarch,
Moralia*, vol. V (Cambridge:  Harvard University Press, 1936).

[64]Ibid.

[65]Ibid., 360 D.

[66]Cf. ibid., 361 E, 362 E.

[67]Mary Douglas, *Purity and Danger:  An Analysis of Concepts
of Pollution and Taboo* (Harmondsworth:  Penguin Books, 1966),
p. 15.

[68]Cf. Douglas in Mary Douglas, ed., *Rules and Meanings*
(Harmondsworth:  Penguin Books, 1973), p. 11.

[69]Recent work in anthropology can provide some suggestive
ideas, but the methods developed to analyze material from small-
scale societies cannot be directly appropriated for the study of
the Hellenistic world, largely because of its much greater complexity.  Rather, the concern with native or indigenous systems
of ordering will be taken as suggestive of a different approach
to familiar data--an approach that will have to be further developed and refined.

[70]Morton Smith, "Prologomena," p. 184.

[71]Moses Hadas in Hadas and Morton Smith, *Heroes and Gods:
Spiritual Biographies in Antiquity* (New York:  Harper & Row,
1965), p. 3.

[72]Koester, "One Jesus," p. 188.

[73]Ibid., p. 187 and Hadas, *Heroes*, p. 3, respectively.

[74]Cf. Koester, "Structure and Criteria," p. 217.

[75]Howard Clark Kee, *Aretalogies, Hellenistic "Lives," and the Sources of Mark* (Berkeley:  Center for Hermeneutical Studies in Hellenistic and Modern Culture, 1975), pp. 1-2; see idem, "Aretalogy and Gospel," *JBL* 92 (1973):  402-422.

[76]Koester, "One Jesus," p. 188.

[77]Cf. Reitzenstein, *HMR*, Steeley, trans., p. 25 (*HMR*[3], p. 25).

[78]For a collection of essays, and a full bibliography, on religious propaganda in the Hellenistic world, see Elisabeth Schüssler Fiorenza, ed., *Aspects of Religious Propaganda in Judaism and Early Christianity* (Notre Dame:  University of Notre Dame Press, 1976).

[79]*Encyclopedia Britannica*, 15th ed. (1975), s.v. "Propaganda," by Bruce Lannes Smith.

[80]Justin, *Dialogue with Trypho*, VII.1-2.

[81]Windisch, *Paulus und Christus*, p. 87.

[82]Henri Hubert, "Magia" in C. Daremberg and E. Saglio, eds., *Dictionnaire des antiquités grecques et romaines* vol. 3, part 2, 1494-1521; passage quoted from p. 1500, col. 1.

[83]Arthur Darby Nock, "Paul and the Magus" in Zeph Stewart, ed., *Essays on Religion and the Ancient World* (Cambridge:  Harvard University Press, 1972), pp. 308-330; passage quoted from pp. 317-318; see also Ramsey MacMullen, *Enemies of the Roman Order* (Cambridge:  Harvard University Press, 1966), pp. 95-127.

[84]Marcel Mauss, *A General Theory of Magic*, Robert Brain, trans., (New York:  W.W. Norton & Company, 1972), p. 32.

[85]Ibid., p. 22.

[86]Morton Smith, *Clement of Alexandria and a Secret Gospel of Mark* (Cambridge:  Harvard University Press, 1973), p. 228.

[87]Tiede, *Charismatic Figure*, p. 98.

[88]See R. Bulmer, "Why the Cassowary is not a Bird" in Mary Douglas, ed., *Rules and Meanings*, pp. 167-193; M. Douglas, "Animals in Lele Religious Symbolism" in *Implicit Meanings: Essays in Anthropology* (London:  Routledge & Kegan Paul, 1975), pp. 27-46.

[89]For example, see Dieter Georgi, "Socioeconomic Reasons for the 'Divine Man' as a Propagandistic Pattern" in Fiorenza,

ed., *Aspects of Religious Propaganda*, pp. 27-42; Walter Burkert, "GOES: Zum griechischen 'Schamanismus'," *Rheinisches Museum für Philologie* n.f. 105 (1962): 36-55.

[90]Peter Brown, "The Rise and Function of the Holy Man in Late Antiquity," *JRS* 61 (1971): 80-101; passage quoted from pp. 80-81.

[91]Ibid., p. 86.

[92]Ibid., p. 92.

[93]Georgi, "Socioeconomic Reasons."

[94]See the representative collection of texts in A.R. Hands, *Charities and Social Aid in Greece and Rome* (Ithaca: Cornell University Press, 1968).

[95]Burkert, "GOES."

[96]On the accuracy of the preservation of Celsus' words see Robert Bader, *Der ALETHES LOGOS des Kelsos* (Stuttgart-Berlin: W. Kohlhammer, 1940); Carl Andresen, *Logos und Nomos: das Polemik des Celsus wider das Christentum* (Berlin: de Gruyter, 1955); and the helpful survey of the whole question of the preservation of Celsus' text in Marcel Borret, *Contre Celse, V: Introduction* (Paris: Les Editions du Cerf, 1976), pp. 9-28. Unless otherwise noted, I will follow Bader's reconstruction. For both Celsus and Origen I will follow the Greek text in Borret, *Contre Celse* and the English translation in Henry Chadwick, trans., *Origen: Contra Celsum* (Cambridge: Cambridge University Press, 1965).

[1]Cf. Reitzenstein, *HMR*, Steeley, trans., pp. 400-401, (*HMR*[3], p. 316); Wetter, *Der Sohn Gottes*, pp. 4-6; Weinreich, "Antikes Gottmenschentum," pp. 649-650; Windisch, *Paulus und Christus*, pp. 55-56.

[2]Notably, Gustave Bardy, "Origène et la Magie," *Recherches de science religieuse* 17 (1928): 126-142; Pierre de Labriolle, *La réaction païenne* (Paris: L'Artisan du livre, 1934), pp. 111-169, esp. pp. 121, 129, 134, 159; N. Brox, "Magie und Aberglaube an den Anfängen des Christentums," *Trierer Theologische Zeitschrift* 83 (1974): 157-180.

[3]Anna Miura-Stange, *Celsus und Origenes: das Gemeinsame ihrer Weltanschauung* (Giessen: A. Töpelmann, 1926), p. 125.

[4]Ibid., pp. 133-135.

[5]Ibid., p. 162.

[6]Ibid., pp. 144-145.

[7]Ibid., p. 158.

[8]Ibid., p. 135.

[9]Cf. CC VII.28, 49, 58, on which see Andresen, *Logos und Nomos*, pp. 138-141, 154, 179, 183.

[10]Cf. Miura-Stange, *Celsus und Origenes*, pp. 125, 142.

[11]Bieler, ΘΕΙΟΣ ΑΝΗΡ, 2: 36.

[12]Cf. Miura-Stange, *Celsus und Origenes*, pp. 106-113; Brox, "Magie und Aberglaube," pp. 164-166.

[13]Cf. Bardy, "Origène et la Magie," p. 142.

[14]Cf. Peter Brown, "Sorcery, Demons and the Rise of Christianity: From Late Antiquity into the Middle Ages" in Brown, *Religion and Society in the Age of Augustine* (New York: Harper & Row, 1972), pp. 119-146; esp. pp. 122-125.

[15]Cf. Apuleius, *Apologia* CII-CIII for his summary of the charges and his defense.

[16]Mauss, *A General Theory of Magic*, p. 28.

[17]Cf. Borret, *Contre Celse*, V: 35-40.

[18]On the figure of the Jew see Andresen, *Logos und Nomos*, p. 22 n.32, pp. 214-215; on such rhetorical figures in general

see Josef Martin, *Antike Rhetorik: Technik und Methode* (München: C.H. Beck, 1974) pp. 292-293 and the literature cited there.

[19]Bader, *ALETHES LOGOS*, pp. 62, 83 notes that the concluding statements of each book summarize their contents.

[20]To the extent that Celsus' remarks on Jesus (and Origen's responses) follow a roughly chronological order, they do preserve something of the biographical form, but Celsus' treatise as a whole does not preserve the biographical form, nor does Origen's.

[21]Marc Lods, "Etude sur les sources juives de la polemique de Celsus contre les Chretiens," *Revue d'historie et de philosophie religieuse* 21 (1941): 1-33.

[22]Cf. Miura-Stange, *Celsus und Origenes*, p. 126 n.1 for an earlier argument against such a source hypothesis.

[23]The points covered by Celsus conform quite closely to the list of rhetorical commonplaces in invective given by M. Caster, *Etudes sur Alexandre ou le faux prophète de Lucien* (Paris: Société d'Edition "Les Belles Lettres," 1938) pp. 84-85.

[24]Cf. Lods, "Etude sur les sources juives;" Miura-Stange, *Celsus und Origenes*, p. 127 n.1; H. Chadwick, *Contra Celsum*, p. 28 n.2; M. Borret, *Contre Celse*, I: 151 n.2.

[25]In comments which seem to be based on the genealogy in Luke 3:23-38 or a parallel tradition Celsus underlines the incongruity of Mary's actual state in life and the pretensions of "the men who compiled the genealogy [and] boldly said that Jesus was descended from the first man and from the kings of the Jews." He claims that "the carpenter's wife would not have been ignorant of it if she had such a distinguished ancestry" (II.32).

[26]Andresen, *Logos und Nomos*, p. 177.

[27]Cf. ibid., p. 227.

[28]Nock, "Paul and the Magus," p. 318.

[29]Cf. Miura-Stange, *Celsus und Origenes*, p. 143.

[30]Brown, "Sorcery, Demons," p. 112.

[31]Ibid.  Though I have adopted Brown's terminology of Single and Double Images, I have tried to extend its utility by applying them to a broader range of phenomena than he treats in his essay. Essentially, I have used Single Image and Double Image to refer to two distinct perspectives, two different ways of looking at things.  The Single Image prizes the static order of things as they are and have been, explicit and literal meanings, and conformity to recognized standards, while the Double Image cherishes dynamic changes and things as they might or should be, implicit, symbolic, and allegorical meanings, and departure from recognized standards.

[32]Ibid., p. 124.

[33]On Panthera see Chadwick, *Contra Celsum*, p. 31 n.3;
Borret, *Contre Celse*, I:  163 n.4.

[34]Cf. Robert M. Grant, *The Earliest Lives of Jesus* (New
York:  Harper & Row, 1961), pp. 121-122.

[35]Grant, *Earliest Lives*, provides a clear and concise survey of the use of such terms.  Though it is not as complex or
as fully developed as the classification of candidates for
divine status, there is in CC an implicit taxonomy of stories,
and of story-tellers.  Grant has illuminated the roots of those
taxonomies in contemporary rhetoric.  Stories can be convincing
(cf. I.28, 67), appropriate (I.68), or true (II.5) on one hand,
or unconvincing (I.32), fictions (I.28, 37, 43), lies (I.32,
II.21), myths in the pejorative sense (I.37, II.58), fantastic
tales (I.68, VI.8), or plain rubbish (II.5).  Celsus and Origen
share the categories of classification in common; there is a
greater number and variety of negative terms.  By impugning
the stories told about candidates for divine status, they intend
to cast doubt on the candidates themselves.  Celsus' comment in
II.30 summarizes their approach:  "But no one gives proof of a
god or son of a god by such signs and false stories (ἐκ . . .
συμβόλων καὶ παρακουσμάτων), nor by such disreputable evidence
(τεκμηρίων ἀγεννῶν)."  A similar procedure is followed in the
comments on the story-tellers, though the set of categories is
even more fragmentary.  In each case, the implicit taxonomy is
subordinated to the primary task of deciding which candidates
for divine status are worthy and which are not.

[36]Cf. N.R.M. deLange, *Origen and the Jews:  Studies in
Jewish-Christian Relations in Third-century Palestine* (Cambridge:  Cambridge University Press, 1976), pp. 69, 98-99.

[37]Miura-Stange, *Celsus und Origenes*, p. 147; compare Chadwick, *Contra Celsum*, p. 386 n.7 who prefers the less obvious
connection with Celsus' remarks on the Pythian priestess in
III.25 and VII.3.

[38]Miura-Stange, *Celsus und Origenes*, p. 163.

[39]In VIII.47 Origen summarizes his method of assessing
stories:  "Let us compare them all with one another, and consider the aim which those who caused them to be written had in
view, and the resulting help or harm, or neither, to those who
were the recipients of the supposed benefits."

NOTES

CHAPTER III

[1] Cf. Grant, *Earliest Lives*, p. 71.

[2] Cf. CC III.18, 46; VI.13; VII.23.

[3] Both Chadwick (*Contra Celsum*, p. 44 n. 3) and Borret (*Contre Celse* I: 204 n. 1) find Origen to be relying on Proverbs 2:5, though not in the LXX version. They both cite a parallel in Clement, *Strom.* I, 27, 2.

[4] Cf. Miura-Stange, *Celsus und Origenes*, pp. 30-33.

[5] The question of the audience of CC is difficult to solve. Origen's remarks in the preface (esp. pref. 6) are directed to his patron Ambrose who had requested a written answer to Celsus' treatise. But while Ambrose is clearly the intended initial *recipient* of CC, it is unlikely that he was the sole intended *audience*. Several distinctions need to be made. The common profile of literary patrons in the Roman empire [cf. Frederic G. Kenyon, *Books and Readers in Ancient Greece and Rome* (Oxford: Oxford University Press, 1951), p. 80; Theodor Birt, *Abriss des Antiken Buchwesens* (München: C. H. Beck, 1913), pp. 317-318; and especially on the dissemination and intended audiences of apologetic literature, V. Tcherikover, "Jewish Apologetic Literature Reconsidered," *Eos* 48 (1956): 169-193, esp. 172] and scattered comments by Origen himself show that the work was destined for a wider audience. It is unlikely, though, that a single audience was envisaged. Origen notes two distinct groups in his preface: those entirely without faith in Jesus and those weak in faith (pref. 6; cf. V.18). Upon closer examination each of those groups appears to divide into two components. Those entirely without faith would include both the "Greeks," represented by Celsus (cf. I.32, 37, 46, 47, 60, 67, II.16, 35, 76), and the "Jews," represented by Celsus' imaginary Jew (cf. I.35, 43, 44, 46, II.34, 55, 58, 76). Each of those audiences is clearly singled out by Origen and some remarks are directed to both Jews and Greeks (cf. I.36, 56, 59, II.75). The divisions of the "weak in faith" group are less obvious. Origen clearly perceived a cleavage between the "multitude" of believers and the "perfect" (cf. I.7, 10, 31, II.63) especially with regard to his interpretation of scripture in CC (cf. I.22, 42, 45, II.9, 24, 69). It thus seems possible that by "weak in faith" Origen meant potential, new, or fledgling Christians or even those who were capable of no deeper understanding. But the overtones of the phrase raise the possibility that Origen may have intended to correct inadequate or erroneous Christian beliefs. Those professed Christians who, wrongly in Origen's viewpoint, advocated positions similar to those of Celsus might have been included in the "weak in faith" group. To use Tcherikover's term, it might then be possible to view CC as an "inner-directed" apology, directed both to those who know no better and to those who should know better.

The information about the use of CC (such as Eusebius' praise of
it at the beginning of his treatise against Hierocles' comparison
of Jesus and Apollonius of Tyana [cf. ch. V]) is not full enough
to determine whether it reached all of the audiences mentioned
or implied by Origen.  But the variety of audiences addressed
by Origen suggests that he did not design his remarks for a narrow constituency.  The breadth of issues covered reinforces that
impression.  The encyclopaedic nature of the work may even furnish a key to its possible use.  As a compendium of common Greek
and Jewish accusations and possible Christian errors along with
their refutations and corrections by an eminent scholar, it may
have served other less erudite exponents of the faith, like Ambrose, as a guidebook in discussions, controversies, and instruction.   It provides responses to a host of charges which had been
made, and would be made again, against the Christian religion.
In response it attempts to demonstrate, on a level accessible
to the multitude, the correct understanding of the Christian
faith.

[6]Cf. Chadwick, *Contra Celsum*, p. 60 n. 1; Borret, *Contre
Celse* I:  257 n.2.

[7]That figure will be discussed more fully in chapter 4.

[8]Cf. p. 189 n. 35 on Celsus' and Origen's taxonomies of
stories and storytellers.  It is interesting to note that Origen
accuses Jews, Greeks (particularly Celsus), and the "weak in
faith" of the same simplistic, erroneous literal-mindedness in
their readings of the scriptures.

[9]Cf. Bader, *ALETHES LOGOS*, pp.13, 64, 71 on II.7 and II.32.

[10]Ibid., p. 61.

[11]On Origen's principle that opposites imply the existence
of each other see Chadwick, *Contra Celsum*, p. 106 n.1; Borret,
*Contre Celse* I:  402-403 n.1.

[12]Cf. Reitzenstein, *HMR*, Steeley trans., pp. 400-401,
($HMR^3$, p. 316).

[13]Richard Reitzenstein, *Poimandres: Studien zur griechisch-
ägyptischen und frühchristlichen Literatur* (Darmstadt:  Wissenschaftliche Buchgesellschaft, 1966, rpr. of Leipzig, 1904 ed.),
p. 222.

[14]Bader, *ALETHES LOGOS*, p. 90.

[15]The place of Jesus among the divine and holy angels is,
of course, also a question of taxonomy, but Origen does not
elaborate on that classificatory scheme in CC.  In CC his aim
seems to be to secure the proper standing of Jesus among the
worthy and unworthy candidates for divine status, rather than
among those who have already been accorded such status, such as
the angels.

[16]But see Hal Koch, *Pronoia und Paideusis: Studien über Origenes und sein Verhältnis zum Platonismus* (Berlin:    de Gruyter, 1932); Henry Chadwick, *Early Christian Thought and the Classical Tradition* (New York:    Oxford University Press, 1966); Henri Crouzel, *Origène et la Philosophie* (Paris:    Aubier, 1962).

[17]Timaeus 28C, cf. Chadwick, *Contra Celsum*, p. 429 n. 1.

[18]Cf. Miura-Stange, *Celsus und Origenes*, pp. 17-20.

NOTES

CHAPTER IV

[1]Cf. CC II.16, 25, 34, 38, 40, 42 for repetition of that theme.

[2]Cf. Chadwick, *Contra Celsum*, p. 86 n.2; Borret, *Contre Celse* I: 342 n. 1.

[3]Cf. CC pref. 2: "Now Jesus is always being falsely accused, and there is never a time when he is not being accused so long as there is evil among men. He is still silent in face of this and does not answer with his voice; but he makes his defence in the lives of his genuine disciples, for their lives cry out the real facts and defeat all false charges, refuting and overthrowing the slanders and accusations."

[4]Cf. CC III.22-25.

[5]Cf. Henry Chadwick, "The Evidence of Christianity in the Apologetic of Origen" in Kurt Aland & F.L. Cross, eds., *Studia Patristica II* (Berlin: Akademie-Verlag, 1957), pp. 331-339.

[6]Cf. I.50, 57, for example.

[7]See note 1 above.

[8]On Origen's paraphrase of Celsus in II.40 cf. Bader, *ALETHES LOGOS*, p. 74 n.4.

[9]Since Origen frequently voices the notion that Celsus appears to have thought that Jesus should not have died an exemplary death, some of what Origen attributes to Celsus in II.40 may be due more to Origen's interpretation of the death of Jesus than to Celsus' criticism of it. On the preservation of Celsus in II.40, cf. Bader, *ALETHES LOGOS*, p. 74 n.4.

[10]Cf. Charles Talbert, "The Concept of Immortals in Mediterranean Antiquity," *JBL* 94 (1975): 419-436.

[11]Ibid., pp. 421-422.

[12]Cf. CC VII.53-57.

[13]Those without faith and those weak in faith seem to be Origen's primary audiences for CC; cf. pref. 6, V.18; Ch. III, p. 191 n.5.

[14]Brown, "Sorcery, Demons," p. 124.

[15]Ibid.

[16]Cf. Frederick W. Danker, "2 Peter 1: A Solemn Decree," *CBQ* 40 (1978): 64-82, esp. p. 64.

[17] Samuel Dill, *Roman Society from Nero to Marcus Aurelius* (New York: The World Publishing Company, 1956, rpr. of 1904 ed.), p. 269.

[18] Jean Gagé, *Les classes sociales dans l'empire romain* (Paris: Payot, 1971, rev. ed.), p. 308.

[19] Ramsey MacMullen, *Roman Social Relations* (New Haven: Yale University Press, 1974), p. 77.

[20] Hands, *Charities and Social Aid*, #27, p. 187. Latin text in H. Dessau, ed., *Inscriptiones Latinae Selectae* (Berlin: Weidmann, 1892-1916), 5 vols. #6595.

[21] Hands, *Charities and Social Aid*, #13, p. 183. Greek text in Gustave Fougerès, "Inscriptions de Mantinée," *Bulletin de correspondence hellénique,* 20 (1896): 125-127.

[22] Hands, *Charities and Social Aid,* pp. 55-56.

[23] Edwyn Bevan, ed., *Later Greek Religion* (Boston: Beacon Press, 1950), pp. 66-67. Greek text in W. Dittenberger, *Orientis Graeci Inscriptiones Selectae*, 2 Vols. (Lipsiae: S. Hirzel, 1903-1905), vol. 1, #458.

[24] Bevan, *Later Greek Religion,* p. 68. Greek text in Victor Ehrenberg and A.H.M. Jones, eds., *Documents Illustrating the Reigns of Augustus and Tiberius* (Oxford: Clarendon Press, 1955, 2nd ed.), #98A.

[25] Whether that is a secondary phenomenon, under the influence of the language of the inscriptions, or a parallel development needs to be investigated.

[26] Cf. Ch. I, pp. 23-25 on the polemical dimensions of Diodorus' classificatory scheme.

[27] Diodorus, I.17.1-2.

[28] Cf. Chadwick, "Evidences," p. 336.

[29] Bevan, *Later Greek Religion*, p. 71. Greek text in Bruno Keil, ed., *Aelii Aristidis Quae Supersunt Omnia* (Berlin: Weidmann, 1898), pp. 81-97.

[30] Bevan, *Later Greek Religion*, p. 72.

[31] Ibid., p. 75.

[32] Ibid.

[33] Ibid., p. 76.

[34] Cf. Eiliv Skard, *Zwei religiös-politische Begriffe: Euergetes-Concordia* (Oslo: Norske Videnskaps-Akademi, 1931), pp. 1-66.

NOTES

CHAPTER V

[1]Cf. Eusebius, *Against Hierocles* I for Eusebius' reliance on Origen.

[2]On the sources and influence of Celsus see the summary in M. Borret, *Contre Celse*, V: 183-198; and see also G. Loesche, "Haben die späteren neuplatonischen Polemiker gegen das Christentum das Werk des Celsus benutzt?," *Zeitschrift für Wissenschaftliche Theologie* 27 (1884): 257-302; Heinrich Otto Schröder, "Celsus und Porphyrios als Christengegner," *Die Welt als Geschichte* 17 (1957): 190-202. Recently, J. Schwartz and J.M. Vermander have reopened the question, arguing for a pervasive influence of Celsus on early Christian apologists; their arguments are conveniently summarized by Borret. Among their articles are: J. Schwartz, "Du Testament de Lévi au Discours véritable de Celse," *Revue d'histoire et de philosophie religieuse,* (1960): 126-145; "La 'conversion' de Lucien de Samosate," *Antiquité classique* 32 (1964): 383-400; J.M. Vermander, "De quelques repliques à Celse dans l'Apologeticum de Tertullien," *Revue des études augustiniennes* 16 (1970): 205-225; idem., "Celse, source et adversaire de Minucius Felix," *Revue des études augustiniennes* 17 (1971): 13-25; idem., "La parution de l'ouvrage de Celse et la datation de quelques apologies," *Revue des études augustiniennes* 18 (1972): 27-42; J. Schwartz, "Celsus redivivus," *Revue d'histoire et de philosophie religieuse* (1973): 399-405. Their arguments do nothing to alter the fact that CC is the fullest and most detailed response to Celsus up to the date of its composition.

[3]Cf. ch. I, pp. 33-36.

[4]Schwartz and Vermander (see note 2, above) have done the most to propose historical connections between Celsus and various Christian apologists. Eusebius (see note 1, above) is clearly dependent upon Origen's treatment of Celsus' attack for his response to Hierocles. Origen knew of Apollonius (cf. CC VI.41), but it is not possible to establish any clear links between Philostratus and Origen. Neither a positive nor a negative identification of the author of the *True Doctrine* with the Celsus mentioned by Lucian in Alex. 1 would materially effect my analysis.

[5]Franz Cumont, "Alexandre d'Abonotichos et le néo-Pythagorisme," *Revue de l'histoire des religions* 86 (1922): 202-210 called attention to the contrast between Lucian's characterization of Alexander and the evident success of the cult he founded. On the background of the cult see Franz Cumont, *Alexandre d'Abonotichos: un épisode du paganisme au II siècle de nôtre ère*, Academie Royale des Sciences, des Lettres et des Beaux-Arts de Belgique: Memoires Couronnés et Autres Memoires, vol. 40, no. 7 (Bruxelles: Academie Royale, 1887); Otto Weinreich,

"Alexandros der Lügenprophet und seine Stellung in der Religi-
osität des II.   Jahrhunderts nach Christus," *Neue Jahrbücher
fur das klassische Altertum* 47 (1912):   129-151; Arthur Darby
Nock, "Alexander of Abonuteichos," *Classical Quarterly* 22 (1928):
160-162; M. Caster, *Etudes sur Alexandre*.  For Lucian I follow
the Greek text and English translation in A.M. Harmon, trans.,
*Lucian*, vol. 4 (Cambridge:  Harvard University Press, 1925).

[6]Cf. CC I.62-64, e.g. and Andresen, *Logos und Nomos*, p. 227.

[7]On the translation of the name and its pejorative connota-
tions see Caster, *Etudes sur Alexandre*, pp. 14-15.

[8]Cf. ibid., p. 20 on the bronze tablets.

[9]The genealogy was apparently designed to make him all the
more attractive to the citizens of the area; cf. ibid., pp. 21-
22; Nock, "Alexander," p. 161.

[10]Cf. Caster, *Etudes sur Alexandre*, pp. 38-40; on the same
processes for opening queries see Hippolytus, *Ref*. IV. 28-42 and
the commentary by R. Ganschinietz in his *Hippolytos' Capitel
gegen die Magier* (Leipzig:  J. C. Hinrichs'sche Buchhandlung,
1913).

[11]See Cumont, *Alexandre d'Abonotichos:  un épisode*, pp. 8-9
on Lucian's motives.

[12]For Philostratus I follow the Greek text and English translation in F.C. Conybeare, trans., *Philostratus, The Life of
Apollonius*, 2 vols. (Cambridge:  Harvard University Press, 1912).

[13]Cf. CC I.62-64, e.g. and Andresen, *Logos und Nomos*, p. 227.

[14]See Jonathan Z. Smith on VA I.6 in "Good News is No News"
in Jacob Neusner, ed., *Judaism, Christianity, and Other Greco-
Roman Cults:  Studies for Morton Smith at Sixty* (Leiden:  E.J.
Brill, 1975) 1:   21-38, esp. 27-28.

[15]Ibid.

[16]In that Philostratus closely resembles Origen whose primary goal also was to move Jesus away from the negative pole of
evaluation.

[17]For φύσις in the sense of "character" see Helmut Koester,
"φύσις, φυσικός, φυσικῶς" *TDNT* 9:   251-277, esp. pp. 254, 270,
275.  For Eusebius I follow the Greek text and English translation in Conybeare, *Philostratus*, vol. 2.

[18]I know of no work which, like Bader and others for Celsus,
attempts to recover the text of Hierocles.

NOTES

CHAPTER VI

[1]Cf. chapter I, pp. 33-36.

[2]Cf. Kee, "Aretalogy and Gospel," p. 421.

[3]Cf. Rodney Needham, "Introduction" in Needham, ed., *Right and Left: Essays on Dual Symbolic Classification* (Chicago: University of Chicago Press, 1973), p. xxxii.

[4]Cf. Burkert, "GOES."

[5]Cf. Georgi, "Socioeconomic Reasons."

[6]Mary Douglas in Douglas, ed., *Rules and Meanings*, p. 11.

[7]Lewis Coser, *The Functions of Social Conflict* (New York: The Free Press, 1956), p. 123.

[8]Douglas, *Purity and Danger*, p. 15.

[9]Hill, *The Sociology of Religion*, p. 163.

[10]Mary Douglas, "Heathen Darkness" in *Implicit Meanings*, pp. 73-82, passage quoted from p. 81.

BIBLIOGRAPHY

Achtemeier, Paul. Review of *The Charismatic Figure as Miracle Worker*, by David L. Tiede. *Catholic Biblical Quarterly* 35 (1973): 559-560.

Andresen, Carl. *Logos und Nomos: das Polemik des Celsus wider das Christentum*. Berlin: de Gruyter, 1955.

Babbit, F.C. Trans. *Plutarch, Moralia*, vol. 5. Cambridge: Harvard University Press, 1936.

Bader, Robert. *Der ALETHES LOGOS des Kelsos*. Stuttgart-Berlin: W. Kohlhammer, 1940.

Bardy, Gustave. "Origène et la Magie." *Recherches de science religieuse* 17 (1928): 126-142.

Betz, H.D. "Jesus as Divine Man." In *Jesus and the Historian*, edited by F. Thomas Trotter, pp. 114-133. Philadelphia: Westminster Press, 1968.

_____. *Lukian von Samosata und das Neue Testament*. Berlin: Akademie-Verlag, 1961.

Bevan, Edwyn, ed. *Later Greek Religion*. Boston: Beacon Press, 1950.

Bieler, Ludwig. ΘΕΙΟΣ ANHP: *Das Bild des "göttlichen Menschen" im Spätantike und Frühchristentum*. 2 vols. 1935 and 1936. Reprint (2 vols. in 1). Darmstadt: Wissenschaftliche Buchgesellschaft, 1976.

Birt, Theodor. *Abriss des Antiken Buchwesens*. Munich: C.H. Beck, 1913.

Borret, Marcel. *Origene: Contre Celse*. 5 vols. Paris: Les Editions du Cerf, 1967-1975.

Brown, Peter. "Sorcery, Demons and the Rise of Christianity: From Late Antiquity into the Middle Ages." In *Religion and Society in the Age of Augustine*, by Peter Brown, pp. 119-146. New York: Harper & Row, 1972.

_____. "The Rise and Function of the Holy Man in Late Antiquity." *Journal of Roman Studies* 61 (1971): 80-101.

Brox, N. "Magie und Aberglaube an den Anfängen des Christentums." *Trierer Theologische Zeitschrift* 83 (1974): 157-180.

Bulmer, R. "Why the Cassowary is not a Bird." In *Rules and Meanings*, edited by Mary Douglas, pp. 167-193. Harmondsworth: Penguin Books, 1973.

Burger, Thomas. *Max Weber's Theory of Concept Formation:
    History, Laws, and Ideal Types*. Durham:  Duke University
    Press, 1976.

Burkert, Walter.  "GOES:  Zum griechischen 'Schamanismus'."
    *Rheinisches Museum für Philologie* n.f. 105 (1962):  36-55.

Caster, Marcel.  *Etudes sur Alexandre ou le faux prophète de
    Lucien*. Paris:  Société d'Edition "Les Belles Lettres,"
    1938.

Chadwick, Henry.  *Early Christian Thought and the Classical
    Tradition*. New York:  Oxford University Press, 1966.

_____. Trans. *Origen:  Contra Celsum*. Cambridge:  Cam-
    bridge University Press, 1965.

_____.  "The Evidence of Christianity in the Apologetic of
    Origen." In *Studia Patristica II*, edited by Kurt Aland
    and F.L. Cross, pp. 331-339. Berlin:  Akademie-Verlag,
    1957.

Conybeare, F.C. Trans.  *Philostratus, The Life of Apollonius*.
    2 vols. Cambridge:  Harvard University Press, 1912.

Coser, Lewis.  *The Functions of Social Conflict*. New York:  The
    Free Press, 1956.

Crouzel, Henri.  *Origène et la philosophie*. Paris:  Aubier,
    1962.

Cumont, Franz.  *Alexandre d'Abonotichos:  un épisode de l'histoire
    du paganisme au II siècle de nôtre ère*. Academie Royale
    des Sciences, des Lettres et des Beaux-Arts de Belgique:
    Memoires Couronnés et Autres Memoires, vol. 40, no. 7.
    Bruxelles:  Academie Royale, 1887.

_____.  "Alexandre d'Abonotichos et le néo-Pythagorisme."
    *Revue de l'histoire des religions* 86 (1922):  202-210.

Danker, Frederick W.  "2 Peter 1:  A Solemn Decree." *Catholic
    Biblical Quarterly* 40 (1978):  64-82.

Dessau, H., ed.  *Inscriptiones Latinae Selectae*. 5 vols.
    Berlin:  Weidmann, 1892-1916.

*Dictionnaire des antiquités grecques et romaines*. s.v. "Magia."
    By Henri Hubert.

Dill, Samuel.  *Roman Society from Nero to Marcus Aurelius*. 1904.
    Reprint.  New York:  The World Publishing Company, 1956.

Dittenberger, Wilhelm.  *Orientis Graeci Inscriptiones Selectae*.
    2 vols. Lipsiae:  S. Hirzel, 1903-1905.

Douglas, Mary.  "Animals in Lele Religious Symbolism."  In
    *Implicit Meanings:  Essays in Anthropology*, by Mary Douglas,
    pp. 27-46. London:  Routledge & Kegan Paul, 1975.

_____.  "Heathen Darkness." In *Implicit Meanings*, pp. 73-82.

_____. *Purity and Danger: An Analysis of Concepts of Pollution and Taboo.* Harmondsworth: Penguin Books, 1966.

_____, ed. *Rules and Meanings.* Harmondsworth: Penguin Books, 1973.

*Encyclopedia of Religion and Ethics.* s.v. "Euhemerism." By J. Geffcken.

*Encyclopaedia Britannica.* 15th ed. (1975), s.v. "Hellenistic Religions." By Jonathan Z. Smith.

_____. 15th ed. (1975), s.v. "Propaganda." By Bruce Lannes Smith.

Ehrenberg, Victor, and Jones, A.H.M., eds. *Documents Illustrating the Reigns of Augustus and Tiberius.* 2nd ed. Oxford: Clarendon Press, 1955.

Evans-Pritchard, E.E. *Theories of Primitive Religion.* Oxford: Oxford University Press, 1965.

Fiorenza, Elizabeth Schüssler, ed. *Aspects of Religious Propaganda in Judaism and Early Christianity.* Notre Dame: University of Notre Dame Press, 1976.

Firth, Raymond. "An Analysis of Mana: An Empirical Approach." In *Tikopia Ritual and Belief*, by Raymond Firth, pp. 174-194. Boston: Beacon Press, 1967.

Fougères, Gustave. "Inscriptions de Mantinée." *Bulletin de correspondence hellénique* 20 (1896): 119-166.

Gagé, Jean. *Les classes sociales dans l'empire romain.* Rev. ed. Paris: Payot, 1971.

Ganschinietz, R. *Hippolytos' Capitel gegen die Magier.* Leipzig: J.C. Hinrichs'sche Buchhandlung, 1913.

Georgi, Dieter. "Socioeconomic reasons for the 'Divine Man' as a Propagandistic Pattern." In *Aspects of Religious Propaganda in Judaism and Early Christianity*, edited by Elisabeth Schüssler Fiorenza, pp. 27-42. Notre Dame: University of Notre Dame Press, 1976.

_____. *Die Gegner des Paulus im 2. Korintherbrief.* Neukirchener-Vluyn: Neukirchener Verlag, 1964.

Grant, Robert M. *The Earliest Lives of Jesus.* New York: Harper & Row, 1961.

Hadas, Moses, and Smith, Morton. *Heroes and Gods: Spiritual Biographies in Antiquity.* New York: Harper & Row, 1965.

Hands, A.R. *Charities and Social Aid in Greece and Rome.* Ithaca: Cornell University Press, 1968.

Harmon, A.M.  Trans.  *Lucian*, vol. 4.  Cambridge:  Harvard
    University Press, 1925.

Hill, Michael.  *A Sociology of Religion*.  New York:  Basic
    Books, 1973.

*International Encyclopaedia of the Social Sciences*.  s.v.
    "Typologies."  By E. Tiryakian.

Kee, Howard Clark.  *Aretalogies, Hellenistic "Lives," and the
    Sources of Mark*.  Berkeley:  Center for Hermeneutical
    Studies in Hellenistic and Modern Culture, 1975.

_____.  "Aretalogy and Gospel."  *Journal of Biblical Liter-
    ature* 92 (1973):  402-422.

Keil, Bruno, ed.  *Aelii Aristidis Quae Supersunt Omnia*.  Berlin:
    Weidmann, 1898.

Kenyon, Frederic G.  *Books and Readers in Ancient Greece and
    Rome*.  Oxford:  Oxford University Press, 1951.

Koch, Hal.  *Pronoia und Paideusis:  Studien über Origenes und
    sein Verhältnis zum Platonismus*.  Berlin:  de Gruyter,
    1932.

Koester, Helmut.  "One Jesus and Four Primitive Gospels."  In
    *Trajectories Through Early Christianity*, by James M.
    Robinson and Helmut Koester, pp. 158-204.  Philadelphia:
    Fortress Press, 1971.

_____.  "The Structure and Criteria of Early Christian
    Beliefs."  In *Trajectories Through Early Christianity*,
    pp. 205-231.

deLabriolle, Pierre.  *La réaction païenne*.  Paris:  L'Artisan
    du livre, 1934.

deLange, N.R.M.  *Origen and the Jews:  Studies in Jewish-Chris-
    tian Relations in Third-Century Palestine*.  Cambridge:
    Cambridge University Press, 1976.

Lods, Marc.  "Etude sur les sources juives de la polemique de
    Celsus contre les Chretiens."  *Revue d'histoire et de
    philosophie religieuse* 21 (1941): 1-33.

Loesche, G.  "Haben die späteren neuplatonischen Polemiker gegen
    das Christentum das Werk des Celsus benutzt?"  *Zeitschrift
    für Wissenschaftliche Theologie* 27 (1884):  257-302.

MacMullen, Ramsey.  *Enemies of the Roman Order*.  Cambridge:
    Harvard University Press, 1966.

_____.  *Roman Social Relations*.  New Haven:  Yale University
    Press, 1974.

Marett, R.R. *The Threshold of Religion*. 4th ed. London:
Metheun & Co., 1929.

Martin, Josef. *Antike Rhetorik: Technik und Methode*. München:
C.H. Beck, 1974.

Mauss, Marcel. *A General Theory of Magic*. Translated by
Robert Brain. New York: W.W. Norton & Company, 1972.

McKinney, John C. *Constructive Typology and Social Theory*.
New York: Appleton-Century-Crofts, 1966.

Miura-Stange, Anna. *Celsus und Origenes: das Gemeinsame ihrer
Weltanschauung*. Giessen: A. Töpelmann, 1926.

Needham, Rodney. Introduction to *Right and Left: Essays on
Dual Symbolic Classification*, edited by Rodney Needham,
pp. xi-xxxix. Chicago: University of Chicago Press, 1973.

Nock, Arthur Darby. "Alexander of Abonuteichos." *Classical
Quarterly* 22 (1928): 160-162.

_____. "Paul and the Magus." In *Essays on Religion and
the Ancient World*, edited by Zeph Stewart, pp. 308-330.
Cambridge: Harvard University Press, 1972.

Oldfather, C.H. Trans. *Diodorus*, vol. 1. Cambridge: Harvard
University Press, 1933.

Olrik, Axel. "The Epic Laws of Folk Narrative." In *The Study
of Folklore*, edited by Alan Dundes, pp. 129-141. Englewood Cliffs, New Jersey: Prentice-Hall, 1965.

Reitzenstein, Richard. *Hellenistische Mysterienreligionen*.
3rd ed., 1927. Reprint. Stuttgart: B.G. Teubner, 1973.

_____. *Hellenistic Mystery-Religions: Their Basic Ideas
and Significance*. Translated by John E. Steeley. Pittsburgh: The Pickwick Press, 1978.

_____. *Poimandres: Studien zur griechisch-ägyptischen
und frühchristlichen Literatur*. 1904. Reprint. Darmstadt: Wissenschaftliche Buchgesellschaft, 1966.

Schröder, Heinrich Otto. "Celsus und Porphyrios als Christengegner." *Die Welt als Geschichte* 17 (1957): 190-202.

Schwartz, J. "La 'conversion' de Lucien de Samosate."
*Antiquité classique* 32 (1964): 383-400.

_____. "Celsus redivivus." *Revue d'histoire et de philos-
ophie religieuse* 53 (1973): 399-405.

_____. "Du Testament de Lévi au Discours véritable de
Celse." *Revue d'histoire et de philosophie religieuse*
40 (1960): 126-145.

Skard, Eiliv. *Zwei religiös-politische Begriffe: Euergetes-Concordia.* Oslo: Norske Videnskaps Akademi, 1931.

Smith, Jonathan Z. "Native Cults in the Hellenistic Period." *History of Religions* 11 (1971): 236-249.

_____. "Good News is No News." In *Judaism, Christianity, and Other Greco-Roman Cults: Studies for Morton Smith at Sixty,* edited by Jacob Neusner, 1: 21-38. Leiden: E.J. Brill, 1975.

Smith, Morton. *Clement of Alexandria and a Secret Gospel of Mark.* Cambridge: Harvard University Press, 1973.

_____. *Jesus the Magician.* New York: Harper & Row, 1978.

_____. "Prologomena to a Discussion of Aretalogies, Divine Men, the Gospels and Jesus." *Journal of Biblical Literature* 90 (1971): 174-199.

_____. "On the History of the 'Divine Man'." In *Paganisme, Judaisme, Christianisme: Mélanges offert à Marcel Simon,* edited by A. Benoit et al., pp. 335-345. Paris: deBoccard, 1978.

_____. Review of *The Charismatic Figure as Miracle Worker,* by David L. Tiede. *Interpretation* 28 (1974): 238-240.

Talbert, Charles. "The Concept of Immortals in Mediterranean Antiquity." *Journal of Biblical Literature* 94 (1975): 419-436.

Tcherikover, Victor. "Jewish Apologetic Literature Reconsidered." *Eos* 48 (1956): 169-193.

*Theological Dictionary of the New Testament.* s.v. "φύσις, φυσικός, φυσικῶς." By Helmut Koester.

_____. s.v. "υἱός (Classical Greek)." By W. Von Martitz.

Tiede, David Lenz. *The Charismatic Figure as Miracle Worker.* Missoula, Montana: Scholars Press, 1972.

Vermander, J.M. "Celse, source et adversaire de Minucius Felix." *Revue des études augustiniennes* 17 (1971): 13-25.

_____. "De quelques repliques à Celse dans l'Apologeticum de Tertullien." *Revue des études augustiniennes* 16 (1970): 205-225.

_____. "La parution de l'ouvrage de Celse et la datation de quelques apologies." *Revue des études augustiniennes* 18 (1972): 27-42.

Weber, Max. "Religious Rejections of the World and their Directions." In *From Max Weber,* edited and translated by H.H. Gerth and C. Wright Mills, pp. 323-359. New York: Oxford University Press, 1946.

Weeden, Theodore J.  *Mark--Traditions in Conflict.*  Philadelphia:
    Fortress Press, 1971.

Weinreich, Otto.  "Alexandros der Lügenprophet und seine Stellung
    in der Religiosität des II.  Jahrhunderts nach Christus."
    *Neue Jahrbücher fur das klassische Altertum* 47 (1912):
    129-151.

_____.  "Antikes Gottmenschentum." *Neue Jahrbücher für
    Wissenschaft und Jugendbildung* 2 (1926):   633-651.

Wetter, G.P.  *Der Sohn Gottes:  Eine Untersuchung über den
    Charakter und die Tendenz des Johannes-Evangeliums.*  Gött-
    ingen:  Vandenhoeck & Ruprecht, 1916.

Windisch, Hans.  *Paulus und Christus:  Ein biblischreligions-
    geschichtlicher Vergleich.*  Leipzig:  J.C. Hinrichs'sche
    Buchhandlung, 1934.